The Best Of *The Mailb*
Primary Editio

Our favorite ideas from the 1992–1996 issues of the Primary edition
of *The Mailbox*® magazine

Editor in Chief
Margaret Michel

Product Director
Kathy Wolf

Editor
Diane Badden

Copy Editors
Lynn Bemer Coble, Karen L. Huffman, Jennifer Rudisill,
Debbie Shoffner, Gina Sutphin

Artists
Jennifer Tipton Bennett, Cathy Spangler Bruce, Pam Crane, Teresa Davidson,
Susan Hodnett, Sheila Krill, Rebecca Saunders, Barry Slate, Donna K. Teal

Cover Artist
Jeannine Lorenz

Typographers
Scott Lyons
Lynette Maxwell

About This Book

Since its publication in 1988, the first *Best Of* The Mailbox®—*Primary* book has become one of the most popular titles available to teachers of grades 1–3 today. In 1994 we presented the second in the series, *The Best Of* The Mailbox®—*Book 2* (Primary Edition), which proved to be another favorite with teachers. Now we're proud to present the newest *Best Of* The Mailbox® book for primary teachers. Inside these covers, you'll find many of the best teacher-tested ideas published in the 1992–1996 issues of *The* Primary *Mailbox*® magazine. Our editors selected these practical ideas from those sent to us by teachers across the United States. We've included many of our regularly featured sections of the magazine plus special teaching units and reproducibles.

©1998 by THE EDUCATION CENTER, INC.
All rights reserved except as here noted.
ISBN #1-56234-214-2

Manufactured in the United States
10 9 8 7 6 5 4 3 2 1

Table Of Contents

BULLETIN BOARDS

Bulletin Boards..

Here's a team that can outshine any of its competition! On white construction paper, duplicate student copies of the pattern on page 23. Have each student cut out a pattern, then decorate the resulting cutout to resemble himself. Provide an assortment of arts-and-crafts supplies that include crayons, yarn, buttons, and scraps of fabric, construction paper, and wallpaper. Mount the cutouts, a student-generated list of "team rules," and the title as shown. Go! Team! Go!

Kathy Lezotte-Zuck—Gr. 1, Ladysmith Elementary School, Ladysmith, WI

If you want your youngsters to go bananas over school, here's the perfect display! On a paper-covered bulletin board, mount a large, three-dimensional tree, a banana-packing monkey, and the title as shown. Then, using colorful markers, have the students write their names on the display. When the project is finished, serve each child one-half of a banana. Then invite your youngsters to talk about their expectations for the new school year.

Susie Petges—Gr. 2, St. Dennis School, Lockport, IL

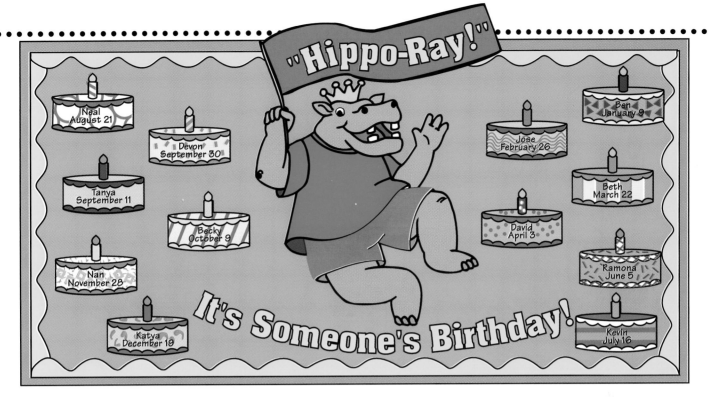

Recognize your youngsters' birthdays in a big way with this year-round display! Mount the title and a large birthday character like the one shown. Write each child's name and birthday on a white, construction-paper copy of the cake pattern on page 24. Then have each child decorate and cut out his birthday cake. Mount the completed cutouts onto the display. Plan to recognize every student's birthday during the school year—even those that occur during the summer months.

Diane Fortunato—Gr. 2, Carteret School, Bloomfield, NJ

Students take great pride in this year-round display that they help make and maintain. A student cuts out, personalizes, and decorates a construction-paper pattern (page 23) to resemble himself. Using a pushpin, he attaches his resemblance to the display. When a child is absent, his cutout is moved by a class helper. When the absent child returns, he signs in at the display and returns his cutout to its original position. Replace the schoolhouse with a pumpkin (or other seasonal cutout) at the start of October.

Christopher D. Brown, Laurens, SC

Create an appetite for learning with this versatile display. Mount the character and title. Have each student trim a construction-paper square into a cookie shape, then personalize and decorate the resulting cutout. On writing paper, have students write their goals for the school year. Mount the cookies and papers as shown. Periodically have students evaluate and rewrite their goals. Or invite youngsters to showcase their best work throughout the year at the display. Now you're cookin'!

Diane Afferton—Gr. 3, Morrisville, PA

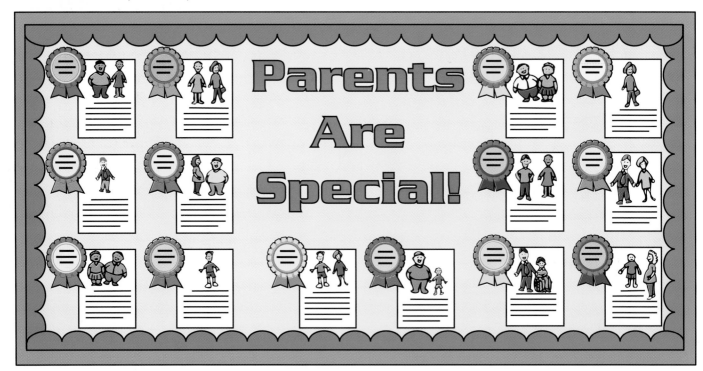

This Open House display is a guaranteed showstopper! Prior to Open House have students write and illustrate paragraphs that explain their parents' special traits. Then, using construction-paper copies of the patterns on page 24, have each student decorate, program (if appropriate), cut out, and attach a ribbon to his project. The resulting display is very impressive!

6   Leigh Anne Newsom—Gr. 3, Greenbrier Intermediate, Chesapeake, VA

This seaworthy display encourages youngsters to follow their dreams. Using the instructions on page 124 (see "Sail On" and "One Man's Big Dream"), have each youngster design a ship and write his biggest dream on a cloud cutout. Next have each youngster cut a bottle shape from dark blue paper, mount his ship atop the resulting cutout, and cover the project with a length of clear plastic wrap. Mount each youngster's ship project and cloud cutout. What a fleet!

Carla T. Jurukov—Gr. 3, John Muir School, Glendale, CA

Invite youngsters to showcase their best work at this nutty display. Mount the character and title. On light brown construction paper, duplicate a student supply of acorn paper toppers using the patterns on page 25. Have each student personalize, decorate, and cut out a paper topper. Then have each student choose a sample of her best work. Display the work samples and paper toppers as shown. Periodically ask students to replace their displayed work with more current samples. That's it in a nutshell!

Spin a web of reading motivation with this "spook-tacular" display. Mount the title and attach a yarn web. Duplicate a supply of circular book-report forms. A student completes one of these reports for each book that he reads. To make a spider, he mounts his report onto black construction paper and trims the paper to create a spider body. Then he uses construction-paper scraps to add legs and other desired features. Attach the completed projects to the web.

adapted from an idea by Ann E. Fausnight, Canton, OH

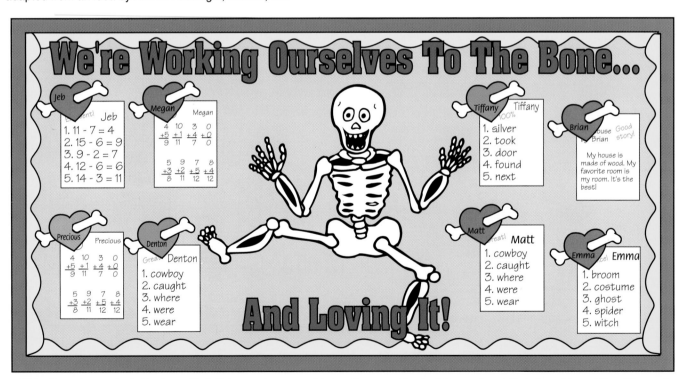

This "spook-tacular" display will delight students and keep them motivated throughout October. Mount the title and a character. (Consider purchasing a silly skeleton cutout with movable limbs.) Have each student personalize, decorate, and cut out a paper topper pattern (page 25) and choose a sample of her best work. Display the work samples and paper toppers as shown. Regularly ask students to replace their work with more current samples.

Toni J. Mongino—Gr. 1, Eckhart School, Trinidad, CO

Branch out with this three-dimensional student-made display! To make the branches, have each youngster cut a large grocery bag down one side and then cut to detach the bottom of the bag. Next have each student flatten and roll the resulting paper to create a tree branch. Using the patterns on page 26, duplicate a supply of fall-colored leaves. Have students cut out and label each leaf with a thankful thought. Mount the branches and leaves in a desired fashion.

Janet Chadwick—Gr. 2, Monte Vista Elementary, La Crescenta, CA

Reinforce your youngsters' Spanish or have fun introducing new Spanish words and phrases with this seasonal display. With your youngsters' input, determine four or more desired categories. Then have each youngster complete an illustration for the category of his choice. Before attaching the students' projects to the display, have each youngster share his illustration and name its category. Magnífico!

Jean Garza—Gr. 2, Country Club School, Farmington, NM

Put your youngsters into a spin over good work! Using the pattern on page 26, have each youngster decorate and cut out a construction paper top. Then invite students to showcase their tops and samples of their best work at the display as shown. For a top-notch Hanukkah display, have each student appropriately decorate his cutout to resemble a dreidel, then display his best work as described.

You'll receive a jolly response when you display these student-made projects. To make a reindeer, bend a clothes hanger into a diamond shape. Stretch one leg of a pair of pantyhose over the hanger, pulling it toward the hook. At the base of the hook, secure the hose with a piece of yarn or string. Cut antlers, eyes, a nose, and other desired decorations from construction paper. Glue the cutouts to the hose. Mount the completed projects and the title as shown.

Vivian Campbell—Gr. 2, Knollwood School, Piscataway, NJ

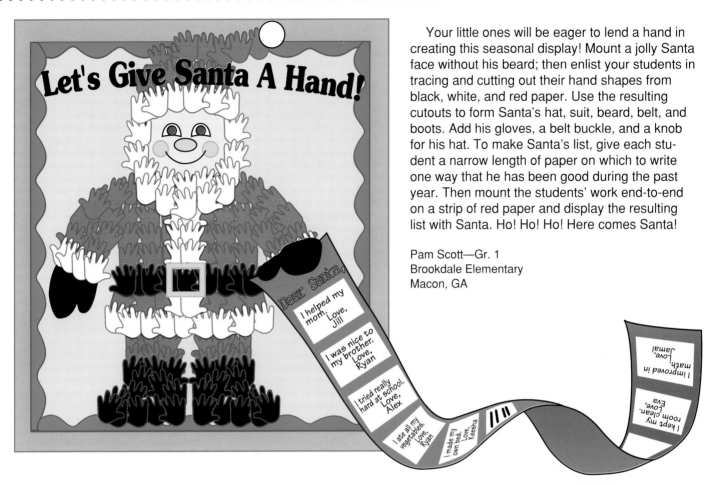

Let's Give Santa A Hand!

Your little ones will be eager to lend a hand in creating this seasonal display! Mount a jolly Santa face without his beard; then enlist your students in tracing and cutting out their hand shapes from black, white, and red paper. Use the resulting cutouts to form Santa's hat, suit, beard, belt, and boots. Add his gloves, a belt buckle, and a knob for his hat. To make Santa's list, give each student a narrow length of paper on which to write one way that he has been good during the past year. Then mount the students' work end-to-end on a strip of red paper and display the resulting list with Santa. Ho! Ho! Ho! Here comes Santa!

Pam Scott—Gr. 1
Brookdale Elementary
Macon, GA

Create a spectacular sight this season with star-studded greenery! Each student traces a star-shaped template on green paper and cuts out the resulting shape. Then she centers and glues a snapshot of herself on her cutout, making sure that one point of the star is directly above her picture. Each student then decorates her star as desired. Provide glitter pens, sequins, rickrack, pom-poms, and other arts-and-crafts supplies for this purpose. Be sure to fashion a star yourself! Then mount the completed projects as shown. Happy holidays!

Renee Fehr—Grs. 1 & 2
Westmoreland Elementary
Westmoreland, KS

Prior to creating these perky penguins, have each youngster write a personal goal for the new year on an eight-inch white construction-paper circle. To make a penguin, cut a five-inch circle and a nine-inch circle from black construction paper. Trim two 3" x 9" strips of black construction paper to resemble penguin wings and two 3" x 2" strips of orange construction paper to resemble penguin feet. Cut facial features from construction-paper scraps; then assemble the penguin. Mount the title and projects as shown. Too cool!

Rona Mendelson—Gr. 3, Estes McDoniel Elementary, Henderson, NV

Display each student's wish for the new year with a lucky penny, and these wishes won't soon be forgotten! Give each child an index card to which you have taped a shiny new penny. Ask the youngsters to write their wishes for the new year on the cards; then mount the cards as shown. Encourage students to make wishes that would have a positive effect on several people.

Maureen Martin, Northport, NY

Join hands for peace with this lovely reminder of Dr. Martin Luther King, Jr.'s dream. On lengths of red, white, and blue bulletin-board paper, have each youngster trace his hand and cut out the resulting shapes. Then mount the cutouts as shown. The dream is still alive!

adapted from an idea by Teresa Fenton, Bomoseen, VT

This eye-catching scene is effortless to assemble. Drape a length of fabric or a bedsheet across the top of a bulletin board (securing it at each corner and in the middle) to make a curtain for your "window." Then, using white chalk and scraps of construction paper, have each student create a winter scene on dark blue paper. Mount the completed projects atop slightly larger pieces of black paper; then attach black-paper windowpanes. Ooooooh! What a sight!

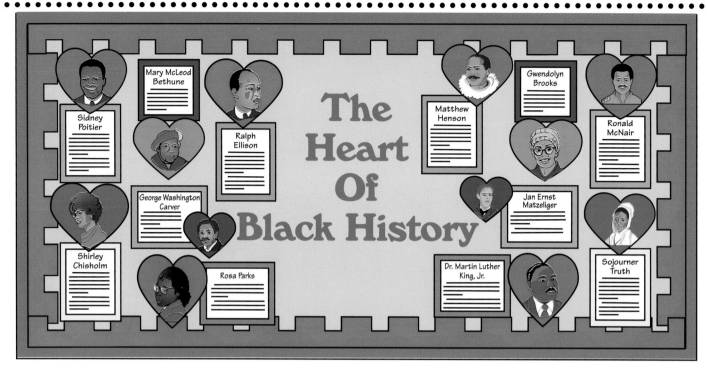

As students create this display, they learn about famous Black Americans. Each student researches a different African American hero or heroine, and writes several interesting facts about him or her. The student mounts his written work atop a slightly larger piece of construction paper. Then he mounts a picture of the famous person he researched on a heart cutout. (The picture may be cut from a discarded periodical, traced and colored by the student, or student-illustrated.) Display the completed projects as shown.

Karen Bryant—Gr. 3, Rosa Taylor Elementary School, Macon, GA

Salute our country's past and future greats! Using the patterns on page 55, enlarge and cut out silhouettes of Lincoln and Washington. With the help of an adult volunteer, have each student create a silhouette cutout of himself. Mount the title and silhouettes as shown. Discuss the achievements of our country's past greats, then invite students to share their future aspirations. Now that's impressive!

Jean Hawkinson—Gr. 3, Mosel-Lakeview School, Howards Grove, WI

Get to the heart of the matter with this eye-catching display. Have each student copy and complete the following sentence on a white construction-paper heart: "I put my heart into _____ because _____." Then—using construction paper, crayons or markers, glue, and a variety of other arts-and-crafts supplies (such as lace, glitter, sequins, feathers, and ribbon)—students decorate their heart cutouts as desired. How sweet it is!

Vickie Genovese, Parkside Elementary, Solon, OH

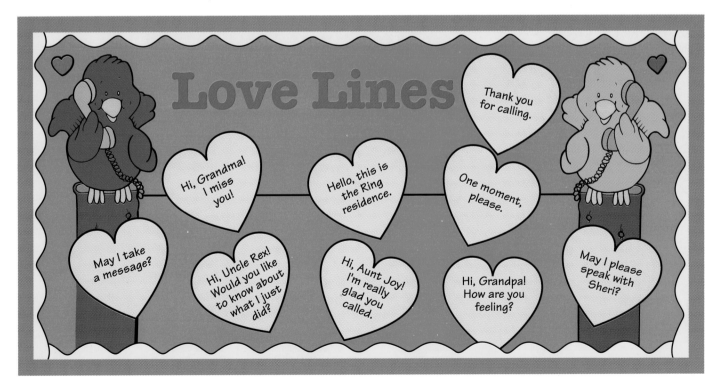

Ring in a collection of heartfelt messages as you promote well-mannered telephone conversations. Follow up a lesson about proper phone etiquette by having each youngster write a well-mannered telephone phrase on a construction-paper heart. Mount the cutouts and characters (pattern on page 27) as shown. For added appeal, use coiled pipe cleaners for the telephone cords and a length of yarn or cord for the telephone wire. "May I ask who is calling?"

Diane Fortunato—Gr. 2, Carteret School, Bloomfield, NJ

Creating this March display is a real breeze! Have each child cut out and personalize a cloud shape. Mount the character, cloud cutouts, and title. Add yarn lengths as desired; then invite students to exhibit their finest work near their cutouts as shown. To keep the display current, encourage students to replace their work as frequently as desired. The forecast for spring is a steady breeze of success.

Lisa Borgo, Gould Avenue School, North Caldwell, NJ

Check out these one-of-a-kind rainbows! Duplicate student copies of the rainbow pattern on page 28. Each student writes his name inside a cloud; then on each band of the rainbow, he writes one or more self-describing adjectives. After he has verified that his adjectives are spelled correctly, he traces over them using a black, fine-tipped marker. Then, using crayons, he colors the rainbow before he cuts out his project. For added razzle-dazzle, have each youngster use a silver glitter pen to outline his cloud and trace over his name.

Diane Fortunato—Gr. 2, Carteret School, Bloomfield, NJ

Motivate students to read, read, read at this one-of-a-kind library! To make each bookshelf, position and attach a strip of black bulletin–board paper as shown. Near the display keep a supply of colorful construction-paper strips in a variety of widths and lengths. After reading a book, a youngster writes his name and the title of the book he read on a strip. He then mounts the strip on the display. Read on!

Vallery McLaughlin, Charles Haskell Elementary, Edmond, OK

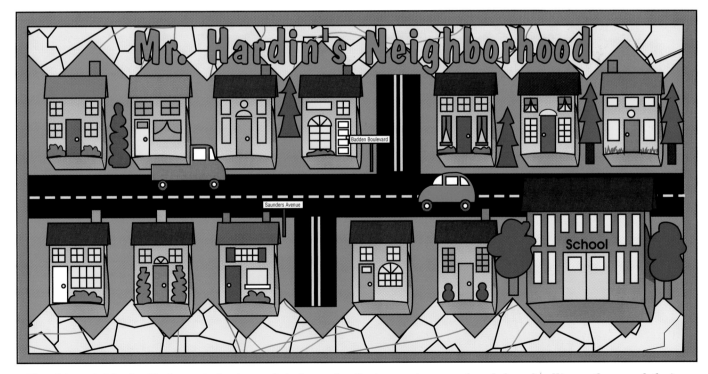

For this neighborly display, students work independently to create paper lunch-bag dwellings, then pool their projects to create a neighborhood. To make a dwelling, partially fill a lunch bag with crumpled newspaper; then fold down and staple the top of the bag closed before decorating the dwelling as desired. Use the same technique to create a schoolhouse from a large-size paper bag that has been spray-painted red. Name the neighborhood for your school principal and use teachers' names for streets. For added fun, cut the border from a discarded road map.

Emily Navidad—Art Educator, Morganton Road Elementary School, Fayetteville, NC

Who knows? Your youngsters' career goals may "egg-ceed" your greatest "eggs-pectations"! Using a variety of art-and-craft materials, have students decorate large egg-shaped cutouts to illustrate their future career goals. Mount the resulting projects and title for all to enjoy.

Chantelle Lockwood, Urbana, OH

Make a splash with this poetry-writing activity and display! Have each student write a poem about rain on a sheet of raindrop-shaped writing paper. Next have each student mount his project atop light blue paper, then trim the colored paper to create an eye-catching border. Mount the title, character, puddle, and raindrop projects as shown. It's the perfect project for a rainy day!

Diane Fortunato—Gr. 2, Carteret School, Bloomfield, NJ

Invite students to lend a hand in preserving the earth! Each student colors and cuts out a copy of the earth pattern on page 29. The student also traces one hand atop a sheet of colorful construction paper; then he cuts out and programs the resulting shape with an earth-friendly tip. Mount the hand cutouts around a large globe cutout. Display a snapshot of each child atop his earth cutout. The title says it all—"Earth: It's In Our Hands!"

Mary Jo Kampschnieder—Gr. 2, Howells Community Catholic, Howells, NE

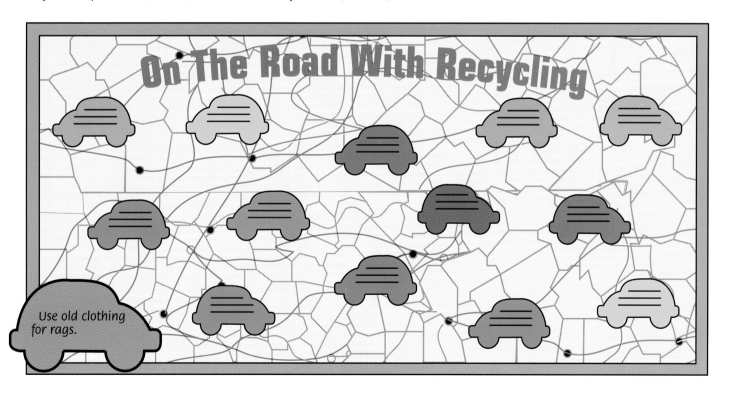

Take a recycling road trip! Cover a display area with discarded road maps and mount the title. Using the pattern on page 29, duplicate a supply of colorful construction-paper cars. Each student cuts out a pattern and writes a recycling suggestion on the resulting car shape. Ask each child to share his recycling tip before you mount his cutout on the display. Vroooom!

Gina Parisi—Gr. 2, Demarest School, Bloomfield, NJ

This eye-catching display may be just the bait to lure your youngsters into unlimited writing practice. Using the patterns on page 27, duplicate, laminate, and cut out a supply of colorful fish. Arrange the fish cutouts on a decorated bulletin board as shown. Using a wipe-off marker, label the fish with student-generated writing topics. Invite youngsters to visit the topic tank and hook up with writing topics at their leisure. When desired, wipe away the programming and brainstorm another fine catch of topics.

Melissa Miller—Gr. 1, Bart-Colerain Elementary, Christiana, PA

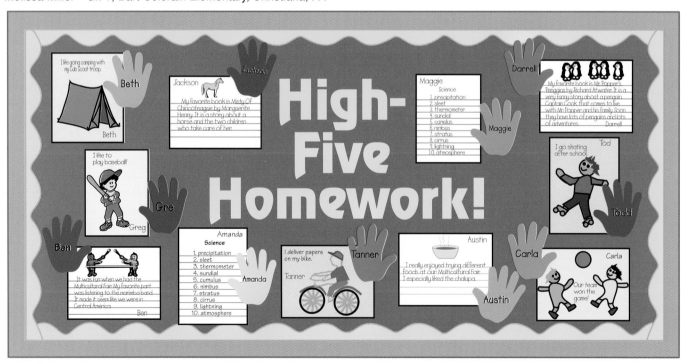

This hip display is sure to create enthusiasm for homework. Enlist the help of your youngsters in preparing a supply of high-five cutouts. To do this, have students trace their hands atop sheets of construction paper and cut out the resulting shapes. When a student's homework merits extra recognition, attach his paper to the display with a personalized high-five cutout. For added fun, give the youngster a high-five yourself!

Diane Fortunato—Gr. 2, Carteret School, Bloomfield, NJ

This May encourage students to set their sights on whatever their hearts desire with this unique display. On a large square of colorful paper, have each student complete the sentence, "One day, just MAYbe...." Have students trim their papers to resemble flower blossoms. Mount the blossoms atop crepe-paper stems and leaves to create a spectacular flower garden!

Debbie Wiggins, North Myrtle Beach Primary, North Myrtle Beach, SC

With a few seeds of encouragement, youngsters can grow a colorful garden of literary accomplishments. Duplicate a supply of construction-paper flowers using the pattern on page 30. Each time a student reads a book, he completes the information on a duplicated flower. Then he uses markers or crayons to add desired details, cuts out the flower, and attaches it to the display. How nice!

adapted from an idea by Diana Curtis, Albuquerque, NM

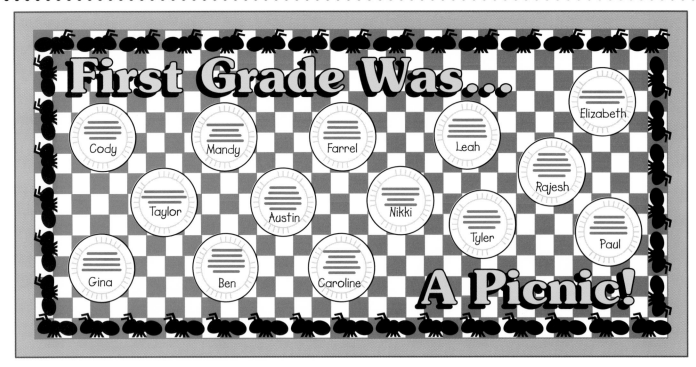

Here's an end-of-the-year display that's sure to create quite a stir! Have each student personalize and program a thin white paper plate with a favorite memory from the past school year. Mount the plates on a checkered backdrop. Add the title and a border of student-designed ants. Now that's a picnic!

Holly L. Davis—Gr. 1, Rural Retreat Elementary, Rural Retreat, VA

Here's a fun way to showcase your youngsters' accomplishments. Mount the title and a decorated clown cutout similar to the one shown. (For a three-dimensional effect, attach a partially inflated red-balloon nose.) On construction-paper circles, have students write sentences describing their greatest achievements of the school year. Attach the programmed cutouts to the clown's bow tie. Isn't a round of applause in order for this outstanding performance?

Jana Jensen, Gillette, WY

Pattern
Use with "Things Go Better With Team-
work!" on page 4 and "Our Class Is Not
Complete Without You" on page 5.

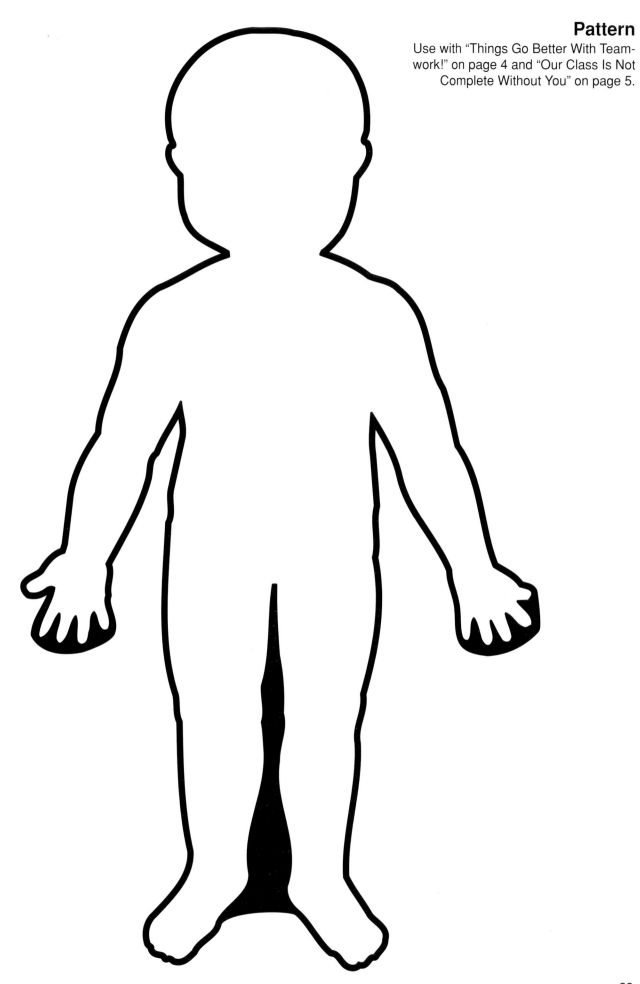

Patterns
Use with " 'Hippo-Ray!' It's Someone's Birthday!" on page 5.

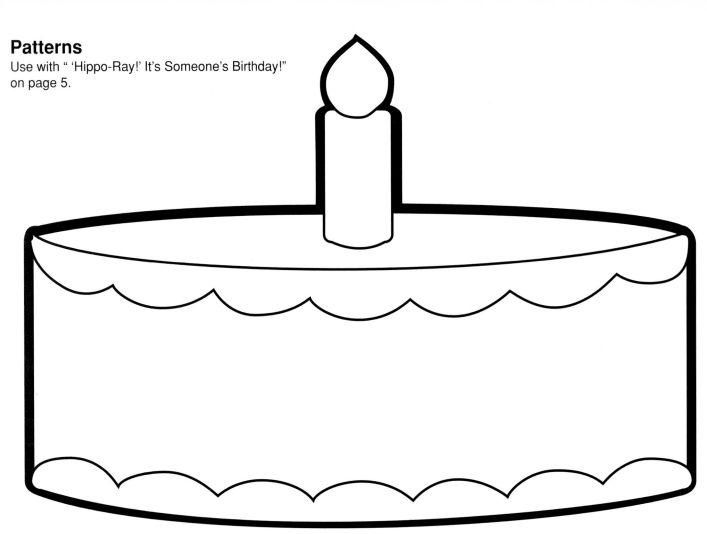

Use with "Parents Are Special!" on page 6.

Use with "We're Working
Ourselves…" on page 8.

Patterns

Use leaves with " 'Tree-mendously' Thankful Thoughts!" on page 9.

Use dreidels with "We're Tops!" on page 10.

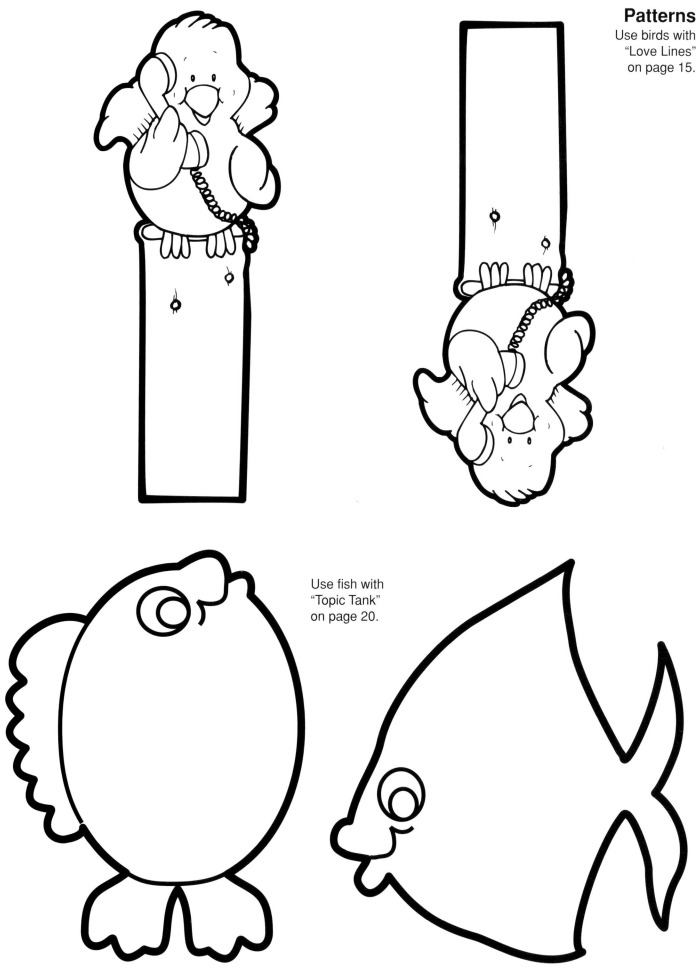

Patterns
Use birds with
"Love Lines"
on page 15.

Use fish with
"Topic Tank"
on page 20.

Pattern

Use with "One-Of-A-Kind
Rainbows!" on page 16
and "A Trail Of Sham-
rocks" on page 63.

Use with "Earth: It's In Our Hands!" on page 19.

Pattern

Use with "Bloomin' Good Books!" on page 21.

Title: _____

Author: _____

I think the best part of the story was _____

_____

_____

_____.

This book was read by

_____.

Arts & Crafts

Foil Collage

For lots of razzle-dazzle, get creative with food coloring, glue, and foil. To make this project, crumple a piece of aluminum foil; then flatten it, leaving it somewhat crinkled. Add a few drops of food coloring to each of several small containers of white glue. Brush a thin, even coat of several colors of tinted glue onto the foil, occasionally allowing the colors to mix. Allow the glue to dry overnight. Cut the foil into small bits and separate the bits by color. Glue the bits to a black construction-paper background in a collage of a distinctive shape. How's that for sparkle?

Cheryl Braida
St. Joseph/St. Mary School
Kingston, Ontario
Canada

Patchwork Elephant

Now who could forget seeing a patchwork elephant? Not many people! To begin, fold and crease a sheet of construction paper four times. Unfold the paper and confirm that the folds created 16 nearly equal sections. Draw lines as indicated in the diagram; then cut on the lines for an elephant shape. Decorate each of the remaining areas (sectioned off by fold lines) differently. Trim the rectangular scrap to make the elephant's ear, and decorate it before gluing it in place. Glue on a gray paper tail. Use a marker to add an eye, and tie some yarn around the elephant's trunk. When displayed prominently at home, these elephants may serve as gentle reminders to students about homework assignments. Don't forget! There's a little homework to do.

Jane B. Buggs—Gr. 2
St. Mary's School
Janesville, WI

Mouth-Watering Nametags

These tasteful three-dimensional nametags are hard to overlook! Using the pattern on page 50, make two tagboard tracers: one of the entire pattern and one of the center portion only. To make a nametag, fold in half a 9" x 12" sheet of green construction paper and an eight-inch square of red construction paper. Trace the larger pattern on the green paper and the smaller pattern on the red paper. Cut on the resulting outlines. Next sandwich the green cutout between the red cutout by aligning the fold and cut lines; then glue the two together. Personalize and decorate both sides of the project. To complete the project, fold the tabs inward and glue one tab atop the other. When the glue is dry, adjust the folds as needed so that the resulting nametag is freestanding. Tape each student's nametag to his desk.

Jolene Pennington—Grs. 1 & 2 , Hutton School, Chanute, KS

Back-To-School Banners

Weave these personalized banners into your back-to-school festivities! To begin, fold a 12" x 18" sheet of construction paper in half, widthwise. Use your ruler to draw a faint line approximately 1 1/2 inches from the open end; then cut a series of 1 1/2-inch-wide wavy lines from the fold to the pencil line. Unfold the resulting loom and set it aside. Next draw a set of 1 1/2-inch-wide wavy lines across the width of another 12" x 18" sheet of construction paper. Number the strips and cut them apart. Then tightly weave the strips through the loom in order. On the last strip that will fit in the loom, trim one side to a straight edge. (See the illustration.) Discard the extra strips and glue the ends of each woven strip in place. To personalize the banner, trace and cut out the letters needed from a third color of construction paper. Glue the letters in a pleasing arrangement on the woven banner.

Dr. Pamela Amick Klawitter—Gifted Instructor
Mt. Nebo, WV

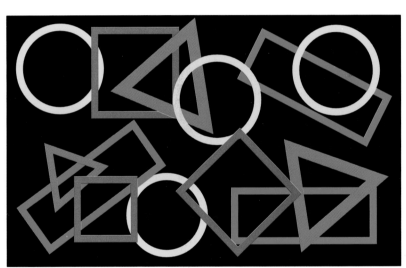

Spectacular Shapes

Watch abstract artwork take shape before your very eyes with this nifty project. Cut each of the following shapes from a different color of construction paper: square, rectangle, circle, equilateral triangle. To begin, fold the square cutout in half. Then, cutting into the fold, cut a slightly smaller shape from the folded paper. Continue in this manner until the center of the fold is reached. Unfold the resulting shapes and set them aside. Repeat this entire procedure with each of the remaining cutouts. Then glue the collection of shapely cutouts on a 9" x 12" sheet of black construction paper in an overlapping fashion. Colorful and spectacular!

Showy Sunflowers

Big and bold, these striking sunflower projects create a stunning display! Begin by cutting a six-inch circle from white construction paper. Using brown tempera paint, sponge-paint the resulting cutout and set it aside. Trace and cut out approximately 30 petal shapes from yellow paper. (If desired, use the patterns on page 51 to create tagboard templates for this purpose.) Glue a row of petals side by side around the back edge of the circle cutout. Glue a second row of petals behind the first, so that their tips can be seen between the existing row. Repeat a third time. To give the project dimension, fold some of the petals forward. Glue a long stem cut from green paper onto the back of the flower; then glue a desired number of leaf cutouts along the stem. Showcase the giant flowers side by side on a bulletin board or wall for an eye-catching garden display.

Rita Andreu—Gr. 3
Sabal Palm Elementary
Ponte Vedra, FL

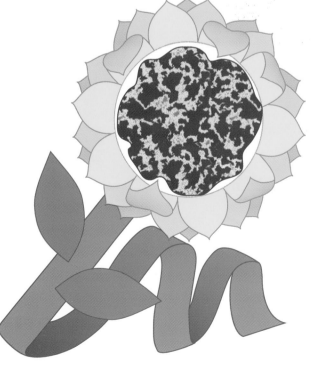

Tree Weavings

Weave some red, orange, and yellow into green paper foliage to bring the first touches of autumn color into your classroom. To make one of these trees, begin by cutting a sheet of green construction paper to resemble the foliage of a deciduous tree. Fold this paper cutout in the middle. Use a ruler to draw parallel lines from the fold to within an inch of the opposite edges of the paper, spacing the lines about one-half inch apart. Cut on the lines; then unfold the paper. Weave 1/2" x 9" strips of red, orange, and yellow paper through the slits in the green paper. Glue the strips' ends to the green paper before trimming away any unattached parts of the strips. Use glue to attach a brown construction-paper trunk cutout to the woven foliage.

Vicki Smith, Murfreesboro, TN

Seasonal Sparklers

These sparklers are sure to dazzle everyone who catches a glimpse of them. To make a sparkler, arrange and press small squares of colored tissue paper between two 6-inch squares of clear Con-Tact® covering. Fold a 6" x 12" sheet of construction paper in half to make a square. Trace a seasonal design (the leaf or pumpkin design from page 51, for example) onto the square. Then, cutting through both thicknesses, cut out the shape. When the shape has been cut away, unfold the remaining frame and cover it with a thin layer of glue. Refold the frame, sandwiching the Con-Tact® covered tissue paper between the two halves. Display these sparklers on classroom windows or other lighted glass surfaces.

Julia Elsen
Thatcher, AZ

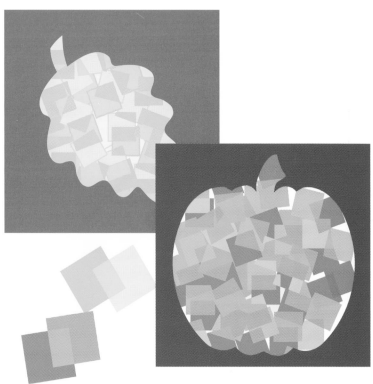

Paper Strip Jack-o'-Lantern

Create jack-o'-lanterns a bit differently this year! To begin, arrange eight orange paper strips (9" x 1/4") as shown on a sheet of black construction paper. Then cut facial features and a stem from scrap paper. Glue the cutouts in place to finish the project. Why are you grinning, Mr. Jack-o'-Lantern?

Kathryn Arena—Gr. 2

"Boo-tiful" Windsock

Want to create an eerie spectacle in your October classroom? These ghostly windsocks may be just what you're looking for. To make a hanger for a windsock, poke a hole in the bottom center of a white paper bag. Tie one end of a yarn length to a paper clip; then insert the other end into the hole from inside the bag. Pull the yarn to the outside of the bag, and loop and knot it. Position the bag so that the hanger is at the top. Flatten the bag; then glue on paper facial features and scallop the bag's opening. Glue eight 12" x 3/4" tissue-paper strips to the inside of the scalloped opening. Hang these windsocks from the ceiling for all to enjoy the specter of poltergeists as they eerily bob and billow in the autumn breeze.

Kathryn Arena—Gr. 2
Steven's Creek Elementary
Martinez, GA

Marvelous Masks

It's the time of year when youngsters are eager to hide their identities behind all kinds of masks. Capitalize on this interest with a mask-making project. To make a mask, begin with a paper-plate half. For the nose area of the mask, cut a v-shaped piece from the center of the straight side. Also cut two eyeholes in the half-plate. Using paint, sequins, feathers, drawings, glitter, buttons, beads, ribbon, yarn, seeds, and other available supplies, decorate the mask. To hold the mask in place, staple the ends of a length of elastic to the sides of the mask. Or glue a tongue depressor or dowel-half perpendicular to the mask so that the mask can be easily held in front of the face.

Jeanine Davy, Immaculate Conception School, Lake Charles, LA

Bat Mobiles

Your classroom will have more bats than a belfry when these mobiles are flitting to and fro in schoolroom breezes. Without changing the shape of the hook or the bottom part, gently bend both sides of a coat hanger downward. Place the hanger near the upper edge of a half-sheet of black tissue paper. Squeeze a thin trail of glue around the hanger; then fold up the lower half of the tissue paper sheet to cover the hanger. Press lightly so the glue will grip the paper all the way around the hanger. The following day, trim the excess paper from the hanger. For wings, glue a few tissue paper strips on each side of the hanger. Complete the mobile by gluing on additional paper features.

To vary this idea, bend a coat hanger into a ghostlike shape. Using a whole sheet of white tissues paper, complete the ghost similarly to the bat.

Cecile Shelter—Gr. 3
Louisiana State University Laboratory School
Baton Rouge, LA

Wad-A-Bodies

How do you transform a wadded-up piece of paper into a work of art? Follow these steps. To make a wad-a-body turkey, wad a 16-inch square of paper into a ball as before. Glue colorful feather cutouts to what will be the back of the turkey. Then cut out and glue on paper wings, legs, and feet. (Patterns are provided on page 52.) Create the turkey's wattle and beak in a similar manner using construction-paper scraps. To finish the turkey, attach adhesive dots for the eyes or glue on construction-paper circles.

Andrea Grubbs Scott—Gr. 2
Walker Elementary School
Springdale, AR

Great Gobblers

Making these tremendous turkeys is a great follow-up to a fall leaf hunt. To make a turkey, cut a large circle from brown construction paper and a small circle from yellow construction paper. Then cut turkey feet from yellow construction paper (pattern on page 52) and a wattle from red construction paper. Use crayons to add facial features to the yellow circle (head) before gluing it to the brown circle (body). Attach the feet and wattle with glue. Complete the turkey by taping real leaves to the back of the brown circle for feathers.

Ruth Foss
Victor Haen Elementary
Kaukauna, WI

Squirrel's Nest

If your youngsters get a kick out of watching squirrels collect acorns, they'll have a lot of fun creating these squirrelly critters. To make an imitation squirrel's nest, begin by rolling down the top of a brown paper bag about two-thirds of the way. Color a white construction-paper copy of the squirrel on page 53, and cut it out along the bold lines. Fold the cutout along the dotted lines so that the squirrel will be two-sided and self-standing. Tape or glue the flaps that are below the squirrel's body to the inside bottom of the bag. Tape or glue leaves to cover the exterior of the bag, and place additional leaves inside the bag around the squirrel. Put a few acorns around the squirrel to represent his personal winter stash.

Peg Meehan, Narragansett, RI

Colorful Corn

This year harvest a bumper crop of colorful Indian corn! Begin with a white construction-paper copy of the patterns on page 54. Using crayons, randomly color blue, purple, red, black, and brown kernels on each ear of corn; then color the remaining kernels different shades of yellow and orange. Cut out the ears of corn and set them aside. Open a brown paper lunch sack. Cut along the side seam; then cut away the bottom of the bag. Fold the resulting rectangle into thirds. Sketch a corn husk on the folded paper and cut on the outline. Slightly crumple the three resulting corn-husk shapes.

To assemble the project, stack the ears of corn. Place two corn husks on the bottom of the stack and one on top. Hold the lower edges of the cutouts together as you slightly fan the tops. When the desired look is achieved, staple the lower edges in place. If desired, fashion a bow from brown paper scraps or raffia, and glue it to the project as shown.

Robin Woodson—Gr. 3, James Poole Elementary, Gilmer, TX

Turkey Sun Catchers

You'll hear lots of ooohs and aaahs from your students as they create these grand gobblers. To make a turkey's tail feathers, begin by coloring a coffee filter with watercolor markers. Fold the filter in half four times. Immerse the point of the folded filter into a bowl of water and watch as the water seeps upward, bleeding the colors. Unfold the filter and set it aside to dry. Cut a turkey body from a brown construction-paper copy of the pattern on page 52. Glue it to the dried filter along with feet, a beak, eyes, and a wattle cut from construction paper. Personalize the turkey if desired.

Laura A. Silver—Gr. 1
Oxford Central School
Oxford, NJ

Native American Moments

If your youngsters are learning about Native American culture, then this art project is an open-ended culminating activity you won't want to miss. Ask each youngster to recall one group of Native Americans to feature in his artwork. Help him in recalling the lay of the land on which this group lives or previously lived. Encourage him to recall the types of shelters and activities that were (are) indicative of the Native Americans that he has chosen. Then guide each student in developing a collage.

In preparation for making a collage, thin glue with water. Brush the thinned glue onto a large sheet of art paper. Place strips of tissue paper on the glue so that they overlap, creating a sky-and-landscape background. Brush on more thinned glue if necessary. Cut dwellings, people, and other objects from construction paper and glue them on top of the tissue-paper background. If desired, crayon or marker details can be added to the collage when it dries. Your students will love the vivid results!

Rebecca English—Gr. 2
Dawson County Primary School
Dawsonville, GA

Arts & Crafts

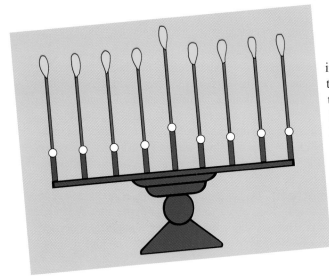

Warm Reminder

Crafted by little hands, this menorah project casts an especially warm, inviting light during Hanukkah. In preparation for making a menorah, position a sheet of construction paper horizontally and draw a centered horizontal line about two-thirds of the way down a sheet of construction paper. Extending upward from the line, draw nine evenly spaced, short, vertical lines, making the fifth one a bit longer than the others. Attach a sticky dot at the upper end of each vertical line. Use a marker to draw a base beneath the horizontal line to complete the menorah. For imitation candles, trim one swab from each of nine Q-tips®. Color each swab stick with a marker; then dip each swab in yellow paint. When the paint has dried, glue each swab to the menorah to resemble a candle. The cheerful glow of this menorah is a warm reminder of the great miracle it represents.

Ellen M. Stern—Gr. 1, Alberta Smith Elementary, Midlothian, VA

Watercolor Wonders

Create a gallery of eye-catching holiday artwork with this quick watercolor technique. For a Christmas tree, practice making a single long stroke near the bottom of your paper with a watercolor-filled, soft pointed brush. This stroke will be the widest part of the tree. From there use the brush to quickly make zigzagging lines that diminish in length as they near the top of the page. Clean and refill the brush before adding the tree trunk and before using the brush to add small droplets of watercolor for multicolored lights. Practice making this tree several times, if desired, before making your final version on art paper. Mount the artwork on contrasting paper.

Vary the use of this technique to create a bright dreidel. Begin by making one long angled stroke. Then make quick zigzag strokes, working downward at an angle to a point. Clean and refill the brush before making the post of the dreidel with a single stroke.

Diana Curtis
John Baker Elementary School
Albuquerque, NM

Festive Wreath

Spruce up your classroom for the holidays with wrapping-paper wreaths. In a parent note, request that each youngster bring to school several scraps of holiday gift wrap and one large bow. You will also need one paper plate and three red pom-poms per student. To make a wreath, cut the center out of a paper plate. Using a tagboard tracer, trace and cut out 15 to 20 holly leaves (patterns on page 54) from gift wrap. Glue the cutouts around the rim of the plate. When the rim is covered with "greenery," glue on three red pom-poms for berries. Add a bow as a cheery finishing touch.

Jeri Daugherity—Gr. 1
Mother Seton School
Emmitsburg, MD

Peppermint Reindeer

It may be made of paper, but this reindeer projects looks so perky that you can practically smell the peppermint. Trace a candy cane shape onto a 12" x 18" sheet of white construction paper. Cut out the shape; then use a crayon or a marker to add stripes. For the reindeer's antlers, trace the shapes of your hands onto brown construction paper, and cut on the outlines. Glue the hand cutouts to the back of the cane cutout. For a nose, glue on a glittered construction-paper circle or a pom-pom. Add an eye to complete the reindeer.

Cheryl S. Johnsen—Gr. 3
East Elementary
Monroe, NC

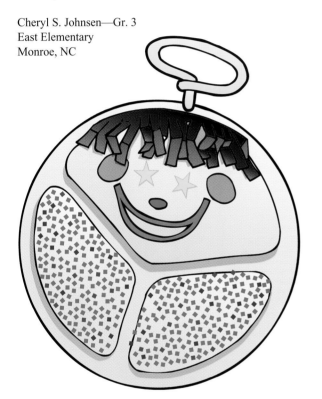

Glittering Angels

Set your room aglow with these cheerful cherubs. Spray paint the bottom a divided paper plate, if desired, before beginning this project. For eyes, attach two large foil stars to the biggest section of the plate bottom. With markers or paint pens, add a smile, rosy cheeks, and a nose beneath the eyes. For hair, crumple fringed construction paper or pull apart pastel cotton balls, and glue them in place. Spread glue on each remaining section of the plate. Sprinkle glitter onto the wet glue. Bend a pipe cleaner to make a halo. Then poke one end of the pipe cleaner through the back of the project at the hairline, and twist it to hold the halo in place.

Marcia Miller
Merritt Elementary
Mt. Iron, MN

Darling Deer

Although your youngsters will want to create an entire herd of reindeer, the most popular one will likely be the most famous reindeer of all—Rudolph! To make a reindeer, begin by folding two sheets of light brown paper in half vertically. Cut one piece of construction paper to create a large heart shape when the paper is unfolded. Turn the heart upside down for the reindeer's head. Then similarly cut two smaller heart shapes from the remaining folded construction paper. Glue these hearts to the back of the head for ears. Fold a darker piece of construction paper in half, cut the paper to create antlers, and glue the antlers behind the reindeer's ears. Embellish this basic reindeer form with paper or button eyes, a circular nose, a drawn-on expression, a tissue-paper topknot, and cutouts to resemble a sprig of holly. Is it just my imagination, or can you actually hear the prancing and pawing of dozens of hooves?

D. Hautala—Gr. 3
Washington Elementary School
Ely, MN

First-Fruits Necklace

Kwanzaa is the African-American holiday reminiscent of traditional African harvests. Since the word Kwanzaa comes from a Swahili term meaning "first fruits," celebrate Kwanzaa this year by making first-fruits necklaces. To make a necklace, cut out three different fruit shapes from red construction paper and three more from green construction paper. From black paper, cut out the shape of Africa. Punch a hole near the tops of all seven shapes. If necessary, refer to a book such as *Kwanzaa* by Dorothy Rhodes Freeman and Dianne M. MacMillan (Enslow Publishers, Inc.) for the African terms, their translations, and the sequence in which they are introduced. Then write one of the principles of Kwanzaa and its translation on each of the seven shapes, putting the African term on one side and its translation on the other. (Since the first principle goes on the black cutout of Africa, either write the first principle and its translation with a white crayon or write them on small pieces of white paper and glue them on.) Tape the ends of a length of thick, black yarn to prevent raveling. Then, in the order shown, thread the labeled shapes onto the yarn along with red, green, and black beads or dyed pasta. Tie the ends of the yarn together, and wear the first-fruits necklace with pride.

The Seven Principles Of Kwanzaa

Umoja—unity
Kujichagulia—being yourself
Ujima—helping one another

Ujamaa—sharing
Nia—having a goal
Kuumba—being creative

Imani—believing

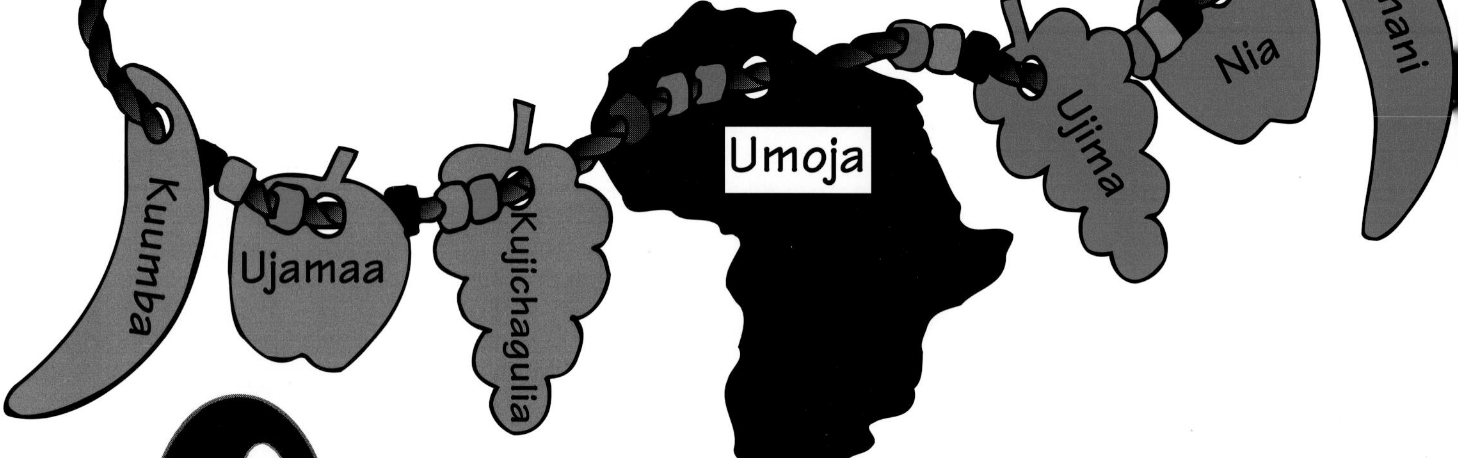

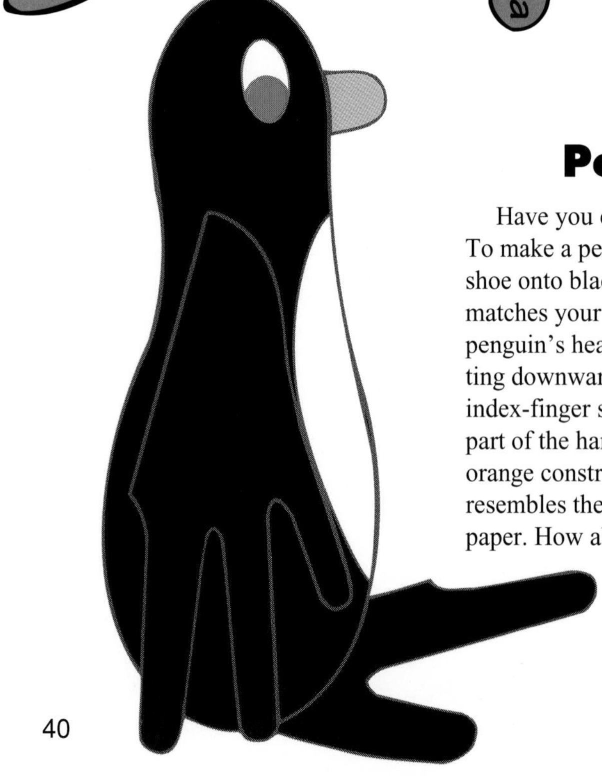

Penguins With A Personal Touch

Have you ever had a personal connection with a penguin? No? Well, here's your chance! To make a penguin, begin by tracing the outline of your hand (fingers outstretched) and your shoe onto black construction paper. Cut along the resulting outlines. Position the cutout that matches your shoe's sole so that the heel of the tracing is at the top and will represent the penguin's head. Use white chalk to color the penguin's belly. Split the hand cutout by cutting downward between the index and middle fingers. Glue the part with the thumb and index-finger shapes to the penguin's body so that it resembles its foot. Attach the remaining part of the hand cutout to the body to represent a flipper. Trace the end of your thumb onto orange construction paper. Cut on the outline and glue the cutout to the penguin so that it resembles the penguin's beak. Finish this proper penguin by attaching an eye fashioned from paper. How about that? You now have a personal connection with a penguin!

Melissa Raleigh—Gr. 1
Whittier Elementary School
Amarillo, TX

Parka Pals

When the temperature drops, slip into this parka project and watch students' interest go up and up. To make a parka pal, trace a circle template that's seven inches in diameter onto skin-toned paper. Cut on the resulting outline. Using markers, glue, scissors, construction paper, and assorted art supplies, decorate the circle to resemble your face. Glue the circle to a paper plate; then glue cotton balls along the outer rim of the plate. Trim to round two corners of a 9" x 12" sheet of construction paper, and draw two lines as shown to indicate the arms of the jacket. Glue this paper to the back of the plate. Complete this project by attaching buttons and/or cotton balls to finish the parka. It's cold outside, but you'd never know it snuggled deep down in your parka!

Deborah Burleson
Silverdale, WA

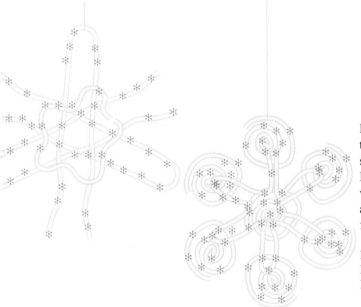

Snowflakes From Spaghetti

Follow these steps to create a flurry of colorful snowflakes. Pour an ample amount of white (or pastel-tinted) glue into a pie tin. Then, working atop a sheet of waxed paper, dip each of several cooked and cooled spaghetti noodles into the glue. Position the noodles in an abstract snowflake shape atop the waxed paper. Sprinkle your completed project with silver glitter and let it dry overnight. If desired suspend the shimmering flakes from the ceiling on lengths of monofilament line. Let it snow!

Karen Lyon—Gr. 1
Lenoir City Elementary
Lenoir City, TN

Dr. King Mobile

Keep Dr. Martin Luther King's dream alive with these patriotic mobiles. To make a mobile, glue a 5 1/2-inch, red construction-paper circle in the center of a 9-inch white paper plate. Color and cut out a copy of the Dr. King pattern on page 56; then glue the cutout in the center of the red circle. Use a blue marker or crayon to outline the rim of the plate as shown and to draw a large cloud shape on a 9" x 12" sheet of white construction paper. Cut out the cloud shape; then write a dream(s) for our world inside the shape. Hole-punch two holes in the top and bottom of the paper-plate project and in the top of the cloud shape. Thread a 12-inch length of red yarn through the holes at the top of the plate and tie the yarn ends. To connect the cloud cutout to the paper plate, thread a 12-inch length of red yarn through the remaining holes; then tie the yarn ends.

My Dream
I dream that the children in Bosnia will have peace.
I dream that the children in Haiti will have clean water.
by Sarah

Barbara S. Johnson—Gr. 1, Greensboro Primary School, Greensboro, GA

Arts & Crafts

Famous Folks

Get to the heart of the matter with this presidential project. Duplicate the patterns on page 55 onto black construction paper; then cut out each presidential profile. Mount each cutout on a 6" x 8" white construction-paper rectangle. Stack the rectangles and trim the edges to create two equal-sized ovals. Mount each oval on a 7" x 9" rectangle of blue paper. Trim each blue rectangle to create an eye-catching border. Cut a large heart shape from a 12" x 18" sheet of red construction paper; then mount one project on each side of the heart cutout. Punch a hole near the top of the project and suspend it from the ceiling.

Judy Goodman
Perryville Elementary
Perryville, MO

Heart To Heart

These valentine keepsakes will surely help youngsters win the hearts of those they love. To make a heart-shape wreath, mix 1/4 cup of school glue with one teaspoon of water; then add 3/4 cup of mixed dried beans. Mold the bean mixture into the shape of a heart on a sheet of waxed paper. When the glue has completely dried, remove the heart-shaped wreath from the waxed paper and spray it with clear acrylic spray. Embellish the completed bean wreath with a ribbon bow.

Tami Fedor—Gr. 1, Lenoir City Elementary, Lenoir City, TN

Haven Of Hearts

Why wait until spring to convert your classroom into a garden-like haven? Enlist the help of your youngsters in gathering a variety of papers and foils for cultivating these fancy flowers. To make a flower, cut out several heart shapes of various sizes from selected papers and/or foils. Decorate some of the cutouts using glitter glue pens, lace, and other craft supplies. Then arrange the heart cutouts into a flower blossom before gluing them in place. If desired, fold some of the hearts in half and glue sparingly along the folds so that the hearts retain a partially folded and dimensional effect. Attach a stem and leaves to complete the project. When the flower designs are dry, display them in clusters around your room.

Beth Jones—Grs. 1 & 2, General Vanier School, Niagara Falls, Ontario, Canada

Hearts Aflutter

These wings of love are just a heartbeat away! To make a butterfly, fold in half a 12" x 18" sheet of red, pink, or purple construction paper. Unfold the paper. Working atop newspaper, place several dollops of white tempera paint on one half of the paper. Refold the paper and gently rub the top of the folded paper with your open palm. Unfold the paper. When the paint has dried, refold the paper. Using a template like the one shown, trace a large heart shape on the folded paper. Cut on the resulting outline and unfold the paper. Attach a construction-paper body and bent pipe-cleaner antennae. Now that's a flamboyant flyer!

Elizabeth McDonald
Lincoln Elementary
Wichita, KS

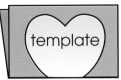

Arts & Crafts

Vivid Valentines

Pretty-as-can-be hearts are magically simple using this technique. Flatten a coffee filter. Fold the filter in half and cut a half-heart shape from it. Unfold the heart shape. Use watercolor markers to add some color to the cutout, intentionally leaving some spaces uncolored. Next place the heart on a stack of paper towels and use a spray bottle to lightly spray it with water. The colors will bleed randomly, creating interesting visual effects.

If desired, use a warm iron to press the heart cutout along with bits of tissue paper between two lengths of waxed paper. (Or use clear Con-Tact® covering.) Trim the waxed paper into a heart shape significantly larger than the filter heart. Use yarn or ribbon to suspend these translucent heart-shaped sparklers from the ceiling.

Lou Coakley—Gr. 3, Evans Elementary, Evans, GA

General George

Create a visual salute to General George Washington with this eye-catching project. To begin, trim the lower corners of a 6" x 9" sheet of pink paper for George's face. Fold an 8" x 6" sheet of white paper in half (to 4" x 6"); then cut an irregular shape through both thicknesses, creating two identical hair pieces. For George's hat, fold a 4" x 12" piece of dark blue paper to 4" x 6". Trim the unfolded end diagonally and cut a V-shaped notch as shown. Unfold the paper and glue a narrow strip of yellow paper to the hat cutout. Glue the face, hair, and hat patterns together. Use paper scraps and crayons to complete George's face and collar. By George, isn't that a dapper guy?

Audrey M. Brenholt—Gr. 1
Roselawn Elementary
Chetek, WI

Loopy The Lion

Here's an art project worth roaring about. On yellow construction paper, duplicate the lion pattern (page 56). To make a lion, cut out the pattern and glue on wrinkled brown paper strips for whiskers. Bend the ears forward where they connect to the head. For the lion's mane, you will need a dozen 1 1/4"x 8 1/2" orange paper strips. Glue together the ends of each strip without folding the strip. To complete the project, glue the strips' ends to the back of the lion's head. This project is a great follow-up activity for any lion-related book.

Chasing Rainbows

Have each of your youngsters welcome spring by fashioning his own double-sided rainbow. To make a rainbow, you will need a rainbow-shaped template. Trace the pattern onto white paper twice, creating two separate rainbow shapes. Using tempera paints in assorted rainbow colors, create two matching rainbows by painting each shape the same. When the paint has dried, cut out the shapes and position the cutouts side by side, painted sides down. Glue several crepe-paper streamers to the ends of each rainbow; then flip over one cutout and align it atop the other so that the painted surfaces are to the outside. Staple the cutouts together, leaving a generous opening at the top; then carefully tuck a desired amount of crumpled newspaper strips in the opening. When the project is sufficiently stuffed, staple the opening closed. Pull apart several cotton balls (or use polyester batting) and glue fluffy clouds at the ends of the rainbow. Suspend the rainbow from monofilament line and watch it dance and twirl in the springtime breezes.

Kimberly Spring—Grs. 2 & 3, Lowell Elementary, Everett, WA

Snakes Alive!

Legend has it that St. Patrick drove all the snakes from Ireland! Besides being fun to make, these colorful snakes are a great topic of conversation. So how did St. Patrick do that, anyway?

To begin, sketch the outline of a snake on a large sheet of white construction paper. Then—using colorful markers, tempera paints, chalks, or crayons—create a series of colorful patterns on the snake's body. Trace the outline of the snake with a black marker; then cut out the project and attach it—along with a piece of your best work—to a good-work display entitled "Snakes Alive! We've Outdone Ourselves!"

Peep! Peep!

You probably won't hear a peep out of your youngsters while they're busy crafting these spring chicks. To make a construction-paper chick, trace both hands and one large egg-shaped template on yellow paper. Cut out the resulting shapes. For movable wings, use brads to attach the hand cutouts as shown. Gently pull forward the finger and thumb portions of each hand cutout to add dimension. Cut two large eyes from white paper. Add pupils using a marker; then glue the eyes in place. For the chick's beak, fold an orange-paper square in half diagonally and glue it on. Also attach two orange-paper feet. Now that's an art project that's all it's clucked up to be!

Connie Carver—Gr. 1
St. Charles School
Parma, OH

I Can't Believe It's A Bunny!

Who would have thought an empty soda can would make such an interesting bunny? Practically no one. That's one of several reasons your youngsters will be happy to hop right into this unique project. To make a bunny, flatten an empty soft-drink can; then spray paint the can white. Using a small brush and black paint, paint inside the can opening. To highlight the bunny's mouth, trace the opening with a red permanent marker. Complete the bunny's facial features by using craft glue to attach wiggle eyes, tagboard teeth, and a pom-pom nose. Trim to round the corners of a narrow strip of white felt for the bunny's ears. Use craft glue to attach the center of the felt above the wiggle eyes. Glue a ribbon bow to the felt. Attach a cotton-ball tail to finish this fine bunny.

Susan M. Stires—Gr. 3, Alamo Elementary, Wichita Falls, TX

Cotton-Ball Beauties

Get ready for Easter with baskets full of pastel cotton balls serving as pretty Easter-egg impostors. To make a basket, fold a 12" x 18" sheet of construction paper in half to a 9" x 12" size. Fold the paper once more, so that the paper is now 6" x 9". On the folded paper, draw a design similar to the one shown. Cut along the lines, trimming through all thicknesses. Unfold the paper entirely. Cut one of the basket shapes so that when the basket is done its opening will be lower (and larger) than the other one. (See the diagram.) Glue narrow strips of fringed green paper so that the fringes will extend above each basket rim when the project is complete. Put glue around the perimeter of one basket shape; then fold the design in half, creating a two-sided basket with a pocketlike opening. Glue colorful cotton balls inside the opening, tucking them attractively among the fringed paper to resemble eggs nestled in grass.

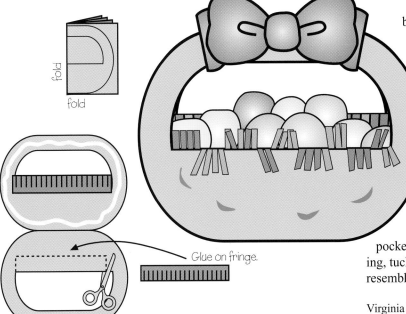

fold

fold

Glue on fringe.

Virginia Mozden, South Lincoln Elementary School, Alliance, OH

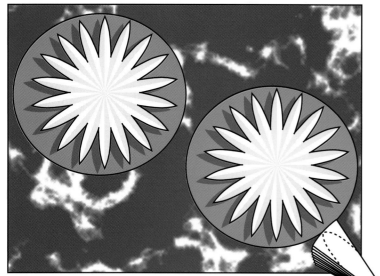

Water Lily Masterpieces

Expect lots of passersby to stop and admire these striking water lily projects. Nearly fill a large aluminum pan with water. Sparingly dribble a few drops of blue oil-base paint into the water. Use a craft stick to swirl the paint. Place a sheet of art paper on the surface of the water; then lift it from the water using tongs. When the paint has dried completely (which may be several days later depending on the paint and the humidity), cut irregular oval-like shapes from green construction paper. Glue the green shapes on the painted paper to represent water lilies. Fold a coffee filter in half repeatedly until it resembles a narrow wedge. Trim the wedge as shown. Unfold the filter, gather and twist it at the center bottom, and glue or staple it to a water lily. Add additional coffee-filter blooms as desired to complete the masterpiece.

Positively Perky Petals

Fill your classroom with these pretty posies for lots of springtime eye appeal. To begin making a flower, cut a 12" x 4 1/2" strip of green construction paper to resemble a flower's stem and leaves. Then color the center of a flattened muffin-tin liner. Place this liner atop two or three other flattened liners. Poke a brad through the muffin-tin liners and through the top of the paper stem. Spread the prongs of the brad to hold the liners in place. Cutting through all thicknesses of the liners, use scissors to repeatedly make snips about 1 1/2 inches in length. Then bend some of the resulting petals forward and "fluff" others to create the dimensional look of a blossom.

Ellen S. Keyster—Gr. 3
Princeville Grade School
Princeville, IL

Tissue-Paper Impressions

Small scraps of colored tissue paper make a big impact on these one-of-a-kind creations. Choose scraps of tissue paper with which to decorate a 5" x 8" sheet of white construction paper. Trim the scraps if necessary and arrange them on the paper. Using water and a small paintbrush, dampen each piece of tissue paper and gently press it into place. Then brush over the arrangement using a glaze of two parts white glue and one part water. When the paper is dry, mount it atop a 6" x 9" sheet of colorful construction paper.

Amy Butler Barsanti—Gr. 1
St. Hilda's and St. Hugh's School
New York, NY

Colorful Collectables

With a little creativity, it's easy to dish up this keepsake gift. Using permanent markers, decorate the face of a white plastic Rubbermaid® dinner plate (available at most department stores). Also sign and date the back of the plate. To seal the artwork, spray the face of the plate with a light coat of clear enamel. There you have it—a decorative plate to brighten Mom's kitchen.

Alice Elaine Fink—Gr. 3
Krebs Public School
Krebs, OK

Coffee-Filter Corsages

Here's a pretty, decorative corsage for a very special lady. Use colorful markers to embellish each of five paper coffee filters. Be creative—anything goes! Coloring a solid band around the rim of each filter adds a nice touch. Stack the decorated filters; then pinch together the bottoms as shown. Bend a five-inch length of green pipe cleaner in half. Slip the pinched portion of the filters between the open ends of the pipe cleaner. Tightly wrap a length of masking or floral tape around the pinched filters, securing the pipe cleaner in place. Carefully pull the coffee filters apart to open the flower. Someone is going to feel very proud to have this corsage pinned to her clothing!

Luddie Johnson
Lake Primary School
St. Amant, LA

Mom's Fan

What mom wouldn't be pleased to receive a pretty decorative fan from her biggest fan—her youngster? To make a fan, begin by accordion-folding a ten-inch square of wallpaper. (More advanced youngsters may glue lace around the perimeter of the wallpaper backing before folding.) Staple the folded wallpaper about one-third of the way up. Fan out both the upper and the lower sections of paper. Glue or staple the sides of the fan together as shown. Attach a ribbon loop to the back of the fan for hanging. Glue a small bow and perhaps a few sprigs of baby's breath on the front of the fan. It's a "fantastic" gift!

Donna Fischer—Gr. 3
Holy Rosary School
St. Marys, OH

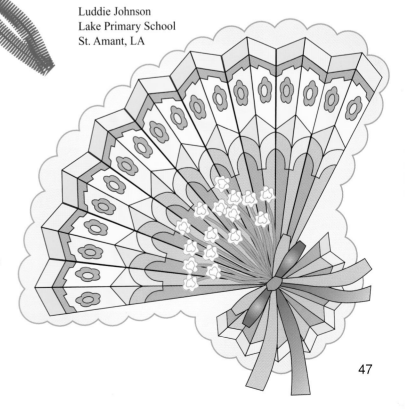

Arts & Crafts

All Aflutter!

These eye-catching butterflies can be created in just a flit and a flutter! Invert a small-size disposable soup bowl; then use colorful tempera paints to paint the bottom of the bowl. While the paint is drying, trim four 4 1/2" x 6" sheets of construction paper to resemble butterfly wings and two 2" x 4" strips of black construction paper to resemble butterfly antennae. Arrange the wing and antennae cutouts so that they achieve the desired results when the inverted bowl is in place. Glue together all overlapping surfaces of the wing and antennae cutouts, creating one large shape. Squeeze a trail of glue around the rim of the bowl; then invert the bowl on the construction-paper shape. Gently press on the bowl until the glue dries. Now that's a colorful flier!

Doris Hautala—Gr. 3
Washington Elementary
Ely, MN

Bask In The Glow

It's the time of year when everyone welcomes the warmth of the sun. Why not bring a bright-and-cozy aura into your classroom by having each student make a paper-plate sun? To make a sun, visualize an imaginative personified design and sketch it onto a paper plate. Then use crayons, markers, or tempera paints to "colorize" the design. To give your design radiant shine and sparkle, consider adding colored glues and clear glitter. Grab your shades! Here comes the sun!

Marsha Black & Michelle McAuliffe
Greensburg, IN

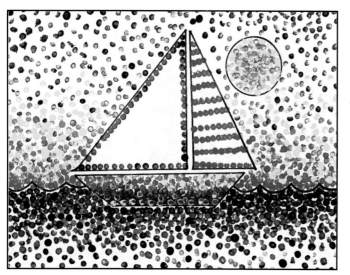

Dots By The Droves

Here's a dot. There's a dot. Everywhere there are dots—more dots! Most of the time an ordinary dot is not thought of as an art tool. But skillful artists have proven that the dot can be as powerful a force in artwork as can a brush stroke. Have your youngsters try their hands at artwork comprised of dots, called *pointillism*. To make a pointillistic picture, begin by drawing a simple design with a marker. Dip a cotton swab in tempera paint and repeatedly press the swab end onto the paper, filling an area of the design with dots. Use additional swabs and other colors of tempera paint to fill the remaining areas of the design. As you work, remember that—from a distance—dots that are placed closer together appear to create darker areas than dots of the same color that are more loosely scattered.

Joan Mary Macey—Art Teacher
Benjamin Franklin School
Binghamton, NY

48

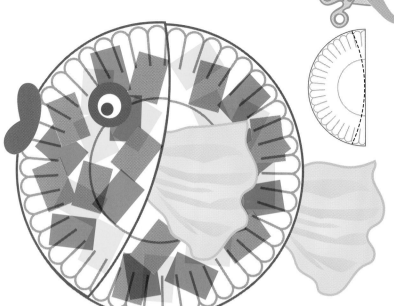

Fishy Fanfare

Decorate your room with a school of colorful fish. Trim half of a paper plate as shown; then invert it atop a regular-size paper plate. Align the outer edges, and staple or tape the two plates together to form the fish's body and gill. Cut a supply of one-inch squares from colorful tissue paper. Using diluted glue and a paint-brush, cover the body and gill with overlapping tissue-paper squares. Allow time for the project to dry. Then cut two seven-inch squares from tissue paper. Gather one end of each square. Tape the gathered end of one square to the back of the fish body for a tail. Tape the gathered end of the remaining square beneath the gill for a fin. Add an eye, a mouth, and other details to the fish using construction-paper scraps. What a catch!

Sunset Silhouettes

To make this impressive sunset, align an 8" x 11" piece of manila paper atop an 8" x 11" piece of white construction paper and staple the two top corners. At the bottom, tear off a narrow strip of the manila paper. Pressing heavily, draw a chalk line along the torn paper edge; then use a facial tissue to rub the chalk downward onto the exposed portion of the white paper. When this step has been completed, tear off another narrow strip of manila paper and repeat the process, using a different color of chalk and a clean portion of tissue. Continue in this manner until you have used the last strip of manila paper. Then remove the staples and the remaining manila paper. Smear the top chalk layer upward to cover any white space at the top of the page. Cut a desired silhouette from black paper and glue it on your colorful sunset. Mount the project on a 9" x 12" sheet of black construction paper.

Karen Saner—Grs. K–1, Burns Elementary School, Burns, KS

Family Ties

Father's Day flattery is on its way with these one-of-a-kind greetings! Begin by cutting a tie-shaped tracer from a 4 1/2" x 12" strip of tagboard. Trace this pattern onto a 4 1/2" x 12" strip of construction paper; then use crayons or markers to decorate the resulting shape. Cut out the tie shape. Then fold a 9" x 12" sheet of construction paper in half and glue the cutout to the front. Inside, use a marker to write a personalized message such as the one shown. Happy Father's Day!

Giovanna Anzelone—Gr. 3
Frank A. Sedita #38 School
Buffalo, NY

Nametag Pattern

Use with "Mouth-Watering Nametags" on page 32.

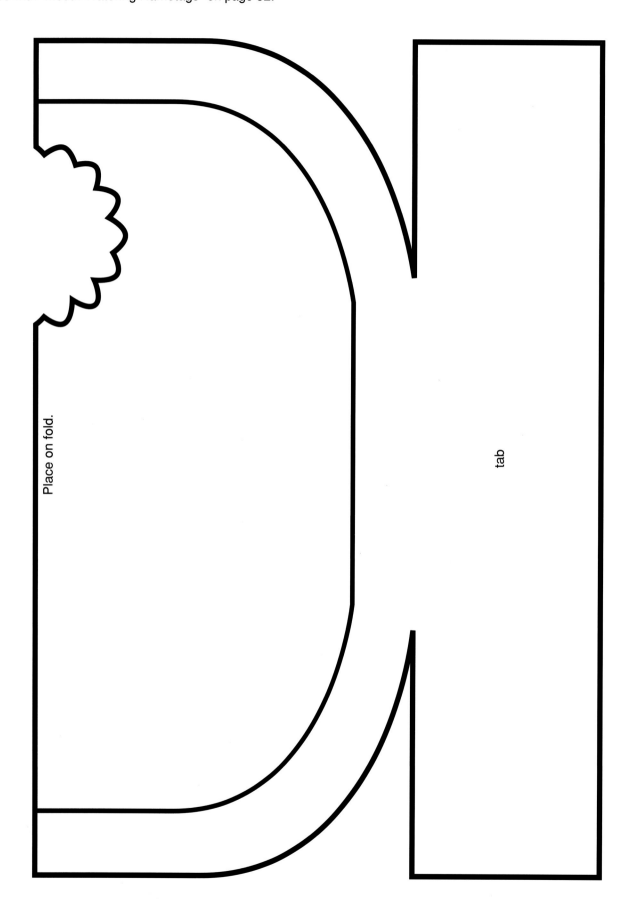

Place on fold.

tab

Use petal patterns with "Showy Sunflowers" on page 33.

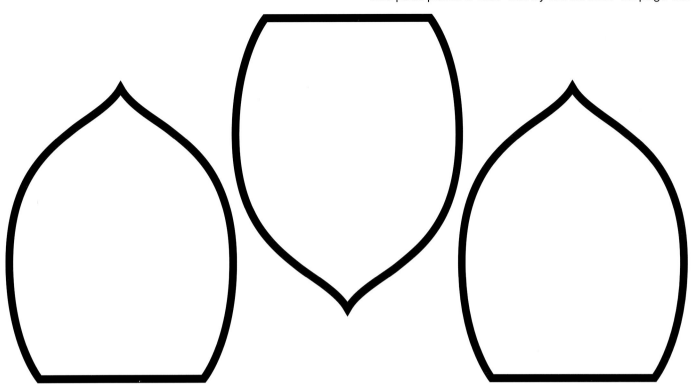

Use the leaf and pumpkin patterns with "Seasonal Sparklers" on page 34.

Patterns

Use the wing pattern with "Wad-A-Bodies" on page 36.

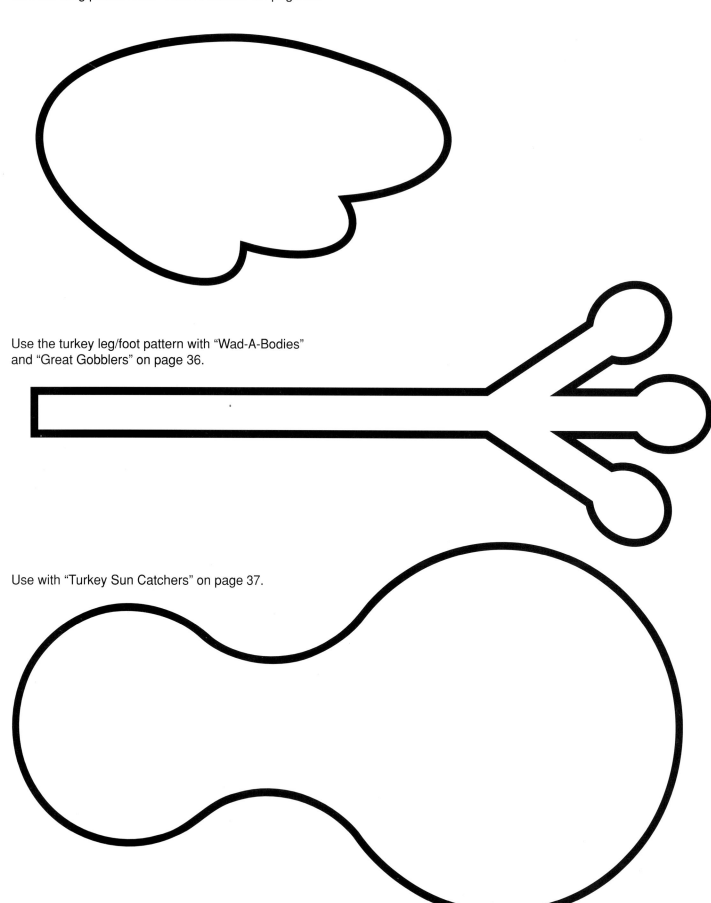

Use the turkey leg/foot pattern with "Wad-A-Bodies"
and "Great Gobblers" on page 36.

Use with "Turkey Sun Catchers" on page 37.

Patterns

Use with "Colorful Corn" on page 37.

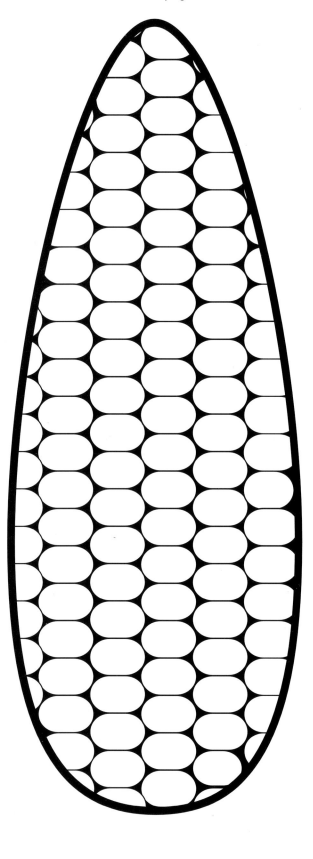

Use holly leaves with "Festive Wreath" on page 38 and "Multiple Meanings" on page 61.

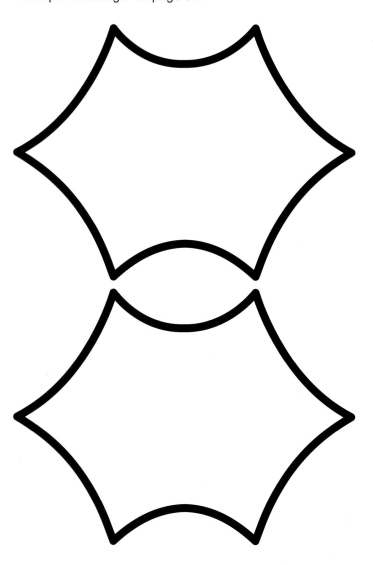

Use the holly berry with "Multiple Meanings" on page 61.

Use with "Past And Future Greats" on page 14 and "Famous Folks" on page 42.

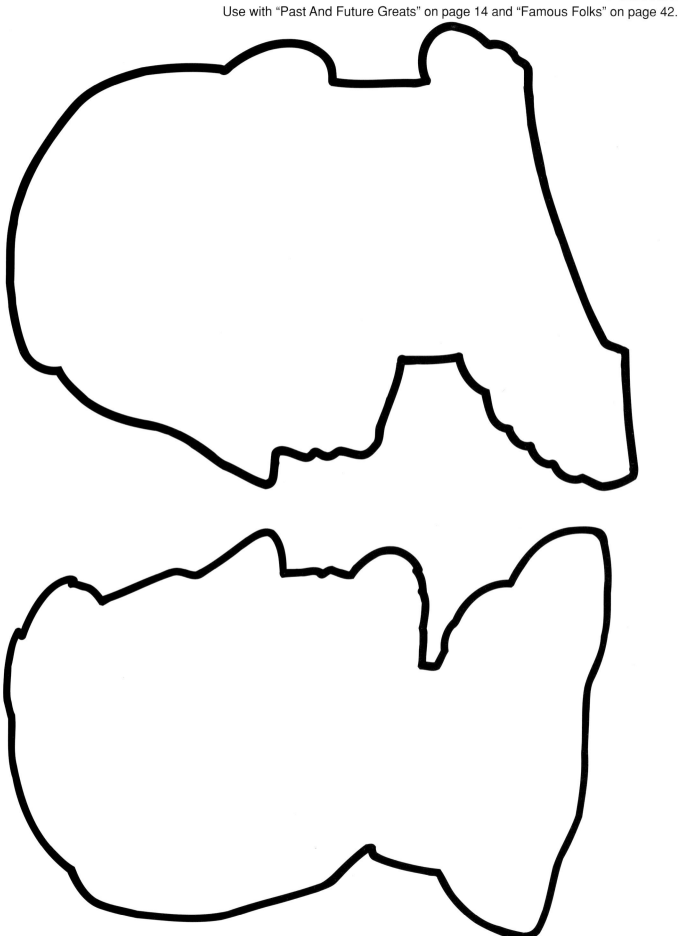

Patterns

Use with "Loopy The Lion" on page 44.

Use with "Dr. King Mobile" on page 41.

Spotlight on Centers

"Classy" Pictures

Students create "classy" pictures at this classification center. On each of several index cards, write a classification such as toys, flowers, babies, transportation, fruits, school supplies, and footwear. Place the cards at a center along with 9" x 12" sheets of construction paper, a supply of discarded magazines, glue, scissors, and crayons or markers. A student chooses a classification card; then he writes his name and the classification on one side of his construction paper. On the opposite side of his paper, he glues magazine pictures that represent the classification.

Jeri Daugherity
Emmitsburg, MD

Countable Caterpillars

Not one youngster will try to wiggle out of doing this center! Remove the lids and thoroughly clean several plastic pill containers. Then place the containers, an ink pad, pencils, crayons, and drawing paper at a center. Add one or more task cards programmed with counting instructions. To make a caterpillar, a student inks the open end of a pill container and stamps a series of adjoining circles on his paper. Reinking the container as needed, he continues stamping circles until his caterpillar is the desired length. After decorating the caterpillar's head, the student sequentially numbers the remaining body sections as described on a task card. He completes his project by coloring a scene around his countable critter.

For practice alphabetizing, program a new task card with a list of letters or words. After a student creates his caterpillar, he uses the programming on the task card to alphabetically label its body.

Betsy Crosson—Gr. 1
Pleasant Elementary School
Tulare, CA

Make a caterpillar with ten or more body sections.
Count by 2's.

Cookie Capers

There's no doubt that this versatile center will attract lots of student interest! Label a supply of seasonal cookie shapes for matching, sorting, or sequencing. Laminate and cut out the shapes; then attach a piece of magnetic tape to the back of each one. Store the cutouts in a nonbreakable cookie canister. Place the canister, a cookie sheet, and an answer key at the center. A student arranges the cutouts on the cookie sheet; then he uses the answer key to check his work. Delicious!

Mary Kay Gallagher—Gr. 1
Seton Catholic School
Moline, IL

Paper Punch Addition

Put some punch into addition-fact practice with this center activity. Place a hole puncher, a pencil, and a supply of construction-paper cards labeled with assorted math facts at a center. A student selects a card; then, using the hole puncher, he punches a set of holes to match each addend. Next he counts the holes and writes the fact answer on the back of the card. Have each student complete a predetermined number of cards.

For a variation, have students label blank cards with math facts and answers, then check their answers by punching the cards. If desired, recycle the colorful paper punches by using them at an art center. Mosaics, anyone?

Susan Menning—Gr. 1
Resurrection School
Arnold, MO

Sizing Up Written Directions

Reinforce reading and following written directions with this hands-on activity. From several colors of 8" x 10" poster board, cut a supply of templates. (See the illustration.) On the templates, above each cut-out area, write a one-sentence direction. A student chooses a template and places it atop a 9" x 12" sheet of paper. He then reads each direction and follows it by drawing in the open area below the sentence. When he has completed both directions, he removes the template and copies the sentences above their corresponding pictures. Following written directions has never been so much fun!

Beverly Bippes—Gr. 1
Humphrey Public School
Humphrey, NE

Pasta With Pizzazz

This partner math center has plenty of "pasta-bilities"! Fill a plastic bowl with three or more different kinds of uncooked pasta shapes. Attach a sample of each pasta shape to a length of laminated tagboard labeled "Pasta Values." Then, using a wipe-off marker, write a desired number value beside each piece of pasta. Place the resulting pasta code, the bowl of pasta, a small scoop, paper napkins, and a supply of blank paper at a center. Each student places a scoop of pasta on a napkin and uses the code to determine its total value. Next he trades pasta with his partner and repeats the activity. The two students then compare their pasta totals. If their totals match, they return the pasta to the bowl. If one or both of the totals do not match, the students together recalculate the value of the pasta scoop(s). To keep the center fresh, reprogram the pasta code each week!

Gina Parisi—Gr. 2, Demarest Elementary, Bloomfield, NJ

Spotlight on Centers

Shoe Swap

This writing center is a real "shoe-in"! Gather several pairs of high-interest adult-size shoes such as cowboy boots, ballet slippers, high-heeled shoes, snowshoes, fishing boots, ski boots, army boots, tap shoes, and high-top sneakers. Place the shoes, a supply of story paper, and crayons or markers at a center. A student slips her stocking feet into a pair of shoes and imagines her life as an adult in these shoes. Then she writes and illustrates a story about one of her adventures.

Krista K. Zimmerman—Gr. 3
Tuckerton Elementary School
Tuckerton, NJ

The Big One
I had a bite. Boy, did I have a bite! My fishing pole was jumping all over the place. I lost my lucky fishing cap, then I lost my fish! But I didn't give up! And the next time...

Piggy Bank Totals

Cash in on money-counting skills with this easy-to-create center activity. In a plastic bank (that has an easy-to-remove stopper), place a desired number of coins. Copy the following question on a length of colorful tagboard: "How much money is in our bank today?" Laminate the resulting sign for durability; then use a wipe-off marker to program the back of the sign to reflect the coin amount in the bank. Display the bank and the sign at a center. A student removes the stopper, empties the bank, and calculates the total value of the coins. After verifying that his total is correct, he returns the coins to the bank and secures the stopper.

Empty the bank at the end of each day. The next morning place a different set of coins in the bank and reprogram the back of the sign accordingly.

Christine Andrus—Grs. 1 & 2, Cessford School
Cessford, Alberta, Canada

All Smiles

Your youngsters will be all smiles as they complete this math and following-directions center. For each student, label a long, narrow paper strip with a series of ten happy faces. (Older students may draw their own.) Create a word bank that randomly features the number words one through ten written in ordinal form and program a set of directions for the students to follow. Laminate the word bank and directions for durability; then place the paper strips, word bank, and directions at a center along with pencils and crayons or markers. A student writes the corresponding ordinal number word above each happy face on his paper strip; then he carefully reads and follows the directions.

Gina Parisi—Gr. 2, Demarest Elementary School, Bloomfield, NJ

Word Bank
second
sixth
fourth
eighth
seventh
first
tenth
third
fifth

first second third fourth fifth sixth seventh eighth ninth tenth

Directions:
1. Draw a red hat on the third face.
2. Color the tenth face yellow.
   face five brown freckles.

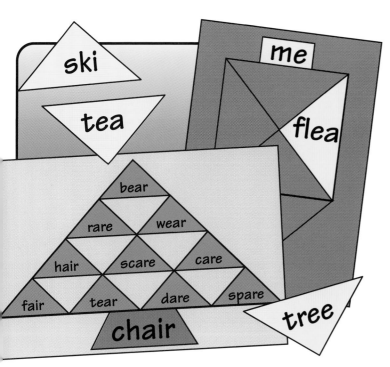

Holiday Puzzlers

'Tis the season for rhyming at this holiday center! For each dreidel puzzle, cut five triangles and a small rectangle from construction paper. Label each puzzle piece with a rhyming word and code the backs of the pieces for self-checking. Make as many puzzles as desired. To create a puzzle board for the center, trace the dreidel shape onto a piece of tagboard as shown; then laminate the puzzle board and pieces for durability. A student makes each dreidel in the set by placing the rhyming pieces atop the puzzle board. To check his work, he flips over the puzzle pieces.

To make a set of Christmas tree puzzles, cut ten triangles and one trapezoid from construction paper for each puzzle.

Angela Choate—Gr. 2
Mustang Trails Elementary
Mustang, OK

Multiple Meanings

A jolly-holly time will be had at this seasonal center! Using the patterns on page 54, duplicate a supply of red berry clusters and green holly leaves. Write a word with multiple meanings on each berry cluster. Then write each meaning of the word on a separate leaf. Laminate and cut out the shapes; then use a permanent marker to program the backs of the cutouts for self-checking. Store the cutouts in a holiday basket. A student matches the holly leaves to the correct berries, then flips the cutouts to check his work. Happy holidays!

Tonya Byrd—Gr. 2
Shaw Heights Elementary
Shaw Air Force Base, SC

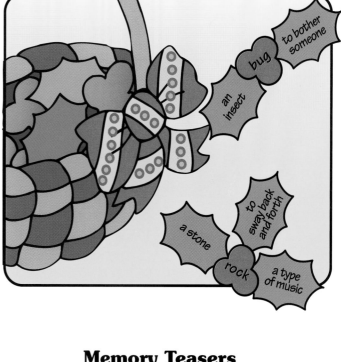

Memory Teasers

This easy-to-make memory center is great any time of the school year. Use markers to prepare a set of symbol sequence cards such as the one shown. Place the cards, markers or crayons, and a supply of paper at a center. A student stacks the cards facedown. To begin the activity, he flips the top card. He studies the card; then he flips it back over. Next, on his paper, the student attempts to re-create the exact sequence of symbols from memory. To check his work, he simply flips the card over again. The student continues in this manner until he has completed all of the provided cards or his center time runs out. Change the cards weekly. In no time at all, you can enlist the help of your young-sters in supplying cards for the center.

61

Spotlight on Centers

Easy Does It!

When you need a learning center at a moment's notice, this sorting center is the perfect solution. Using a marker and pieces of masking tape, label each section of a muffin tin to correspond with a desired sorting skill. Then place the tin and a basket of objects (for sorting) at the center. Suggestions include:

- Label each section with numerals or number words. Supply the exact number of counters needed.
- Label each section with a color word. Provide an assortment of appropriately colored buttons.
- Label each section with an amount of money. Supply the correct coins needed to make each amount.

Susan Voss—Gr. 1
Knapp School
Michigan City, IN

Colorful Kisses

You can bet students will experience sweet success at this alphabetizing center! Using the pattern on page 66, cut two or three candy-kiss shapes from tagboard. Use one of the resulting templates to trace five candy-kiss shapes onto six different colors of construction paper for a total of 30 shapes. Program each color-coded set of five kisses with words for alphabetizing. Laminate the construction-paper shapes and cut them out. Place the cutouts in a basket. Display the basket, the tagboard tracers, crayons or markers (optional), and a supply of paper at the center. A student sorts the cutouts by color and alphabetically arranges the words in each set. To make his answer sheet, the student uses a template to trace six chocolate-kiss shapes onto a sheet of paper. Then he copies each alphabetized set of words onto a different shape. For easy checking, have students color-code their answer sheets to match the cutout sets. (See illustration.) Present candy kisses to the students who satisfactorily complete the center!

Jeri Daugherity
Emmitsburg, MD

Colorful Creations

Add a touch of color to your writing center! Duplicate the crayon pattern on page 66 onto several colors of construction paper. Program each crayon with a color-related writing activity (such as the ones shown); then laminate and cut out the crayons. Display the crayon cutouts in a discarded crayon box along with a supply of writing paper. A student chooses a crayon and completes the corresponding task on a sheet of writing paper. If desired, also provide crayons and a supply of construction paper at the center. A student can decorate his work and then mount it atop a sheet of matching construction paper.

Shelley Clayburn—Resource
Clinton Elementary
Lincoln, NE

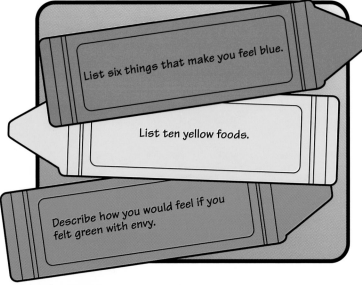

A Trail Of Shamrocks

Check out this gold mine of multiplication practice! Duplicate 20 construction-paper shamrock shapes. Sequentially number the shamrocks and program each shape with a different multiplication fact. Laminate and cut out the shapes; then use the resulting cutouts to make a trail of shamrocks that lead to a center. Place a supply of blank paper at the start of the shamrock trail. At the end of the trail (the center), place a rainbow-shaped answer key (pattern on page 28) and a pot of wrapped butterscotch candies. A student numbers her paper from 1 to 20, then copies and answers each fact along the trail on her paper. When she arrives at the center, she uses the answer key to check her work. When her checking is done, she helps herself to a candy nugget!

Julie A. Decker—Gr. 3
St. Anthony School
Loyal, WI

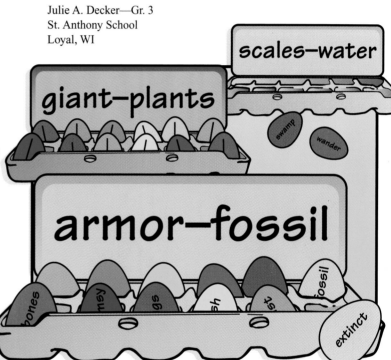

"Dino-mite" Guide Words

Hatch a new interest in guide words at this "dino-mite" center. You will need three egg cartons and 36 construction-paper dinosaur eggs. Label each egg with a dinosaur-related word. Laminate the eggs for durability before cutting them out. Next arrange the egg cutouts in alphabetical order before dividing them into three groups of 12 eggs each. Open each of the three egg cartons and clearly label the inside of each lid with a guide-word pair that corresponds to one of the three egg groups. Finally store the egg cutouts in a large resealable bag. A student uses the guide words to sort the dinosaur eggs into the proper egg cartons. If desired, use a permanent marker to code the backs of the cutouts for self-checking. There's no doubt that this center will be a HUGE success!

Dianne Neumann—Gr. 2
Frank C. Whiteley School
Hoffman Estates, IL

On Location

Review vocabulary and reinforce mapping skills at this versatile center. At a center location, design a grid like the one shown. Write ten vocabulary words on individual word cards and attach the cards to intersecting lines on the grid. Number ten slightly larger cards from one to ten. Write the vocabulary word meanings on these cards. Place the larger cards, pencils, and a supply of paper at the center. A student numbers his paper to ten. To complete the activity, he reads each large card and locates the corresponding vocabulary word on the grid. On his paper he writes the vocabulary word and its grid location. If desired, provide an answer key for self-checking. Students love the unique format of the center, and the center is also a snap to reprogram.

Karen Smith—Gr. 2
Cumru Elementary School
Shillington, PA

63

Spotlight on Centers

Tasty Treasure

Ahoy, mateys! There's pirate treasure to be estimated, sorted, graphed, and tallied at this tasty center! Decorate a large box with a removable lid to resemble a treasure chest. Then, using sandwich bags and curling ribbon, package a treasure of 12–16 small assorted gumdrops (jewels) for each student, making certain that each treasure contains no more than six of any one color. Store the gumdrop treasures in the decorated treasure box; then place the treasure box, crayons or markers, and student copies of page 67 at a center. Each student chooses a bag of booty from the treasure box and uses it to complete the provided center activity. When his paperwork is done, the student asks a matey to check his calculations and sign the bottom of his paper in the space provided. Suggest that each student give his matey a few gumdrop jewels to thank him for his assistance. The rest of the booty is his to eat!

Jennifer Gibson, Pawleys Island, SC

Puppy Love!

These adorable pooches are simply irresistible! Using the pattern on page 68, duplicate and sequentially number several colorful construction-paper puppies. Laminate and cut out the shapes. For math reinforcement use a wipe-off marker to program each puppy's body with a different math problem. Write the corresponding answers on the puppies' ears. Fold each ear forward along the dotted line and crease it. Place the programmed cutouts and a supply of blank paper at a center. A student copies and solves each of the problems in order on his paper. To check his work, he peeks under each puppy's ear. When appropriate, wipe away the programming and label the pooches for additional skill reinforcement.

Beth H. Thomas—Gr. 2
Brunson Elementary School
Brunson, SC

Round And Round

Top off your school year with this easy-to-make center! Notify your students' parents that you are in need of clean snap-on and twist-on lids in a variety of sizes. Store the lids you receive at a center along with a supply of pencils, colorful markers, and white art paper. A student traces several lids on his paper in an overlapping design. Then he uses the markers to decorate each of the resulting spaces differently. Students enjoy the creative opportunity, and the colorful results are striking.

Diane Fortunato—Gr. 2
Carteret School
Bloomfield, NJ

Here's The Scoop!

These ice-cream cones are piled high with skill reinforcement opportunities. Using the patterns on page 66, duplicate several construction-paper cones and ice-cream scoops. Label each cone shape with a math answer, a rhyming word, a pair of guide words, or a vowel sound. Then program three or four paper scoops to correspond to each cone. Laminate and cut out the pieces; then use a permanent marker to program the backs of the cutouts for self-checking. Store the cool cutouts in a resealable plastic bag at a center. A student sorts the scoops atop the cones, then flips the cutouts to check his work. Delicious!

Linda Anne Lopienski, Asheboro, NC

Mystery Objects

This critical-thinking center is sure to pique your youngsters' curiosity! From magazines cut an assortment of colorful pictures of objects. Snip each picture into two parts. Place one part of each picture in a manila envelope. Store the envelope in your desk. Mount and number the remaining picture pieces on a sheet of colorful tagboard as shown. Laminate the resulting poster for durability; then display the poster and a supply of writing paper at a center.

A student carefully studies each partial picture before writing his prediction in the following manner: "I think object number one is a _____ because _____." When all students have completed the center, reveal the envelope containing the missing picture parts. With your students' help, piece together the pictures and reveal the mystery objects.

Dianne Neumann—Gr. 2
Frank C. Whiteley School
Hoffman Estates, IL

Box Lid Math

Warning: If you're trying to keep a lid on math skills, avoid this center! To make the center, you will need one shoebox lid, a construction-paper rectangle sized to fit snugly inside the lid, and two paper clips. Program the rectangle with a grid of desired numerals for adding, subtracting, multiplying, or dividing. Laminate the grid for durability and place it inside the box lid. Place the box lid, paper clips, and a supply of paper at a center. A student sets the two paper clips atop the grid. Next he scoots the clips around the grid by maneuvering the box lid. When the clips come to rest, he copies the numerals under the clips on his paper and performs the specified math operation. He continues in this manner until he has solved a predetermined number of problems.

Susan Reinagel—Gr. 3
Kelso, MO

Patterns

Enlarge and use the candy kiss pattern with "Colorful Kisses" on page 62.

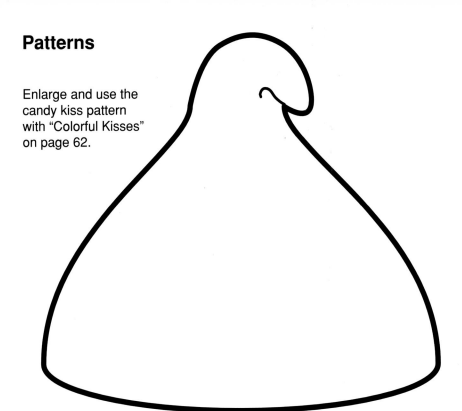

Use the crayon pattern with "Colorful Creations" on page 62.

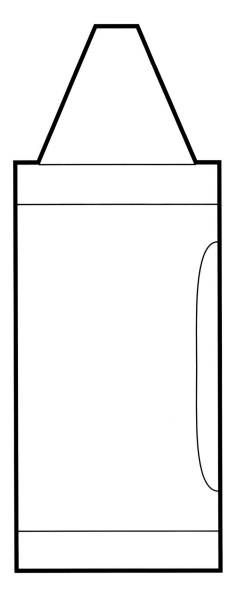

Use the cone and scoop patterns with "Here's The Scoop!" on page 65.

Pirate Treasure

1. Look closely at your bag of treasure.
   How many gumdrop jewels do you think are in the bag?
   Write your estimate on the line. _____

2. Open your bag of treasure. Graph your gumdrop jewels.

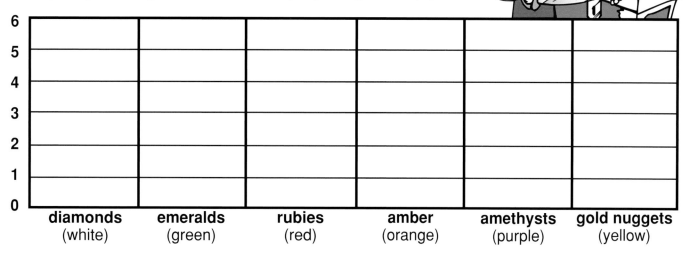

	diamonds (white)	emeralds (green)	rubies (red)	amber (orange)	amethysts (purple)	gold nuggets (yellow)
6						
5						
4						
3						
2						
1						
0						

3. Use your graph. How many of each jewel do you have?

   _____ diamonds   _____ emeralds   _____ rubies

   _____ amber   _____ amethysts   _____ gold nuggets

4. Which jewel do you have the most of? _____

5. Which jewel do you have the fewest of? _____

Find the sums.

a. diamonds + emeralds = _____

b. gold nuggets + diamonds = _____

c. amber + gold nuggets = _____

d. rubies + diamonds = _____

e. amber + rubies = _____

f. rubies + emeralds = _____

g. amethysts + diamonds = _____

h. emeralds + amber = _____

Calculations checked by Matey _____.

Pattern

Use with
"Puppy Love!"
on page 64.

Fire Safety

by

cover
emblem

matches

Name _____

Cooking Up A Paragraph

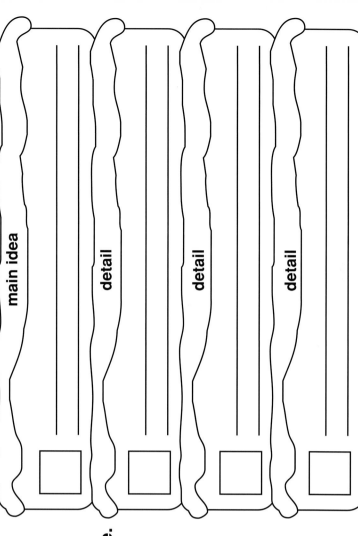

Recipe For A Paragraph

topic: _____

details: _____
_____
_____

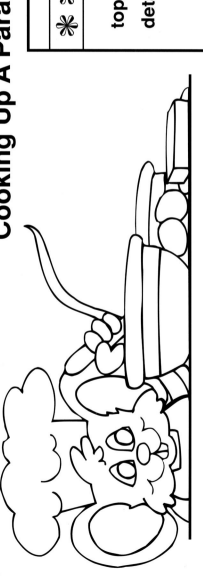

main idea _____

detail _____

detail _____

detail _____

Write a **topic** for your paragraph on the recipe card.

Then write three **details** about your topic on the card.

On the top layer of the cake, write a **main idea sentence.**
(Remember that a main idea sentence tells the point
that you want to make about your topic.)

Then write one sentence about each detail on each cake
layer.

Number the boxes to show the order that you will write
these sentences in your paragraph.

Write your paragraph on another sheet of paper.
Use this sheet as a guide.

Getting Kids Into Books

Boost your youngsters' self-esteem and reading motivation with this reading project. Ask each student to select a book he has recently read that he feels other children would enjoy. Then have each youngster review his selected book by writing and illustrating a paragraph about it. Laminate the completed projects and bind them into an eye-catching booklet. If possible, take a class field trip to a local children's bookstore and present the booklet to its owner. (Suggest that the book be displayed so that potential customers may refer to it for reading suggestions.) Or present the booklet to your school librarian and suggest that she use it in a similar manner. Each month enlist the expertise of your young readers to create another booklet of reviews.

Sheila R. Chapman—Gr. 1, Elm Street School, Newnan, GA

Amazing Grace
Written by Mary Hoffman

This is a wonderful story about a girl who discovers she can do anything she puts her mind to!

Reviewed by Maurice Zin

Oftentimes when new books are added to a classroom library collection, they appear to go unnoticed. To increase students' interest in these new arrivals, enlist student volunteers to read and review the books for their classmates. Each review should include a brief description of the main character, the setting, and the plot, and the reviewer's opinion of the book. Set aside time for students to share their written reviews with their classmates. To keep parents up-to-date on newly purchased books, publish the student-written reviews in your weekly newsletter.

Patsy Higdon—Gr. 3, Glen Arden Elementary School, Arden, NC

Encourage students to read at home with a collection of thematic book bags. Decorate each of several canvas bags for a different theme. Then, inside each bag place a collection of theme-related books, a stuffed animal (if appropriate), and a writing journal. In the journal include a list of the bag's contents, a parent letter of explanation, a suggested follow-up activity or project for each book, and a supply of blank writing pages for parent- and student-written comments. Once the bags are ready, establish a checkout system and invite students to each take a bag home for one week. When the students return the bags, ask them to share their favorite books from the bags and any projects or activities that they completed at home. Students will eagerly await their turns to take home these special bags of books.

Rachel McDaniel—Gr. 3, Sullivan Village Elementary School, Lawton, OK

Alexander & The Terrible, Horrible, No Good, Very Bad Day
by Judith Viorst

Turn students on to reading and boost their comprehension skills with this riddle-writing activity. Have each child glue four library card pockets onto a 9" x 12" sheet of construction paper and label the paper with the title and author of the book he has read. After slipping an index card into each pocket, he programs the top of each card and its corresponding pocket with one of the following questions: "Where am I?", "Who am I?", and "What am I?" Each card is then removed and programmed with a clue. (See the illustration.) He then codes the backs of the cards for self-checking. Bind the riddle pages into a class booklet for all to enjoy. If desired, have students compile thematic riddle booklets or riddle booklets spotlighting individual authors.

Kathy Seals—Gr. 3, Park Lane Elementary, Lawton, OK

Ho! Ho! Ho! This reading activity is perfect for the holiday season. Have each youngster read a book of his choice. Then challenge all students to write letters to Santa convincing him that the books they read should be packed on his sleigh and delivered to other boys and girls around the world. Each letter should include the book's title and author, a summary about the book, and several reasons why the book would make a great Christmas gift. Remind students that letters containing descriptive details and specific reasons will help Santa decide which books to pack. Happy holidays!

Kimberly A. Spring—Gr. 2, Lowell Elementary, Everett, WA

Book Bingo

I read a biography.	I read a fiction book.	I read a make-believe book.	I read a mystery book.	I read a nonfiction book about animals.
I read an excellent book.	I read a nonfiction book.	I read a book by Beverly Cleary.	I read a book about a mouse.	I read a book about friendship.
I read a fairy tale.	I read a book about the ocean.	Free Reading	I read a nonfiction book.	I read a folktale.
I read a book about pets.	I read a book by Mem Fox.	I read a book by Bill Peet.	I read an animal story.	I read a book about dinosaurs.
I read a folktale.	I read a funny book.	I read a mystery book.	I read a book by Eric Carle.	I read a fiction book.

Motivate students to read a variety of books with this easy-to-make game. Program all but one square of a blank bingo grid with a different reading challenge. Label the remaining square "Free Reading." Duplicate a class supply of the resulting cards on construction paper and distribute them to your students. Explain that Book Bingo is played like bingo with the following exception: to cross off a square in Book Bingo, a player must meet the reading challenge written in the square. (Ask students to list the book titles they read on the backs of their Book Bingo cards.) Reward each winner with a small prize or special privilege. If desired, challenge interested players to continue reading for Book Bingo Blackout. Reward a player who meets every challenge on his card by letting him choose a paperback from your classroom library. Now that's reading motivation!

Christy Meyer, Honolulu, HI

Your youngsters are going to love this idea! At the beginning of each week, ask three or four children to choose a predetermined number of picture books from the school library for storytime reading. Store the books in a large basket or box. Each day choose books from the basket to read aloud during storytime. After a book has been shared, place it on display so that it can be read and enjoyed by the students during their free time. Students beam with pride when their book selection is read.

Tina R. Roher—Gr. 3, Haviland Grade School, Haviland, KS

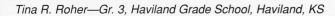

Getting Kids Into Books

Try this approach to encourage even your most reluctant readers to read. Attach a card similar to the one shown to a high-interest, easy-to-read book. Display the book in your reading center. Ask students to read the featured book during their free time, then sign their names on the card. Several weeks later, reward each reader who signed the card with a sticker that corresponds to the book. Display an assortment of books with cards all year long. Your students' interest in reading is sure to soar!

Christine Andrus—Gr. 2, New Cessford School, Cessford, Alberta, Canada

Earn a

Read this book and sign your name.

Frog And Toad Are Friends

Kevin
Zach
Katie

The One In The Middle Is The Green Kangaroo

Here's a great way to stimulate interest in reading. Display an eye-catching sign-up sheet for the Lunch Bunch—a lunchtime book-sharing group. Each time a student reads a "chapter book" (children's novel), he may sign up for the Lunch Bunch. When five students are listed, determine what day the youngsters will meet for lunch. Remind each student in the group that on this day he will need the book that he read and a sack lunch. At lunchtime, take the bunch to a special location (such as outside under a tree or in the library) to eat their lunches and share their books. Students will love this special forum for sharing the books that they've read.

Debbie Patrick—Gr. 3, Filbert Street Elementary, Enola, PA

Pique your youngsters' reading motivation with theatrical book presentations! Invite all interested colleagues to join the fun. On the day of the event, each participating teacher comes to school dressed as a different storybook character. Each teacher must also have prepared a five- (or ten-) minute dramatic presentation of a book that features her character. At a designated time, each teacher enacts her book dramatization for her students. After the allotted time, each participating teacher rotates to the next classroom along a predetermined route. In addition to being highly entertaining, the performances encourage students to seek out a variety of new and exciting books.

Mary Kay Covington—Gr. 3, Woodstone Elementary, San Antonio, TX

Ms. Frizzle

Who am I?
1. Arthur
2.
3.
4.

Pique students' interest in books with this motivational activity. Post a collection of pictures featuring characters from a variety of children's books. Number the pictures for reference; then challenge students to identify the characters. If desired, have each student record his answers on a duplicated answer sheet. Several days later, invite students to name the characters. Once a character has been identified, personalize his picture and share information about the book(s) that features this character. Make these books available for youngsters to read.

Peggy Hart—Instructional Specialist, Fort Worth, TX

LITERATURE

A Treasury Of Favorite ABC Books

Snuggle up with this collection of ABC books and related activities. Straight from our subscribers to you—these classroom favorites promise to please.

A: My Name Is Alice

Written by Jane Bayer & Illustrated by Steven Kellogg
Dial Books For Young Readers, 1984

The alliterative text of this alphabet book is sure to capture your students' attention—as will the parade of animals that grace the book's pages. From *A* to *Z*, animal couples are introduced by their names, their point of origin, and the wares they sell. The text is based on a playground game the author played as a child. If you really want to impress your students, demonstrate the playground game. All you'll need is a rubber ball and a bit of ball-bouncing prowess! Then follow up by asking each student to create an alliterative verse that features his name and that follows the pattern established in the book. These verses can be written, illustrated, and compiled into a classroom book. Or they can be chanted on the playground as part of ball-bouncing, hand-clapping, or jump-rope games.

Theodora Gallagher—Gr. 1, Carteret School, Bloomfield, NJ
Shirley Gillette—Reading Specialist, Lafe Nelson School
Safford, AZ

Alphabears: An ABC Book

Written by Kathleen Hague & Illustrated by Michael Hague
Holt, Rinehart and Winston; 1984

In this delightful book, rhyming text and adorable teddy bears introduce students to the letters of the alphabet. To make an endearing display or a charming classroom version of the book, begin with student copies of the teddy-bear pattern on page 84. Have each student cut out and glue a bear pattern on story paper. Then using scraps of construction paper, wallpaper, and fabric; yarn; crayons or markers; and other arts-and-crafts supplies, have each student dress up his bear and create background scenery. Suggest that students create artwork that reflects their personal interests. Next ask each child to write about this teddy bear that shares his name. Younger students can dictate the information to an adult. Display the projects with the title "Meet Our Alphabears!" or bind your students' work into a "bear-y" special ABC book.

Maggi Eichorn—Gr. 1, Parker School, Tolland, CT

To reinforce rhyming skills, challenge students to create rhyming verses for an ABC book entitled "Alphakids." In turn, have each child share her special qualities and interests with her classmates. This can be in a large-group or small-group setting. After each child's turn, the group members work together to create a rhyme for that child. When each child in the group has a rhyme written on story paper, the group members illustrate their own rhymes. Alphabetically compile the completed projects into a class book.

Rosemary A. Shannon—Gr. 1, Wyomissing Hills Elementary,
Wyomissing Hills, PA

The Extinct Alphabet Book

Written by Jerry Pallotta & Illustrated by Ralph Masiello
Charlesbridge Publishing, 1993

Each page of this intriguing alphabet book features information about a creature that no longer exists. And as if that isn't interesting enough—the author and illustrator have included a few more surprises! For example, on the *B* page the trees spell a two-word message that challenges the reader to find the author. (His photo is neatly camouflaged on a later page.) Or turn the U page upside down and find the profile of a rock-and-roll legend. Without a doubt, this book merits several careful readings and examinations.

This ABC book also packs a powerful message about extinction. Discuss extinction and how it might be prevented in the future. To draw your students' attention to creatures that are nearing extinction, have each child create a page for "An Endangered Alphabet Book." Or have students create a research-based ABC book on a current topic of study such as rain-forest animals or famous Americans.

Ritsa Tassopoulos—Gr. 3, Oakdale Elementary, Cincinnati, OH

On Market Street

Written by Arnold Lobel & Illustrated by Anita Lobel
Greenwillow Books, 1981

A day spent on Market Street results in 26 very interesting purchases—from apples to zippers! After a few readings of the book, put your students' memories to the test! Read the story again, but this time read just the alphabet letters and let the students recall the merchandise that was purchased. Some students may even be up to the challenge of recalling all 26 purchases!

For a fun writing and drawing activity, have each child create his own alphabetical shopping spree along a street of his own choosing. With unlimited budgets, students are likely to make some unusual purchases!

Christy Meyer, Honolulu, HI

Dr. Seuss's ABC

Written & Illustrated by Dr. Seuss
Random House, Inc.; 1963

Just what the doctor ordered—an ABC book that's fun through and through! After a few oral readings of this Beginner Book, students will be ready to create alphabet books of their own. Before students begin to write, have them identify adjectives in the text. Discuss how the descriptive words enhance the doctor's story. Then give each student a blank, 28-page booklet in which to compose his alphabetical masterpiece. To make a 28-page booklet, fold 14 sheets of blank duplicating paper in half; then staple the folded paper between construction-paper covers. If desired, have students use crayons or markers to underline the adjectives in their stories.

Suzanne Albaugh—Gr. 2, Wintersville Elementary
Wintersville, OH

A Little Alphabet

Written & Illustrated by Trina Schart Hyman
Morrow Junior Books, 1993

In this tiny volume, each letter of the alphabet is illustrated with a child playing with or using objects that begin with the featured letter. For example, sharing the spotlight with the letter *A* is a child *artist*, the *arm* of the artist, *acorns*, an *apron*, an *avocado*, *apples*, an *artichoke*, an *anemone*, and an *ant*. Students will love the challenge of naming all of the pictured items. List the words on tagboard strips—one strip for each alphabet letter. (A glossary provides the items pictured on each page.) When you have completed one strip for every letter, distribute them to your students. Ask each youngster to use the words on his strip to craft a story about the child pictured on the alphabet page. When the students have completed their writings, revisit the book and have each student read his story aloud when the appropriate alphabet letter is displayed.

Agnes Tirrito—Gr. 2, Kennedy Elementary School, Texarkana, TX

Handsigns:
A Sign Language Alphabet

Written & Illustrated by Kathleen Fain
Chronicle Books, 1993

This one-of-a-kind book is both an alphabet book and an introduction to American Sign Language. The easy-to-follow format presents 26 full-color illustrations, each revealing at least one animal that begins with the featured alphabet letter. On each alphabet page, an inset picture of a human hand shows how to sign the letter. A foreword provides information on the history of sign language and how it is used today, and a glossary gives information about each animal shown. Students will enjoy signing the alphabet letters and learning about a colorful menagerie of animals.

Elouise Miller, Lincoln School, Hays, KS

Chicka Chicka Boom Boom

Written by Bill Martin, Jr., and John Archambault
Illustrated by Lois Ehlert
Simon And Schuster Books For Young Readers, 1989

This lively alphabet rhyme—in which all the letters of the alphabet race each other up a coconut tree—proved to be a favorite among our subscribers!

Acting out this alphabet rhyme is a must! Have each child cut out and decorate a different alphabet letter. Or have each child design a large poster-board letter that can be worn. During an oral reading of the story, each child stands and displays her artwork when her letter is mentioned. When all of the letters tumble from the tree, the students chant, "Chicka chicka boom boom!" and drop to the floor. At the end of the story, have students trade letters and repeat the activity. Before long students will be retelling the story without any help from their teacher. Chicka chicka boom boom!

Justine A. White—Gr. 1, Southside Elementary, Cleveland, TX
Marcia Dosser—Gr. 1, University School, Johnson City, TN

This coconut caper is a great way to evaluate your students' knowledge of the alphabet. Display a large coconut-tree cutout on a bulletin board entitled "*Chicka Chicka Boom Boom.*" Staple 26 coconuts in the tree—each one bearing a different lowercase letter. Along the bottom of the display, staple 26 more coconuts—each one bearing an uppercase letter. As you point to each of the lowercase letters, ask a different student to point to the corresponding capital letter.

Kelley Russell—Interim Teacher, Rogersville City School
Rogersville, TN

Boom! Boom! A few bumps, bruises, and other minor injuries result when the alphabet letters fall to the ground. Read the story to your youngsters and draw their attention to the condition of the letters after they tumble from the tree. For a fun art activity, have each child choose a different alphabet letter. Then—using colorful paper, markers or crayons, and scissors—each youngster creates a cutout of his slightly shaken letter. For added fun, give each child a small bandage to use. When the projects are done, have each student mount his letter in the top of a classroom coconut tree! Chicka! Chicka!

Linda Stroik—Gr. 1, Bannach Elementary School, Stevens Point, WI

Imagine the view from the top of a coconut tree! That's what youngsters do as they complete this follow-up activity. On light green construction paper, duplicate student copies of the treetop on page 84. Distribute the copies and have each student write a different alphabet letter in the first blank. Then ask each student to finish his sentence. The word(s) he writes must begin with his assigned letter. Next give each student a strip of brown construction paper and a 9" x 12" sheet of construction paper. A student cuts out his treetop; then he cuts a tree trunk from the brown paper. He glues both cutouts on the sheet of construction paper. Next he uses crayons or markers to embellish his tree and to illustrate what his letter saw. Compile the personalized projects in alphabetical order between a poster-board cover entitled "*Chicka Chicka Boom Boom* retold by _____'s Class."

Maxine Bergman—Gr. 1, Loretto Elementary School
Jacksonville, FL

From coconuts to continents! For a unique geography lesson, label one coconut cutout for each alphabet letter. Divide students into small groups. Give each group a world map or atlas and an equal number of coconuts. Challenge the groups to write on each coconut the name of a country that begins with the programmed letter. On the back of the coconut, the group writes the continent where the country is located.

To display the students' work, label a paper palm tree for each of the seven continents. Mount the trees on a bulletin board entitled "From Coconuts To Countries To Continents." Then, beginning with coconut A and proceeding in alphabetical order, have different group members present the programmed coconuts. To do this, a student names the country on the coconut, finds the country on a world map or globe, and attaches the coconut to the appropriate tree.

adapted from an idea by Marcia Dosser—Gr. 1

Q Is For Duck: An Alphabet Guessing Game

Written by Mary Elting and Michael Folsom
Illustrated by Jack Kent, Clarion Books, 1980

Actually *Q* is for quack—but since ducks quack, that means *Q* is for duck! It won't take long before your youngsters will be experts at figuring out this zany book. As you can tell, this ABC book reinforces more than just beginning sounds. It's great for building logical-thinking skills as well. After reading the book with your class, charge them with the enjoyable task of developing a book that is similarly patterned. Younger students can create sentences and illustrations for individual letters. These projects can be compiled alphabetically into a class book. Older students can create individual books by writing and illustrating sentences for each alphabet letter. As the lesson draws to a close, you may find that students are dedicating a letter to you: *F* is for teacher because teachers make learning *fun*!

Michelle Higley—Gr. 2, St. Thomas Aquinas, Lansing, MI

Alligator Arrived With Apples: A Potluck Alphabet Feast

Written by Crescent Dragonwagon
Illustrated by Jose Aruego and Ariane Dewey
Macmillan Publishing Company, 1987

From Alligator's apples to Zebra's zucchini, a multitude of alphabetical animals and foods celebrate Thanksgiving with a grand feast. After students have heard this deliciously entertaining story, they'll be hungry to create a class version of the tale. To do this, have each child design a page that features his name and the food he is bringing to the feast. Challenge students to maintain the alliterative pattern the author used. Compile the completed pages into a one-of-a-kind class booklet.

Betsy Meyer—Gr. 1, Pulaski Academy, Little Rock, AR

Old Black Fly

Written by Jim Aylesworth & Illustrated by Stephen Gammell
Henry Holt And Company, Inc.; 1992

The old black fly may pester the characters of this book, but he'll undoubtedly win quite a few fans in your class. As you read the book to your students, invite them to join in on the refrain: "Shoo fly! Shoo fly! Shooo!" For a high-interest verb lesson, have students identify the verb used on each alphabet page. List these verbs and ask students to examine the completed list for a common factor; then guide them to discover that the verbs are all past tense. Next have the students provide the present tense of each listed verb. Then reread the story with your students. In addition to supplying the refrain, have them supply a present-tense verb for each alphabet page.

Judy Chunn—Grs. 2–3, Westminster School, Nashville, TN

Keeping up with a busy fly can be challenging! But when this project is completed, students will have no trouble at all! Give each child a small construction-paper booklet containing 30 blank pages. Ask each student to write "Old Black Fly retold by [student's name]" on the front cover; "Buzz, buzz, buzz" on the first page; and "It's been a very bad day" on the second page. In the top, outside corner of the third page, the student writes "A." Then on the page she draws and colors an apple pie, writing the words "apple pie" below her illustration. On the fourth page she writes "B" in the top, outside corner; then she draws and colors a baby on the page and writes the word "baby" beneath her illustration. The student continues in this manner for each of the remaining alphabet letters. Then she writes "Buzz, buzz, buzz" on the first of the two remaining pages and "Swat!" on the final page. Suggest that students refer to their books as they retell the fly's story for their friends and family.

adapted from an idea by Linda C. Buerklin—Substitute Teacher
Monroe Township Schools, Williamstown, NJ

Patterns

Use with *Alphabears: An ABC Book* on page 80.

Use with *Chicka Chicka Boom Boom* on page 82.

_____ climbed to the top of the coconut tree to see

_____

_____.

Happy Birthday, Tomie dePaola!

Since his childhood, Tomie dePaola has dreamt of touching the lives of others. DePaola once said, "It's a dream of mine that one of my books, any book, any picture, will touch the heart of some individual child and change that child's life for the better." DePaola has written and/or illustrated almost 200 books, including *The Art Lesson*, which is somewhat autobiographical. The selection of *Strega Nona* as a 1976 Caldecott Honor Book is among his numerous awards and honors. The critically acclaimed success and continued popularity of his books make it apparent that dePaola is indeed realizing his dream.

Tomie dePaola's birthday is September 15. If your youngsters develop a special fondness for dePaola's books, consider having them make a group birthday card and mailing it to the author in care of The Putnam & Grosset Group, 200 Madison Avenue, New York, NY 10016. Happy birthday, Mr. dePaola!

The Art Lesson
Published by G. P. Putnam's Sons

Although you can never be certain just how many dePaolas are in your class, you can be fairly confident that this story will strike an inspiring chord with many of your little ones. Before reading *The Art Lesson* aloud, explain to your students that the author and the book character have several things in common, such as: a dad who was a barber, Irish grandparents, an Italian grandmother, an art teacher named Beulah Bowers, and the desire to be a REAL artist. Then read the story while wearing an apron that has one or more pockets which have been filled with elements from the story. Some of the things you may want to tuck into the apron pockets include: a comb (representing Tommy's dad's barber shop), a fruit (representing his grandparents' grocery store), a flashlight (like the one Tommy used under the sheets), large chalks (like the ones the art teacher had), a box of 64 crayons (like the one Tommy received for his birthday), and a box of eight crayons (like the school crayons). As you are reading the story aloud, pull each prop from the apron at the appropriate moment to bring the story alive. Later, ask each child to design a special award for himself as a tribute to his particular talents or skills.

Kelly Pflederer—Gr. 2
Academy Of The Sacred Heart, St. Charles, MO

Even when he was a kindergartner, Tommy knew that he wanted to be a REAL artist when he grew up. And he knew that REAL artists don't copy! As your students will see when you've finished a reading of *The Art Lesson*, Tommy *did* grow up to be a real artist. Have students think about what they would really like to be when they grow up. Encourage each student to write about these dreams. When it's time to send these papers home, accompany them with a description of the story and the assignment that the youngsters completed. In the note, encourage each parent to put the paper away with other mementos. After many years have passed, parents can enjoy rereading their children's ambitions and seeing how they relate to their current talents.

Deb Marciano Boehm—Gr. 2, Woodridge School, Cranston, RI

Tom
Published by G. P. Putnam's Sons

In his newest autobiographical picture book, dePaola champions the special relationship he had with his grandfather, after whom he is named. Youngsters will enjoy the mischievous bond between grandfather and grandson. This story is a treasure!

Strega Nona

Published by Simon And Schuster
Books For Young Readers

This follow-up activity for dePaola's Caldecott Honor Book, *Strega Nona*, is a great tie-in with your letter-writing unit. Read aloud *Strega Nona;* then ask each of your youngsters to imagine that he is one of the townspeople from the story. Have him decorate the blank side of a lined 5" x 8" index card to resemble a postcard showing a town landmark. On the other side of the card, have him write a fictitious address for Strega Nona at a friend's house, along with a plea for Strega Nona to hurry home to help with the mess that Big Anthony made. If desired, bind the student-made postcards into a booklet titled "Come Quick, Strega Nona!" for students' enjoyment.

Cheryl Sergi—Gr. 2, Greene Central School, Greene, NY

Strega Nona will be an instant hit with your youngsters, but so will these follow-up activities. After reading the story to your students, give each student a helping of long, chilled spaghetti seasoned with a touch of Italian salad dressing. In turn, have each student pose for a photograph that will show his favorite spaghetti-eating technique. Some students may neatly down their carefully twirled forkfuls of spaghetti, while others may exhibit unusual eating styles such as spaghetti "slurping." On a bulletin board, display the developed pictures along with student-made pasta art. Heighten the element of fun by unveiling this display on a day when spaghetti will be served for lunch.

Christina Boyd—Librarian K–3
Wilson Elementary, Collinsville, OK

Readers are led to believe that Strega Nona has very unorthodox methods for making pasta. Ask youngsters to think about how someone makes spaghetti. Have each student write the process in his own words. Then have each student copy the directions—one per strip—onto narrow strips of manila paper, and write his name on the back of each strip. To store the strips, have each student glue the edges—but not the top—of a black pot cutout to a sheet of paper. Instruct students to slide the spaghetti-making direction strips into their pots for storage. Encourage students to take turns sequencing the strips of their classmates.

Lisa Vanderburg—Grs. 3 and 4, Everett Elementary, Paris, TX

Strega Nona's Magic Lessons

Published by Harcourt Brace, Publishers

In this book, Strega Nona is teaching her magic secrets to two young girls—one of whom is actually Big Anthony in disguise. Read aloud *Strega Nona's Magic Lessons;* then use the story as the basis of ongoing integrated lessons. Begin by having students decorate large cardboard cutouts to resemble Strega Nona's house. At first, have students use the cutouts as the backdrop for a reenactment of the story. Then use the cutouts as room dividers to perpetuate the Strega Nona theme. Later have each student cut a pot shape from black tagboard or poster board. Working in cooperative groups, have the students look through copies of *Strega Nona's Magic Lessons* in search of nouns. Make a cumulative list of all the nouns identified; then have each child select a few nouns to write on oval "pasta" cutouts and suspend on thread beneath his pot cutout. On another day, have students search for verbs or adjectives to add beneath their pots. Soon there'll be pasta everywhere!

Sandy Greensfelder—Gr. 1
Naples Elementary, Naples, Italy

Strega Nona Meets Her Match

Published by G. P. Putnam's Sons

In her latest adventure, it looks as if old-fashioned Strega Nona is going to be upstaged by a modern-thinking healer. When Strega Amelia comes to town, she brings more than gossip. Soon she has set up her own shop and is using the latest modern gadgets to treat Strega Nona's regular customers! It looks like Strega Nona's met her match, unless she has her own *cure* for Strega Amelia!

The Popcorn Book

Published by Holiday House

Put the "Yum!" into a reading of *The Popcorn Book* with this suggestion. In advance, prepare for this story by bagging some popcorn for each child. Then, before you begin reading, ask students to only eat a kernel of popcorn each time the word *popcorn* is mentioned in the book. Since the word *popcorn* occurs repeatedly in the story, youngsters can enjoy a great healthful snack while you read. When the totally yummy story is done, permit students to munch out on any remaining popcorn leftovers.

Leigh Anne Newsom—Gr. 3
Greenbrier Intermediate School, Chesapeake, VA

There's lots to learn—including history and science—between these covers. So read *The Popcorn Book* aloud; then make popcorn using a recipe from the book. Have students measure the amount of unpopped popcorn used to prepare the recipe. Then have them measure the popped corn and compare the two measures. Since such a delicious atmosphere has been set, have students write popcorn-related poetry or make a contribution to a class big book while they munch and crunch. Or have them string the excess popped corn to make jewelry. For a social studies tie-in, have students use a globe or maps to locate each of the geographic areas mentioned in the book.

Jane Ursida, Ozone Park, NY

THE
POPCORN
BOOK
by
Class 2J

Fin M'Coul: The Giant Of Knockmany Hill

Published by Holiday House

Fin M'Coul's work on the Giant's Causeway (a true natural wonder in Northern Ireland) is interrupted by the nasty giant Cucullin. But Fin's lovely wife Oonagh soon comes to the rescue. Read the story aloud, stopping before Oonagh's plan is revealed. Have your youngsters brainstorm how Oonagh could help her husband. Explain that this is a fairy tale, so no idea is too far-fetched to be woven into the story. Ask for volunteers to continue the story. Once students have given several possible endings, read the remainder of the book. Find out which ending is the favorite of your youngsters.

Deb Marciano Boehm—Gr. 2, Woodridge School, Cranston, RI

In *Fin M'Coul: The Giant Of Knockmany Hill,* Oonagh works a charm by braiding thread into a bracelet, an anklet, and a circle pin. Students thoroughly enjoy her clever plot to undo the mean-spirited Cucullin. After reading the story to youngsters, have each student make a bracelet similar to the one Oonagh made. To make a bracelet, knot together three different-colored strands of embroidery floss. Tape the knotted end to a tabletop. Braid the three strands of floss together; then knot the loose end. Remove the tape. Wrap the braided embroidery floss around a wrist and tie it in place. Wouldn't it be nice if this bracelet assured that the wearer could not fail at what he attempted? Find out what your youngsters would choose to do, if they knew they could not fail.

Patricia McClune—Librarian K–6
Brownstown Elementary, Brownstown, PA

The Mysterious Giant Of Barletta

Published by Harcourt Brace Jovanovich, Publishers

A little old Italian woman and a giant's statue pair up to defend the town of Barletta from the army of an enemy. Zia Concetta, the woman, divulges the plan only to the statue. The rest of the locals hide from the approaching army. After having students locate Italy on a map, read *The Mysterious Giant Of Barletta,* stopping before Zia's plan is revealed. Have students think of ways that the old lady and a statue of a giant could defeat an entire army. Then continue reading the story. After-ward, talk about different kinds of onions. Be sure to mention that one kind of onion is actually named the Barletta onion. If desired, have students bring in onions for making French onion soup in a Crock-Pot®.

Deb Marciano Boehm—Gr. 2

Little Grunt And The Big Egg: A Prehistoric Fairy Tale

Published by Holiday House

Making a few unusual preparations before you share this story with your students can lead to BIG fun when the story's done. In advance, use tempera to paint an egg-shaped watermelon to resemble a dinosaur egg. Hide it somewhere on the school grounds. Read *Little Grunt And The Big Egg* to your students; then explain that something that resembles a dinosaur egg has been spotted at school. Ask students to write speculative stories about the appearance of the egg and what it contains. Then have students search until they find the imitation dinosaur egg. When all the hubbub about the dinosaur egg has begun to fade away, serve the watermelon to the students for a snack.

Kelly McCaller—Gifted And Talented
Oakland School, Greenwood, SC

Pancakes For Breakfast

Published by Harcourt Brace Jovanovich

Today's youngsters—accustomed to supermarket and fast-food fare—may be surprised to realize just how hard it can be to round up the ingredients for pancakes. When "reading" this story with your youngsters, pause when the lady is on the way back with the syrup, and ask youngsters what will happen next. Turn the page and have students comment on the destruction by the pets and the lady's chances of having pancakes this particular morning. Then finish the story. Using the book's recipe, have students prepare pancakes. While they're feasting on these flapjacks, have youngsters contrast their pancake-making experience to that of the lady in the story.

Quite A Character!

If your students are studying the works of Tomie dePaola, they'll have a great time selecting and describing a dePaola character for this activity. After students are familiar with several of dePaola's books, ask each student to select his favorite character. Then provide him with a shield cutout that has been visually divided into several sections. In each

section, have the student write something different about the character. For example, one section might be used to record special talents of the character, another might be used to tell about the character's occupation, and yet another might be used to tell how the character probably feels in a particular story. If desired, encourage each student to decorate his shield with designs that are befitting of the character. When each student has completed a shield, have him read the information on his shield to his classmates without divulging the name of the character. Find out how many of your students recognize the character from the student's descriptions.

Lisa Vanderburg—Grs. 3 and 4
Everett Elementary, Paris, TX

How Do They Compare?

Once your youngsters are familiar with several of Tomie dePaola's books, they can use Venn diagrams to compare and contrast his books. Ask students to choose two books at a time to compare. For example, you could begin by comparing *Nana Upstairs & Nana Downstairs* and *Now One Foot, Now The Other*. First read both stories. Then draw a Venn diagram on the board and have students name elements that are shared by the stories and elements that are unique to each story. Have students examine several of dePaola's books in this manner. Are there more similarities than they might have first believed, or more differences?

Lisa Vanderburg—Grs. 3 and 4

Dimensional Display

Strega Nona, one of Tomie dePaola's most popular characters, was known to have a pasta pot that overflowed. If your display areas are overflowing with dePaola-related projects, consider this alternative display. Have each student bring to school a square or nearly square lidded box, or provide a box for each student. Instruct students to cover their boxes with colorful paper. Then have them attach some of their projects onto the sides of the boxes. The character shields described in "Quite A Character!", the Venn diagrams described in "How Do They Compare?", and the pasta-filled pots described in the third paragraph under *Strega Nona* (page 86) are examples of projects that would look great on the sides of these boxes. Stack the boxes for a three-dimensional display that all your students can take pride in.

Lisa Vanderburg—Grs. 3 and 4

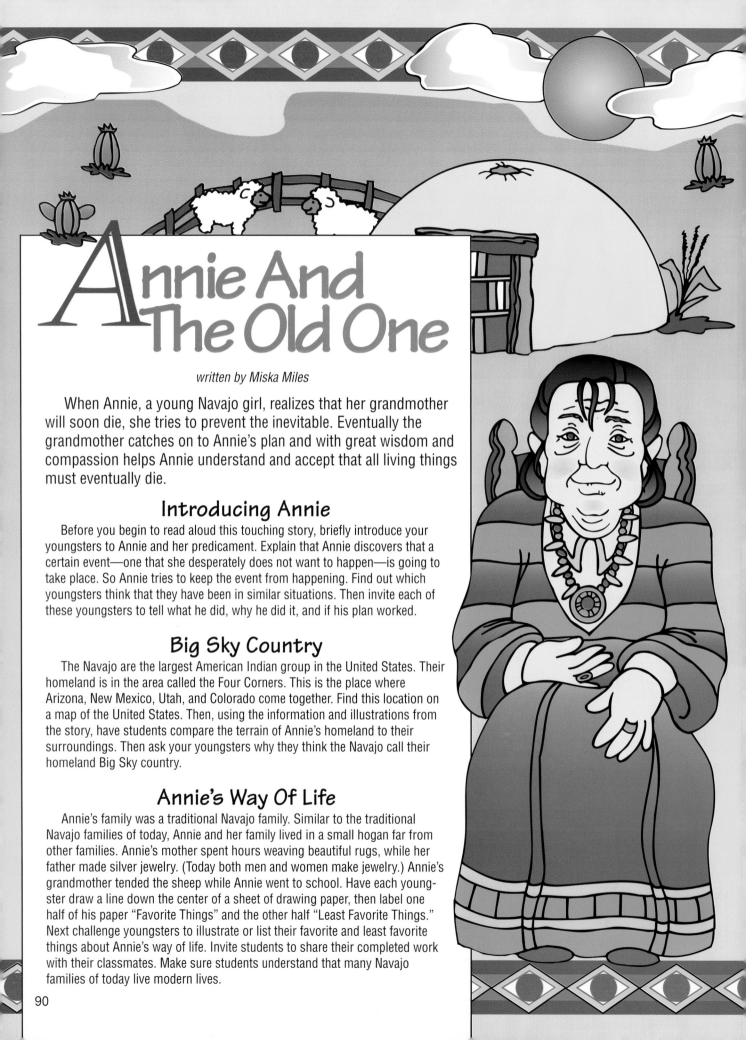

Annie And The Old One

written by Miska Miles

When Annie, a young Navajo girl, realizes that her grandmother will soon die, she tries to prevent the inevitable. Eventually the grandmother catches on to Annie's plan and with great wisdom and compassion helps Annie understand and accept that all living things must eventually die.

Introducing Annie

Before you begin to read aloud this touching story, briefly introduce your youngsters to Annie and her predicament. Explain that Annie discovers that a certain event—one that she desperately does not want to happen—is going to take place. So Annie tries to keep the event from happening. Find out which youngsters think that they have been in similar situations. Then invite each of these youngsters to tell what he did, why he did it, and if his plan worked.

Big Sky Country

The Navajo are the largest American Indian group in the United States. Their homeland is in the area called the Four Corners. This is the place where Arizona, New Mexico, Utah, and Colorado come together. Find this location on a map of the United States. Then, using the information and illustrations from the story, have students compare the terrain of Annie's homeland to their surroundings. Then ask your youngsters why they think the Navajo call their homeland Big Sky country.

Annie's Way Of Life

Annie's family was a traditional Navajo family. Similar to the traditional Navajo families of today, Annie and her family lived in a small hogan far from other families. Annie's mother spent hours weaving beautiful rugs, while her father made silver jewelry. (Today both men and women make jewelry.) Annie's grandmother tended the sheep while Annie went to school. Have each youngster draw a line down the center of a sheet of drawing paper, then label one half of his paper "Favorite Things" and the other half "Least Favorite Things." Next challenge youngsters to illustrate or list their favorite and least favorite things about Annie's way of life. Invite students to share their completed work with their classmates. Make sure students understand that many Navajo families of today live modern lives.

Stories Of Long Ago

Annie enjoyed sitting at her grandmother's feet and listening to stories about times of long ago. Find out if grandparents or other older adults share stories of long ago with your youngsters. For a fun classroom event, have students invite older adults to school for a storytelling festival. On the day of the festival, position the storytellers in quiet locations around the school. Then divide your youngsters among the storytellers. After 15 minutes, have each group rotate to the next storyteller along a predetermined route. To guarantee smooth transitions and to relieve storytellers of any disciplinary concerns, have a parent volunteer accompany each group of students. When each group has visited each storyteller, have students, storytellers, and parent helpers gather in your classroom for refreshments.

A Navajo Upbringing

Knowing how to cook fry bread and how to weave on a loom were two things that Annie was expected to learn as a young Navajo girl. Find out why your youngsters think Annie was not interested in weaving. Also find out why they think Annie was ready to weave at the end of the story.

For a fun follow-up, sample some fry bread. Enlist the help of your youngsters in measuring the needed ingredients.

To make 4 large or 12 small servings of fry bread, you will need:

> 1 cup self-rising cornmeal
> 3/4 cup buttermilk
> 1 egg
> 1 tablespoon sugar

Mix the ingredients together. Then, using an electric fry pan or a skillet and a hot plate, fry the batter in a thin layer of hot oil as students watch from a distance. Before serving it, cool the fry bread atop paper towels or napkins.

Kim Hodge, Tifton, GA

Weaving Tales

These student-made minibooklets are great for creative-writing activities. To make a booklet, first fold a 4" x 12" strip of white construction paper as shown. Decorate the front covers of the booklet to resemble a Navajo weaving; then punch holes along each fold. Loop a four-inch length of yarn through each hole as shown to make fringe. Inside the booklet staple several 3" x 5" sheets of blank paper.

Challenge students to complete one of the following creative-writing activities in their booklets:

- Write and illustrate your favorite part of the story.
- Write and illustrate a different ending for the story.
- Write and illustrate a story that Annie might one day tell to her grandchild.

Carller Jones—Gr. 3, Waycross, GA

Thinking About The Story

Challenge your students' critical-thinking skills with the following questions:

1. Annie did several things to try to delay the weaving of the rug. Do you think Annie should have been punished for these things? Explain your answer.
2. Why do you think the Old One wanted to have each member of the family choose a gift before she died?
3. Do you think the Old One will die as soon as the rug is woven? Explain your answer.
4. Would you like to have Annie for a friend? Why or why not?
5. How do you think Annie's life will change when her grandmother dies?

Weaving Words

Read each clue.
Choose a matching word from the word bank.
Write the word in the puzzle.

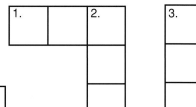

Across

1. the opposite of young
6. an American Indian people
7. Annie was her granddaughter
12. to take more time than needed
13. a precious stone

Down

2. a dry, sandy area
3. a covering used for warmth
4. a group of animals that stay together
5. a traditional Navajo home
8. a hill with steep sides and a flat top
9. a desert plant
10. a cliff
11. a frame on which weaving is done
12. the end of life

Word Bank

bluff	desert
dawdle	cactus
death	herd
blanket	grandmother
loom	hide
old	Navajo
turquoise	mesa
hogan	

Season's Readings!

Peek through the festive windows, past the colorful decorations, and into any holiday celebration, and you'll find the ingredients that make each holiday observance unique. With this impressive collection of holiday favorites, you and your youngsters can explore a variety of customs, beliefs, and celebrations from near and afar.

books reviewed by Deborah Zink Roffino

Hanukkah

A Great Miracle Happened There: A Chanukah Story

Written by Karla Kuskin & Illustrated by Robert Andrew Parker
Published by Willa Perlman Books

Brilliantly intertwining a contemporary story, Hanukkah facts, and ancient history has resulted in one superb picture book. Names and customs from antiquity come to life for children of every faith as they discover the chronicle of the miracle of lights.

In the story, Uncle Mort comments that maybe what makes a holiday a holiday is a combination of past history and present meaning. Ask students to recall the history of Hanukkah, then discuss how it is celebrated today. Repeat this procedure with two or three other familiar holidays. Find out what your youngsters think Uncle Mort meant. Could Uncle Mort be right?

The Gift

Written by Aliana Brodmann & Illustrated by Anthony Carnabuci
Published by Simon & Schuster Books For Young Readers

Set in Europe, this exquisite Hanukkah story gently reminds the reader that giving can bring immeasurable joy. Velvety paintings and a smooth story blend to set a reflective mood as a young girl ponders how to spend the five-mark piece that Father has given her for Hanukkah. She chooses an unlikely present that brings joy not only for her, but also for a little band of townsfolk, tied together only by the silver ribbons of the season.

Discuss the joy that the young girl and others received in exchange for the gift she chose. Ask youngsters to describe how they feel when they give gifts to others. Then discuss the difference between a store-bought gift and a gift from one's heart. For a heartfelt writing activity, have each student write and illustrate a story entitled "The Best Gift I Ever Gave." Compile the stories into a class booklet for all to enjoy.

In The Month Of Kislev: A Story For Hanukkah

Written by Nina Jaffe & Illustrated by Louise August
Published by Viking

Striking, bold prints with luminous colors decorate this lovely holiday folktale from Eastern Europe. The narrative is first-class storytelling, and the wry twist at the end makes this a coveted Hanukkah treat every year: a lesson of wisdom and charity.

Place some loose change in a small cloth bag or a cotton stocking; then shake the pouch of coins at the conclusion of the story. Find out what thoughts come to your students' minds. Discuss how the wisdom of the rabbi helped the merchant realize his selfishness. On the chalkboard write a student-generated list of ways that your students could add joy to the holidays of less fortunate people. As a class, act upon one or more of the suggestions.

Hanukkah Lights, Hanukkah Nights

*Written by Leslie Kimmelman &
Illustrated by John Himmelman
Published by HarperCollins Publishers*

A colorful, primary interpretation of one family's celebrations over the eight nights of the Festival Of Lights. This simple book stresses family love and togetherness more than the holiday's history, although a more detailed explanation of the holiday is on the final page.

Brighten your classroom with these dazzling, student-made menorahs. To begin, sponge-paint a menorah shape on white art paper using sponges that have been cut into narrow rectangles. When the paint is dry, mount the picture onto a slightly larger sheet of colorful construction paper. Light each candle by wrapping a tissue-paper square around a pencil eraser, dipping it in glue, and pressing it onto the top of the candle.

The Uninvited Guest And Other Jewish Holiday Tales

*Written by Nina Jaffe & Illustrated by Elivia
Published by Scholastic Inc.*

Prefaced with a brief but illuminating history of each holiday, this keepsake has seven stories that span the Jewish calendar, including Hanukkah. These tender stories touch the heart with the easy, comforting narration of a master storyteller. The characters are brushed by magic, the unexpected, and the unexplained; but the tales all end with the reassurance that miracles happen in every season.

"Hannah The Joyful" is the enchanting tale that accompanies the history and customs of Hanukkah. Hannah, a Hebrew woman with great joy, overcomes a series of obstacles by using her wit and never losing sight of her beliefs. Because Hannah shared her feelings of joy and gladness with each and every person she met, Hannah was called "Hannah The Joyful." Ask students to consider what qualities they consistently display around others. Near the top of a sheet of drawing paper, have each child write a phrase that describes himself. Below the phrase have each student draw and color a self-portrait. Display the completed projects on a bulletin board entitled "The Season's Finest!"

Becky The Thoughtfu

Christmas

Hark! A Christmas Sampler

*Written by Jane Yolen &
Illustrated by Tomie dePaola
Published by G. P. Putnam's Sons*

Accompanied by the feisty paintbrush of Tomie dePaola, America's story lady Jane Yolen offers this charming collection of legends, traditions, tales, poems, and songs from every corner of the world. Readers learn how children from many cultures celebrate the birth of the Christ Child. This book is full of Christmas magic as new and classic offerings alternate to bring forth a superior assembly of Christmas enchantment.

Packed with a seemingly endless supply of seasonal offerings, this volume can be referred to time and again throughout the holidays. Fill a spare moment with a silly poem about Santa, a rousing chorus of "We Wish You A Merry Christmas," or a Christmas legend.

Christmas Eve At Santa's

*Written by Alf Prøysen &
Illustrated by Jens Ahlbom
Published by R & S Books
Distributed by Farrar, Straus and Giroux*

This fresh Christmas story from Norway finds Santa's own kids pretty lonely on Christmas Eve. Somebody else's pop comes to the rescue, proving that there's a lot of Santa in every daddy. This translation of the late Alf Prøysen's heartwarming narrative gives Santa an authentic Norwegian look, but the meaning of the holiday remains universal.

Students will have a jolly time writing these letters to Santa. In their letters, challenge students to persuade Santa to spend Christmas Eve in their homes. Remind them that Santa will be most concerned about his Christmas Eve responsibilities and that before he can consider their invitations he will need to know how they plan to have his Christmas gifts successfully delivered. And of course it probably wouldn't hurt to mention in their letters that they've been terrific students this year!

Too Many Tamales

Written by Gary Soto &
Illustrated by Ed Martinez
Published by G. P. Putnam's Sons

This precious Christmas story sparkles with lavish, full-page paintings that welcome readers into a loving, Hispanic American home. Maria plunges into a bowl of dough to the elbows, but it's not cookie dough; it's *masa*, for the traditional tamales that give the dinner a truly Hispanic taste. While customs may vary, the traits of children are universal. Maria's curiosity mixes generously with her absentmindedness and yields a bath of trouble. And it is Mother whom she "kneads" when it seems as if the problem is insurmountable.

With the help of a loving family, Maria's precarious situation concludes happily—even after the failed attempt to eat her way out of trouble! For a fun writing activity, have students create imaginary autobiographical versions of Maria's story. To do this, have each student choose a favorite holiday food that he and his family enjoy and identify a household treasure that he wishes were his own. As he writes his story, the student creates a predicament for himself; then he explains how he successfully overcomes the situation with the help of his family and loved ones. When the tales are written and illustrated, set aside time for students to share them with their classmates.

The Christmas Carp

Written by Rita Törnqvist &
Illustrated by Marit Törnqvist
Published by R & S Books
Distributed by Farrar, Straus and Giroux

With delicate watercolors that feature the aged buildings of Prague, the busy marketplace, and all the Christmas customs of Eastern Europe, this poignant tale recounts a holiday that young Thomas spent with his grandpa. No turkey, ham, or goose in this tale, for the traditional dinner is carp. Thomas befriends the substantial fish and complicates the plans for a holiday supper.

Prior to reading this endearing holiday tale, assist your youngsters in locating Prague on a world map. Tell students that you are going to read a story about a young boy who spends Christmas in Prague with his grandpa. Tell them the title of the book. Then, using the book title and the map location as clues, ask students to predict how this young boy's Christmas holiday may differ from their own. At the conclusion of the story, evaluate the predictions, leaving only those that were accurate. Then list other differences your students noted during the story.

Near the end of the story, Thomas makes a difficult, yet wise decision. Ask students to explain why the decision was so difficult to make. Find out if they agree with Thomas's decision and if they think Thomas would have made the decision without his grandpa's encouragement. Conclude the activity by unveiling a poster like the one shown. Provide colorful markers; then invite each student to write a wish on the chart. Display the completed project for all to enjoy.

Happy Holidays! Make A Wish!

I wish I could save the rain forests. Josh

I wish I had a baby brother. Carlos

I wish I had a trampoline! Anna

I wish I had a dog. Petra

Mickey's Christmas Carol

Adapted from the film by Jim Razzi
Published by Disney Press

No one portrays an old-fashioned English Christmas better than Charles Dickens, with the carols, the holly, the goose, and the snow. And Disney does Dickens so well that its retelling is almost as famous as the original. In this written version, based on the Disney film, the timeless story of compassion's triumph over greed comes to life for youngsters.

After hearing Jim Razzi's rendition of this classic tale, your youngsters will be more than delighted to view the Disney video of the same title. This entertaining production features a special cast of Disney characters including Mickey Mouse as Scrooge's humble employee, Bob Cratchit, and Scrooge McDuck as Ebenezer Scrooge himself. In addition to the video presentation, engage your youngsters in a class goodwill project. One example would be to ask students to donate items to be given to a local charity. Suggest items such as outgrown clothing, toys that are no longer played with, and canned food items. Have students deposit their donated items in a large gift-wrapped box in the classroom. Before delivery (or pickup) of the donations, write a holiday greeting on a giant length of bulletin-board paper. Have students color and autograph the banner. Roll the completed banner into a scroll and securely tie the scroll with a length of curling ribbon before tucking it inside the gift-wrapped box.

Christmas Trolls

Written & Illustrated by Jan Brett
Published by G. P. Putnam's Sons

Wrapped snugly in furry warmth against the frosty Scandinavian air—as only the rare artistry of Jan Brett can depict—young Treva finds her holiday decorations disappearing. The hairy culprits are up to Christmas mischief, as the traditional trimmings of a Northern European holiday border each reverberant page.

This is not the first time Treva has had trouble with trolls *(Trouble With Trolls)*, but this time a friendship develops that is filled with the spirit of Christmas. Ask students what the trolls learned from Treva. Then find out what they think Treva learned from the trolls. Emphasize that acts of kindness are the most valuable gifts of any holiday season. Then have each student make a special gift of kindness for a family member. To make the gift, fold a half sheet of drawing paper in half; then, keeping the fold at the bottom, decorate the outside of the folded paper to resemble gift wrap. Inside the folded paper, describe the kindness that will be shared. Refold the paper and punch a hole near the top margin. Thread a one-foot length of curling ribbon through the hole and tie the ends in a bow. From a smaller scrap of paper, design a gift tag. Then use a dab of glue to attach the gift tag to the gift. If desired, place extra supplies at a center and encourage students to make additional gifts of kindness for their family members and friends.

Pancho's Piñata

Written by Stefan Czernecki and Timothy Rhodes &
Illustrated by Stefan Czernecki
Published by Hyperion Books For Children

Deftly applying fancy to facts, this lively fable is a heartwarming explanation of Mexican Christmas customs, such as the precious *piñata*. Stylized folk art sparkles on every page, providing further details of the village of San Miguel, its inhabitants, and its traditions such as the *posada*, or Christmas Eve procession.

Making a piñata is the perfect follow-up activity to this delightful book. Two piñata-making activities are shown at the right. If you have several days, consider engaging your youngsters in making star-shaped piñatas. If time isn't in your favor, colorful paper-bag piñatas can be created in one or two days.

Paper-Bag Piñatas

To make a paper-bag piñata, stuff a paper lunch bag about two-thirds full of crumpled newspaper. Drop a few wrapped candies in the bag; then fold about two inches of the top of the bag to the outside. Set the bag aside. Working with several four-inch-wide strips of colorful tissue paper, fringe each strip by cutting one-inch-wide slits along one side of the paper. Glue the uncut edge of the tissue-paper strips around the bag, starting at the bottom of the bag and working upward. Overlap the fringed edges as you go. When you reach the top of the bag, use a hole puncher to punch a series of holes around the folded edge, at about one-inch intervals. Thread a two-foot length of heavy string or twine through the holes; then close the top of the bag by carefully pulling together the ends of the string. Tie the bag closed. Use the remaining string to suspend the piñata. To complete the project, glue several one-inch-wide tissue-paper streamers to the bottom of the bag.

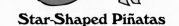

Star-Shaped Piñatas

Follow these steps to make a star-shaped piñata.

1. Inflate and tie off a medium, round balloon.
2. Brush a mixture of three parts school glue and one part water onto a section of the balloon. Apply small squares of newspaper to cover the glue. Continue gluing on additional paper squares until the balloon is completely covered.
3. For added strength, glue on two or three more layers of paper, with at least two hours of drying time between the addition of each layer.
4. Snip the rim of a cone-shaped paper cup, bend the rim pieces outward, and glue the rim pieces to the balloon opposite the knot.
5. Glue four other similarly cut cone-shaped paper cups around the balloon. Allow for drying time.
6. Brush a thinned glue mixture onto the balloon and the cups, and apply small squares of colorful tissue paper to the entire piñata.
7. Glue strips of tissue paper to the points of the piñata cones.
8. Tie yarn around the balloon knot for suspending the piñata.
9. To fill the piñata, cut a slit near the top and poke a few wrapped candies inside.
10. Patch the opening with tissue paper and enjoy!

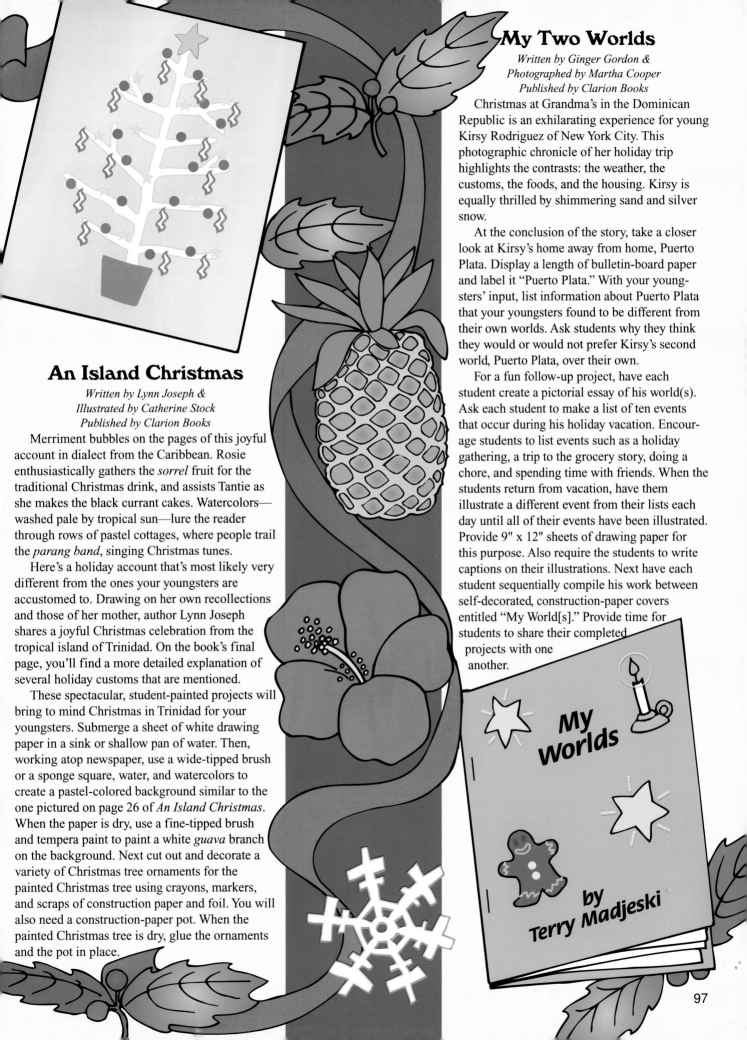

An Island Christmas

Written by Lynn Joseph &
Illustrated by Catherine Stock
Published by Clarion Books

Merriment bubbles on the pages of this joyful account in dialect from the Caribbean. Rosie enthusiastically gathers the *sorrel* fruit for the traditional Christmas drink, and assists Tantie as she makes the black currant cakes. Watercolors—washed pale by tropical sun—lure the reader through rows of pastel cottages, where people trail the *parang band*, singing Christmas tunes.

Here's a holiday account that's most likely very different from the ones your youngsters are accustomed to. Drawing on her own recollections and those of her mother, author Lynn Joseph shares a joyful Christmas celebration from the tropical island of Trinidad. On the book's final page, you'll find a more detailed explanation of several holiday customs that are mentioned.

These spectacular, student-painted projects will bring to mind Christmas in Trinidad for your youngsters. Submerge a sheet of white drawing paper in a sink or shallow pan of water. Then, working atop newspaper, use a wide-tipped brush or a sponge square, water, and watercolors to create a pastel-colored background similar to the one pictured on page 26 of *An Island Christmas*. When the paper is dry, use a fine-tipped brush and tempera paint to paint a white *guava* branch on the background. Next cut out and decorate a variety of Christmas tree ornaments for the painted Christmas tree using crayons, markers, and scraps of construction paper and foil. You will also need a construction-paper pot. When the painted Christmas tree is dry, glue the ornaments and the pot in place.

My Two Worlds

Written by Ginger Gordon &
Photographed by Martha Cooper
Published by Clarion Books

Christmas at Grandma's in the Dominican Republic is an exhilarating experience for young Kirsy Rodriguez of New York City. This photographic chronicle of her holiday trip highlights the contrasts: the weather, the customs, the foods, and the housing. Kirsy is equally thrilled by shimmering sand and silver snow.

At the conclusion of the story, take a closer look at Kirsy's home away from home, Puerto Plata. Display a length of bulletin-board paper and label it "Puerto Plata." With your youngsters' input, list information about Puerto Plata that your youngsters found to be different from their own worlds. Ask students why they think they would or would not prefer Kirsy's second world, Puerto Plata, over their own.

For a fun follow-up project, have each student create a pictorial essay of his world(s). Ask each student to make a list of ten events that occur during his holiday vacation. Encourage students to list events such as a holiday gathering, a trip to the grocery story, doing a chore, and spending time with friends. When the students return from vacation, have them illustrate a different event from their lists each day until all of their events have been illustrated. Provide 9" x 12" sheets of drawing paper for this purpose. Also require the students to write captions on their illustrations. Next have each student sequentially compile his work between self-decorated, construction-paper covers entitled "My World[s]." Provide time for students to share their completed projects with one another.

La Nochebuena South Of The Border

Written & Illustrated by James Rice
Published by Pelican Publishing Company, Inc.

All the trappings of a Mexican celebration are described in this bilingual account of *Papá Noel's* visit on Christmas Eve. *Fruta* and *dulces* for the *piñata* and the *fiesta* are all prepared. But no red fur and reindeer or cookies and milk for this jolly old elf; it's *serape* and *sombrero* and *café con leche*. Lots of cultural information is included in the well-sketched scenes.

With English and Spanish text appearing on each page, this south-of-the-border rendition of " 'Twas The Night Before Christmas" has endless learning possibilities. And the humorous antics—both written and illustrated—add to its literary appeal. A comparison to the original version may be in order. Or consider transferring the text to transparencies so that you can practice chorally reading the piece with your brood. Whichever you choose, this is one holiday selection that's sure to be requested time and time again!

A Christmas Surprise For Chabelita

Written by Argentina Palacios &
Illustrated by Lori Lohstoeter
Published by BridgeWater Books

Young Chabelita's mother must leave Panama to teach in a distant city. Even though she doesn't mind the hours she spends with *Abuelita* and *Abuelito*, the little girl longs for *Mamá*. As Christmas approaches, Chabelita prepares her recitation for the school program—never knowing that her present will come early this year, for Mamá is in the audience. Resonant paintings offer glimpses into Latin American life.

Chabelita's story parallels a childhood memory of the author. As a young girl, author Argentina Palacios was raised by loving grandparents while her mother taught in a different city. And she, too, learned a poem that told the story of Little Red Riding Hood. Invite students to talk about special times they've spent with their grandparents, parents, or other family members. Some students may even like to share experiences they've had that are similar to Chabelita's and the author's. Wrap up the discussion by challenging students to memorize favorite poems. With the assistance of your media specialist, display in your classroom a collection of poetry books owned by your school library. Then, once a week, on an established day and at a predetermined time, invite students to recite favorite poems. Encourage students to invite their loved ones to the weekly presentations.

Panama-born Argentina Palacios has recently translated Chabelita's story into her native language. The Spanish version, *Sorpresa de Navidad para Chabelita*, is also published by BridgeWater Books.

A Southern Time Christmas

Written by Robert Bernardini &
Illustrated by James Rice
Published by Pelican Publishing Company, Inc.

Northern kids often forget that many American children don't look for snow on Christmas morning; but they still search the skies for Santa. In this merry, loose parody of " 'Twas The Night Before Christmas," Santa sheds his heavy coat and feasts on chicken and dumplings and grits to help him make it through that long night down South. Jim Rice's famous pen scratches out droll sketches full of color.

At the end of this playful takeoff of the classic poem, a good ol' Southern roar is in store. So bundle your youngsters up and head outdoors. Be sure to check the skies before puffing up your chests one and all, and bellowing, "Santa, come back here! Come back here tonight!" Check the skies one more time before returning inside, just to be sure.... Once you're settled inside, have students contemplate snacks for Santa. Find out their opinions about what Santa might like to snack on when he visits their town or city. List all suggested snack items on the board; then take a student poll to determine the top ten snacks. Copy and post the resulting list of "Top Ten Santa Snacks" for others in your school to enjoy.

Author Robert Bernardini knows that snowy conditions are not necessary to understand and celebrate the true meaning of Christmas. While his sequel, *Southern Love For Christmas*, is not as closely focused on the South, it carries a strong message for youngsters: *Loving and caring for one another are what the true spirit of Christmas is all about.* Be sure to include this title in your collection of seasonal readings.

Top Ten Santa Snacks

1. cookies
2. milk
3. cake
4. crackers and cheese
5. pizza
6. popcorn
7. carrot sticks
8.

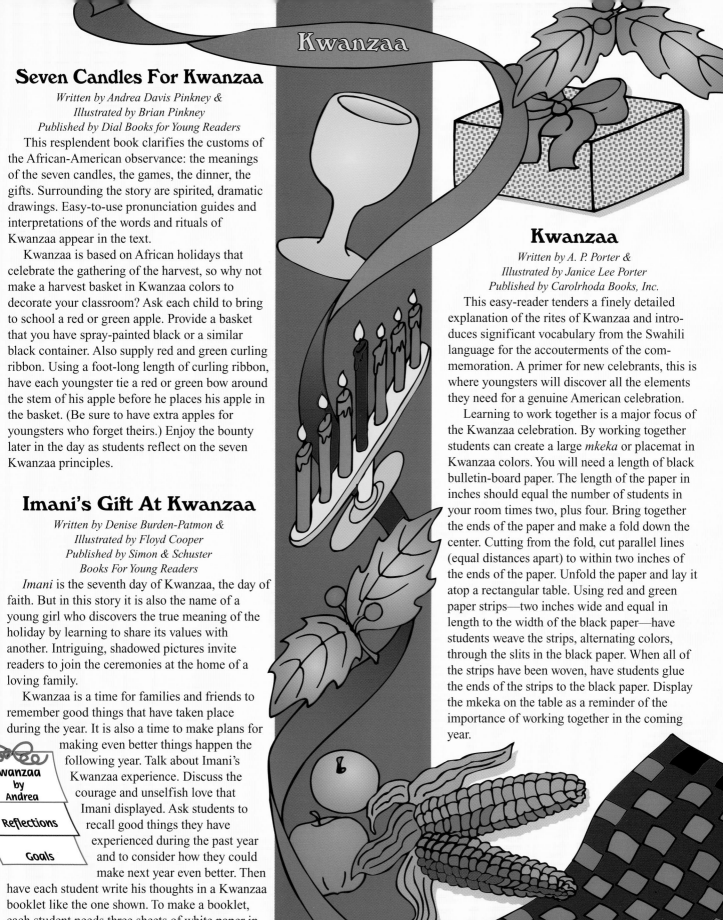

Seven Candles For Kwanzaa

Written by Andrea Davis Pinkney &
Illustrated by Brian Pinkney
Published by Dial Books for Young Readers

This resplendent book clarifies the customs of the African-American observance: the meanings of the seven candles, the games, the dinner, the gifts. Surrounding the story are spirited, dramatic drawings. Easy-to-use pronunciation guides and interpretations of the words and rituals of Kwanzaa appear in the text.

Kwanzaa is based on African holidays that celebrate the gathering of the harvest, so why not make a harvest basket in Kwanzaa colors to decorate your classroom? Ask each child to bring to school a red or green apple. Provide a basket that you have spray-painted black or a similar black container. Also supply red and green curling ribbon. Using a foot-long length of curling ribbon, have each youngster tie a red or green bow around the stem of his apple before he places his apple in the basket. (Be sure to have extra apples for youngsters who forget theirs.) Enjoy the bounty later in the day as students reflect on the seven Kwanzaa principles.

Imani's Gift At Kwanzaa

Written by Denise Burden-Patmon &
Illustrated by Floyd Cooper
Published by Simon & Schuster
Books For Young Readers

Imani is the seventh day of Kwanzaa, the day of faith. But in this story it is also the name of a young girl who discovers the true meaning of the holiday by learning to share its values with another. Intriguing, shadowed pictures invite readers to join the ceremonies at the home of a loving family.

Kwanzaa is a time for families and friends to remember good things that have taken place during the year. It is also a time to make plans for making even better things happen the following year. Talk about Imani's Kwanzaa experience. Discuss the courage and unselfish love that Imani displayed. Ask students to recall good things they have experienced during the past year and to consider how they could make next year even better. Then have each student write his thoughts in a Kwanzaa booklet like the one shown. To make a booklet, each student needs three sheets of white paper in the following sizes: 5 1/2" x 8 1/2", 6 1/2" x 8 1/2", 4 1/2" x 8 1/2"; red and/or green curling ribbon; a red, a green, and a black crayon; scissors; access to a hole puncher; and a pencil.

Kwanzaa
by
Andrea

Reflections

Goals

Kwanzaa

Written by A. P. Porter &
Illustrated by Janice Lee Porter
Published by Carolrhoda Books, Inc.

This easy-reader tenders a finely detailed explanation of the rites of Kwanzaa and introduces significant vocabulary from the Swahili language for the accouterments of the commemoration. A primer for new celebrants, this is where youngsters will discover all the elements they need for a genuine American celebration.

Learning to work together is a major focus of the Kwanzaa celebration. By working together students can create a large *mkeka* or placemat in Kwanzaa colors. You will need a length of black bulletin-board paper. The length of the paper in inches should equal the number of students in your room times two, plus four. Bring together the ends of the paper and make a fold down the center. Cutting from the fold, cut parallel lines (equal distances apart) to within two inches of the ends of the paper. Unfold the paper and lay it atop a rectangular table. Using red and green paper strips—two inches wide and equal in length to the width of the black paper—have students weave the strips, alternating colors, through the slits in the black paper. When all of the strips have been woven, have students glue the ends of the strips to the black paper. Display the mkeka on the table as a reminder of the importance of working together in the coming year.

Charlie And The Chocolate Factory
Written by Roald Dahl

The one thing Charlie Bucket longed for more than anything was a Golden Ticket that would entitle him to a tour of Willy Wonka's Chocolate Factory and a lifetime supply of chocolate. "Many wonderful surprises await you!" read the invitation on the much-coveted Golden Tickets. And that is exactly what's in store for Charlie Bucket and your youngsters!

ideas by Lisa Leonardi

The Man Behind The Story
Roald Dahl: 1916–1990

It's interesting to note that Roald Dahl did not intend to become a writer. His writing career began quite accidentally when a reporter from *The Saturday Evening Post* arranged to interview Dahl about his experiences as a World War II fighter pilot. Dahl had jotted down his ideas in the form of a story, and it was Dahl's story that appeared in print. This incident launched Dahl's writing career.

Much of Roald Dahl's writing reflects adventures he experienced as a boy. In writing *Charlie And The Chocolate Factory*, Dahl drew upon memories of a neighborhood sweetshop, and recollections of testing and rating chocolate inventions for a well-known chocolate manufacturer. To learn more about Dahl's childhood adventures—and misadventures—read *Boy: Tales Of Childhood* (Puffin Books, 1986).

Spoiled Rotten

Augustus Gloop, Veruca Salt, Violet Beauregarde, and Mike Teavee were all spoiled children who, with the help of their parents, routinely got their own way. Ask your students if they think it's possible for a child to have everything he wants. Then ask each child to think of five things he really wishes he could have. Next ask the youngsters if these are the same things they would have wished for last year. Discuss why a person's wants change. Invite students to share their opinions about whether youngsters should or should not be able to have their way all or most of the time.

Five Golden Tickets

However slim Charlie's chances were, he was lucky enough to find a Golden Ticket. Use this exercise to explore the concept of probability with your youngsters. You will need two gift bags labeled "Bag 1" and "Bag 2," ten gold construction-paper tickets, and 75 white construction-paper tickets. Under the watchful eyes of your youngsters, place five gold tickets in each bag. Then place 25 white tickets in Bag 1 and 50 white tickets in Bag 2. Scramble the tickets in each bag.

First ask students to decide from which of the two bags they think they would have a better chance of drawing a golden ticket and why. Lead students to understand that since Bag 1 has the same number of golden tickets as Bag 2, but it has less tickets in all, the chances of drawing a golden ticket from Bag 1 are greater. Then let each student take a turn drawing a ticket from each bag. Record the results on graphs. (Be sure the tickets are returned to the proper bags and the contents of each bag are scrambled after every turn.) When the exercise is complete, help students analyze the results.

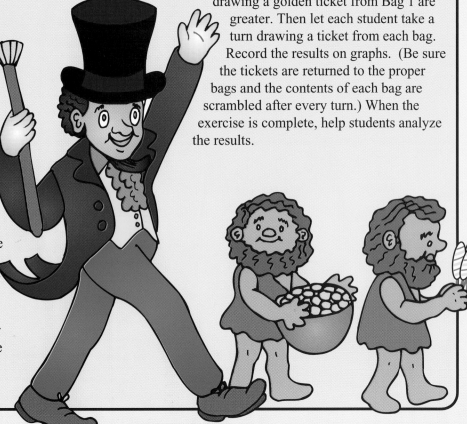

Keeping Ahead Of The Competition

It will be very challenging for Charlie to fill the shoes of Mr. Willy Wonka. He'll need to be very clever, indeed! Find out if your youngsters think they could keep the chocolate factory one step ahead of its competition. Working in pairs, challenge students to create new candy machines for the factory that would produce never-before-heard-of, savory, sweet confections. Students can illustrate their machines on drawing paper or construct models of the machines using modeling clay, cardboard boxes and tubes, craft sticks, pipe cleaners, and other building materials. Also ask each student pair to develop an advertisement for its new candy invention. When the twosomes are ready to unveil and "sell" their new candy creations, invite a neighboring classroom to share in your youngsters' sweet success!

Revolting Recipes

Listening to candy names like Toffee-Apple Trees, Lickable Wallpaper, Eatable Marshmallow Pillows, and other creative confections will have your youngsters wishing for a taste of the sweet stuff. You can make their wishes come true with *Roald Dahl's Revolting Recipes* (Penguin Books, 1994). This unique cookbook features 31 recipes from Dahl's books, and ten of those tasty treats are referenced to *Charlie And The Chocolate Factory*. So whether your class is in the mood for Willy Wonka's Nutty Crunch Surprise or Hot Ice Cream For Cold Days, you're bound to find at least one revolting recipe to whet your youngsters' appetites!

From Cacao Beans To Chocolate

If you're looking for a rich research project, try investigating chocolate! *Chocolate* by Jacqueline Dineen (Carolrhoda Books, Inc.; 1991) offers an excellent look at the history of chocolate, where it comes from, and how it's made. *Let's Visit A Chocolate Factory* by Catherine O'Neill (Troll Associates, 1988) also provides youngsters with a firsthand look at a real-life chocolate factory. Let your youngsters show off their chocolaty knowledge on a classroom cacao tree. Display a large tree cutout on a bulletin board entitled "Flavorful Facts About Chocolate." Add several green leaves near the top. Next to the display, provide a supply of red, yellow, gold, and light green construction paper and a tagboard tracer cut into the shape of a cacao pod. Invite students to record facts about chocolate on pod cutouts; then attach their facts to the tree.

Willy Wonka's Glass Jar

Sweeten up your classroom estimation jar by renaming it Willy Wonka's Glass Jar. Fill the jar with one kind of candy. Give the candy a Wonka name such as Everlasting Gobstoppers, Exploding Candy, or Rainbow Drops. After all students have submitted their estimations for the number of candies in the jar, count the candy and determine which student had the most accurate estimate. Then give each student one piece of candy and send the remaining candy home with the winner. Refill the jar with a different kind of candy—one that has a Willy Wonka name, of course!

Oompa-Loompas

Wonderful workers, musical, and mischievous—that's how Willy Wonka described the Oompa-Loompas. What he didn't mention is that they sing exactly what's on their minds! Talk about each of the four songs the Oompa-Loompas sang. Use the songs to discuss the unflattering characteristics of each of the children who left the chocolate factory in disgrace. Lead a friendly class debate about the author's motives for these characterizations. What was he trying to say about gum chewers? spoiled children? overeaters? television addicts? children not minding their parents? rudeness to others? Ask students to explain why Charlie was chosen to inherit the factory. Then divide students into small groups and have each group create an Oompa-Loompa song about either Charlie, Willy Wonka, or Grandpa Joe. After the songs are written, have a sharing time for the student groups to read their songs. Or for fun, ask each group to sing its song to a familiar tune!

Book Versus Video

Invite your students to an afternoon at the movies! The video *Willy Wonka & The Chocolate Factory* is just as scrumptious to watch as the book is to read, yet offers several differences from which to build an exciting activity on comparing and contrasting. After listing the differences between the book and the video, ask students why they think these differences exist. Students may be surprised to discover that Roald Dahl wrote the screenplay for the movie, too.

"Wonkamania" Day!

As a culmination to this appetizing read-aloud, plan a "Wonkamania" Day! A day or two in advance of the event, present each youngster with a golden ticket invitation. Inform students that they must have their tickets with them to participate! Then gather a top hat and a gold-topped walking cane (or something similar) and work your magic by integrating sweets into activities you've planned for the day. Here are a few savory suggestions you might like to consider:

- Have students write and illustrate an ABC book of candy inventions.
- Complete a taste comparison between three or four different candy treats; then create a class graph that shows which of the four candy treats was most favored by your youngsters.
- Let your students finger-paint with chocolate pudding.
- Brainstorm a class-generated list of foods that are made from or with chocolate. Have each youngster choose his top ten favorites and list them in alphabetical order.
- Have each student write and illustrate a news article about the greatest chocolate story ever told.
- Make a chocolate cookbook. Ask each student to contribute one wacky recipe.
- Set aside some time for singing! Invite students to choose songs they think the Oompa-Loompas might enjoy.

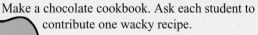

A Golden Ticket Invitation

Entitles you to admittance to "Wonkamania" Day

Date: February 9

Place: Your classroom

Time: 8:15 A.M.

Many wonderful surprises await you!

More Chocolaty Read-Alouds

Chocolate-Covered Ants by Stephen Manes (Scholastic Inc., 1990)
Two brothers make a bet about eating chocolate-covered ants in this hilarious account of one boy's recipe for disaster.

Mary Marony And The Chocolate Surprise by Suzy Kline (G. P. Putnam's Sons, 1995)
Second-grader Mary Marony resorts to cheating to be sure that she gets a golden ticket in her candy bar. The results of her dishonesty surprise Mary and the whole second-grade class. A perfect follow-up to *Charlie And The Chocolate Factory*.

The Chocolate Touch by Patrick S. Catling (Bantam Books, Inc.; 1984)
John Midas discovers that his sweet dream come true (being able to turn everything his lips touch into chocolate) has its bitter side.

Chocolate Fever by Robert Kimmel Smith (Dell Publishing Company, 1994)
Henry Green loves eating chocolate—morning, noon, and night. But a case of chocolate fever teaches Henry that there can be too much of a good thing!

Name _____

Picture-Perfect

Make a picture chart.
Read each clue; then draw the matching
    picture on the chart.
Color your drawings.

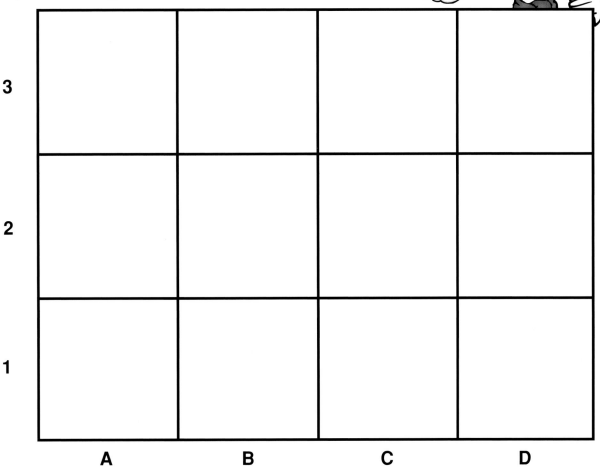

Clues

In C-1, draw what the Bucket family eats for breakfast.
In D-3, draw what the Bucket family eats for dinner.
In B-1, draw what Charlie gets every year for his birthday.
In A-2, draw what is made at the factory where Mr. Bucket worked.
In D-2, draw what Mr. Bucket read to find out about the Golden Tickets.
In C-3, draw what Charlie wants to find in his candy bar.
In A-1, draw what Augustus eats all day.
In C-2, draw what Veruca's father shelled at his factory.
In B-2, draw what Violet puts behind her ear at mealtimes.
In A-3, draw what Mike watches day and night.
In B-3, draw what Grandpa Joe gave Charlie.
In D-1, draw what Charlie found in the snow.

Note To Teacher: Use this activity after completing chapter ten.

Bravo For Beverly Cleary!

Henry Huggins, Ramona Quimby, Ralph S. Mouse, and Muggie Maggie are just a few of Beverly Cleary's endearing storybook characters. Her books have become the favorites of many young readers, and in the classroom they rank as first-rate read-alouds. To complement your best-loved books from Cleary's outstanding collection, pick and choose from these classroom-tested suggestions.

Meet The Author

As a child growing up in Oregon amidst two world wars and economic hardships, Beverly Cleary longed to read honest stories of real kids and their true-life experiences. Later, as a children's librarian, Cleary found herself frustrated in her search for interesting, easy-to-read books that would speak to the average, ordinary child. Finally she decided to fill the void by writing her own children's books. Her first book, *Henry Huggins*, was published in 1950. To date Cleary has penned more than 30 books for young readers.

For a most delightful and accurate portrayal of Beverly Cleary as a child, a teenager, an adult, and a writer, read her autobiography *Beverly Cleary: A Girl From Yamhill* (William Morrow And Company, Inc.; 1988).

The Mouse And The Motorcycle

A mouse can't ride a motorcycle! But as Keith—the motorcycle's owner—soon discovers, this mouse isn't just any mouse!

Vroom! Vroom! Here's a creative-writing activity that's sure to get your students' wheels turning! Ask each child to pretend that he is the proud owner of a brand-new motorcycle. He may keep the bike for two weeks. Suggest that each child choose a travel destination and a riding partner (if desired), then write and illustrate a story about his motorcycle adventures. Vrooooooooooooom!

Jeannette M. Sweet
Newport Beach, CA

Trying to choose a favorite scene from *The Mouse And The Motorcycle* may be the most difficult part of this follow-up activity! Once students have made their selections, ask each child to re-create his favorite scene in the form of a diorama. Give each child a small empty box (a shoebox works well), and make available an assortment of construction paper and craft supplies such as fabric scraps, glitter, sequins, and pipe cleaners. Set aside small portions of time on each of several days for students to work on their projects. When the dioramas are complete, invite each youngster to present and explain the scene he depicted in his diorama.

Betty Kobes—Gr. 1
West Hancock Elementary
Kanawha, IA

The Mouse And The Motorcycle diorama by Luke

Ramona Quimby, Age 8

There are trials and triumphs aplenty as Ramona Quimby, age 8, enters third grade.

When a hard-boiled egg fad begins at school, Ramona joins right in! But she's soon sorry that she did! After reading this portion of the story aloud, discuss the term *fad* with your youngsters. Ask students to brainstorm trends that are currently popular. Record their ideas on a chart labeled "What's Hot!"; then discuss how and why certain fads become popular and others do not. Follow up this discussion by challenging each student to design a poster that introduces a new fad. On a given date, encourage each child to share his fabulous new fad with his classmates!

Laura Lee Powers & Lisa Donahoo—Gr. 3
Bryant Elementary
Mableton, GA

For a lively discussion, ask students to talk about Ramona's relationship with her teacher, Mrs. Whaley. Find out how your students think Ramona rates as a student and how Mrs. Whaley rates as a teacher. For added fun, find out how your students think Ramona would adjust to a classroom taught by teachers featured in other books, such as Ms. Frizzle (Magic School Bus series), Viola Swamp or Miss Nelson *(Miss Nelson Is Missing!)*, or Mrs. Green *(The Teacher From The Black Lagoon)*. Conclude the discussion by having students write and illustrate want ads seeking the perfect teacher for Ramona.

Laura Lee Powers & Lisa Donahoo—Gr. 3

> ☆ **Wanted** ☆
> Nice, friendly teacher with lots of patience for an imaginative, high-spirited 8 year old!

After seeking advice from her father on how to "sell" her book to her class, Ramona decides to write her book report in the form of a television commercial. Your youngsters will enjoy selling their favorite books in the same way! Ask each youngster to create a poster that he feels will hook readers on his favorite book. Remind students that the name and author of the books they are selling must be featured on their posters. Display the resulting advertisements in a prominent location where passersby might also be "sold" on your youngsters' reading suggestions!

Tracy Hutcheson—Gr. 2, Featherstone Elementary
Woodbridge, VA

Ramona can provide plenty of writing motivation for your youngsters! Her experiences are fun, yet so true-to-life that children easily relate to them. The following prompts are sure to get your youngsters writing!

- After reading about Ramona's first day of third grade, ask students to write about their most recent first-day-of-school experiences. You may find that your youngsters' impressions of their first day of school are somewhat different than you recall!
- Follow up chapter three by asking students to write about their most embarrassing moments.
- When Ramona and Beezus prepare Sunday dinner for their parents, it turns into quite an experience. Ask students to write about a time they tried to prepare a meal for their families. Or have students plan meals (with cooking instructions) that they would like to prepare for their families.
- At the conclusion of the book, the Quimbys are astounded by the kindness of an older gentleman. Ask the students to write about a time that an act of kindness took them by surprise, or about a time that they have surprised others with an act of kindness.

Barbara Rumsey
John Kennedy Elementary
Batavia, NY

Ramona And Her Father

When Mr. Quimby unexpectedly loses his job, Ramona takes an active hand in the challenges that develop.

Your students are sure to get down to business when you present them with this creative challenge! To begin ask students to recall Ramona's desire for a million dollars—an amount of money that was sure to solve all of her family's financial problems. Then challenge each student to create a make-believe business that she thinks would earn her a million dollars. Have each child design a 4" x 8" business card for her million-dollar business. Explain that each business card should include the name of the business, a catchy slogan that explains what the business produces or what service it provides, the student's name, and a business phone number. Then in turn have each entrepreneur display her business card as she explains her enterprise to her classmates.

Jennie Mehigan—Gr. 3
St. Hilary School
Akron, OH

When Ramona crafts a crown from burrs, she ends up in a very sticky situation. But when your youngsters create these crowns, they'll end up with one-of-a-kind headpieces and a better understanding of some real-life math skills. In advance set up a classroom store from which crown decorations (such as sequins, feathers, ribbon, lace, and imitation jewels) will be sold. To make a crown, a student colors and cuts out a construction-paper copy of the crown pattern on page 108. He then takes a predetermined amount of play money to the store and buys the crown-making supplies he desires. (Each student should tally his purchases and determine the amount of change he is due.) Then he adorns his crown cutout with his purchases. Help each youngster secure his crown to the center of an 18" x 1 1/2" tagboard strip. Adjust the ends of the headband until the crown fits snugly on the child's head; then remove the crown and staple the head-band ends in place. There you have it! A crown like no other!

Peggy Wolke—Gr. 1
Graham North Elementary
Rosewood, OH

Ramona Forever

Ramona is back! And she has lots of surprises headed her way—a new job for her father, a wedding, and a new little Quimby!

What would be the perfect name for the newest Quimby? No doubt your youngsters will have an idea or two! On chart paper, record a student-generated list of names, sorting them into girl names and boy names. Narrow the list of names to the top five favorites in each category. Then, for added fun, ask student volunteers to find the meanings of the listed names in a book of baby names. Keep the class list of names posted until the name of the newest Quimby is revealed in the final chapter of the book.

Fran Rizzo—Gr. 3
Brookdale School
Bloomfield, NJ

102

Muggie Maggie

Maggie is far from thrilled about having to learn cursive writing. In fact, she decides she absolutely won't do it! Will Maggie ever change her mind?

Mrs. Leeper devises a plan! She writes cursive notes about Maggie; then she asks Maggie to deliver them to other teachers. Just as Mrs. Leeper had hoped, Maggie's curiosity gets the better of her and she peeks at the notes. Like Maggie, your youngsters are likely to be curious about the notes that you and other teachers write to one another. Build on that curiosity by asking each student to choose a teacher and write a note that he feels the selected teacher might write to a colleague. Increase the challenge by asking students to exchange and respond to each other's notes.

Kelli A. Thomas—Gr. 3
Otis Elementary School
Fremont, OH

Dear Ms. Thomas,
You won't believe what happened! Jason's pet snake got loose this morning! The kids went wild. Remember play practice at 1:00.
Mrs. Leeper

Oops! Maggie didn't mean to spell her name "M-u-g-g-i-e." It was just her awful handwriting. But when her classmates see her mistake, they begin to call her "Muggie Maggie." If only she had written more carefully! Help your students learn the value of writing their own names carefully by having them purposely write their names carelessly. Ask each student to write various letters within her name incorrectly. For example, Sally might make her *a* look like an *i*. Then she would write her name as "Silly Sally." Plan to let students share their mistaken identities aloud.

Kaye Schilling—Gr. 3
Lake Cable Elementary
Canton, OH

To reinforce cursive skills, get students reading your cursive writing! Each morning write an intriguing question or comment on the chalkboard. Ask the students to read the sentence to themselves; then ask a volunteer to read the sentence aloud. If desired invite students to respond to the sentence in their journals. As students begin to improve their own cursive writing and reading abilities, leave cursive notes of praise on their desktops.

Pam Williams—Gr. 3
Dixieland Elementary
Lakeland, FL

Wow! I can read this!

A Tour Of The Neighborhood

Through her wonderful stories, Cleary re-created her childhood neighborhood, moved it several blocks to Klickitat Street, and peopled it with lovable yet true-to-life characters. The result is a high-interest neighborhood that's perfect for reinforcing the concepts of neighborhood and community. Once your students are familiar with several of Cleary's books, have them work together to create a mural-size map of the neighborhood featured in Cleary's books. When the class project is complete, students can conduct neighborhood tours in which they share favorite events and humorous anecdotes about the neighborhood.

Patricia White—Librarian & Susan Gerritz—Gr. 3
Ventura Park Elementary School
Portland, OR

Pattern

Use with *Ramona And Her Father* on page 106.

Freckle Juice
by Judy Blume

Andrew Marcus wishes he had freckles—lots of freckles. In fact, he longs to look like his classmate, Nicky Lane, who is covered with freckles. At school, Andrew is so preoccupied with Nicky's freckles that he has difficulty concentrating. But just how far is this second grader willing to go to get freckles of his own?

ideas by Jennifer Overend

Introducing...Judy Blume

Judy Blume is a well-known author of children's books. As a child, she was curious about life and wished that more children's books were written about real-life issues. As an author, Blume recognizes the problems and fears that children face, and she believes that children "have a right to read about themselves." She describes herself as a people person and enjoys writing books about people, relationships, and feelings. Other entertaining titles written by Judy Blume include *Tales Of A Fourth Grade Nothing, The Pain And The Great One,* and *The One In The Middle Is The Green Kangaroo.*

Personality Panorama

Here's an activity that gives your students a peek into the personalities of the main characters. Label a large sheet of construction paper for each of the following characters: Andrew, Sharon, Nicky, Miss Kelly. Then display the resulting posters. After reading each chapter, have students dictate words and phrases that describe the characters and their actions throughout the chapter. Write each description on the appropriate poster.

As a follow-up activity, have students make character displays of their *Freckle Juice* friends. To make a display, accordion-fold a 6" x 18" strip of construction paper into four equal sections. Next fold in half four 4" x 5" white construction-paper rectangles. From the folded papers, cut paper-doll figures to resemble Andrew, Sharon, Nicky, and Miss Kelly. Decorate the resulting cutouts; then glue them to the accordion-folded paper as shown. Using the classroom posters as references, name and describe the characters below the cutouts. Showcase the completed projects in your classroom or school library.

Focus On Freckle Juice

Your freckle-juice fanatics will flip over this fun-filled cooperative-learning activity. At the completion of chapter 2, divide students into small groups. Ask each group to brainstorm a list of possible freckle-juice ingredients. Next give each group a stack of cards labeled with verbs such as *shake, blend, stir, boil, add,* and *chop.* In turn, the students in each group draw cards from the stack and incorporate the verbs and the ingredients into a freckle-juice recipe. When the recipes are completed, have each group use markers to copy its recipe onto a large recipe card cut from bulletin-board paper. Display the freckle-juice recipe predictions for all to see.

Pay Attention, Andrew

With Nicky (and his freckles) seated directly in front of him, Andrew finds concentrating in school downright difficult. Have your children brainstorm distractions that make it difficult for them to concentrate in school (such as noisy classmates, being hungry, or thinking about recess). List each suggestion on the chalkboard. Pair students and assign a distraction to each pair. Then have each twosome write a paragraph that tells how to overcome the distraction. Compile the pages of advice into a class booklet entitled "How To Concentrate In School."

Who Has Freckles?

It's all fun and freckles with this comparative graphing activity. In advance draw and label two poster-board graphs as shown. To begin, display the graph titled "Freckle Facts." In turn, have each student write her name in the column that best describes the amount of freckles she has. Then, beside the first graph, display the graph labeled "Freckle Fantasies." Have each child, in turn, write her name in the column that describes the amount of freckles she wishes that she had. Ask students to compare the results of the two graphs and share their observations. Conclude the activity by having students determine where Andrew and Nicky might write their names on the graphs.

Freckle Facts

Nichlaus		
Tressa	Sophie	
Katie	Marty	
Ian	Kiesha	
Caroline	Chris	
Ashley	Stacie	David
Leon	Todd	Jared
no freckles	some freckles	lots of freckles

Freckle Fantasies

		Nichlaus
Sophie		Leon
Marty	Jared	Tressa
Stacie	Chris	Katie
David	Ian	Kelsha
Todd	Caroline	Ashley
no freckles	some freckles	lots of freckles

Freckles For 50 Cents

Andrew purchased Sharon's freckle-juice recipe for 50 cents. Ask students to recall how many weeks' worth of allowance Andrew spent on his purchase (five weeks); then challenge students to determine how much allowance Andrew earned per week. For a fun math activity, give each student an advertisement insert that features items that youngsters would find appealing. Have each student cut one item and its price from his insert, then attach his cutout(s) to a 9" x 12" sheet of construction paper. When all of the purchases are glued in place, have each student answer the following questions on his paper: How many weeks of allowance would Andrew need to save in order to buy this item? How many weeks would it take to buy the item if Andrew earned 25¢ per week (50¢ per week)? How would you be able to buy this item?

Extra! Extra! Read All About It!

Just think of the talk around Andrew's school when he arrived with blue freckles! Have your youngsters imagine that they are reporters for Andrew's school newspaper. Duplicate student copies of the open newspaper form on page 111. Have each child fill in the date and then write a headline such as "Second Grader Develops Blue Spots!" or "Spotted Boy Enters Second Grade." Then have each child write an article and color a picture describing this amazing event. Allow students to be reporters and share their articles with the class.

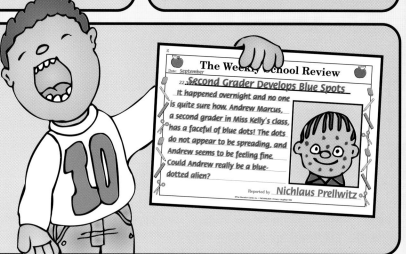

The Weekly School Review

Date: September

Second Grader Develops Blue Spots

It happened overnight and no one is quite sure how. Andrew Marcus, a second grader in Miss Kelly's class, has a faceful of blue dots! The dots do not appear to be spreading, and Andrew seems to be feeling fine. Could Andrew really be a blue-dotted alien?

Reported by *Nichlaus Prellwitz*

It's A Treat To Be Unique

Andrew learned, with Miss Kelly's help, that everyone is special just the way he is. Encourage students to focus on their unique qualities and characteristics such as freckles, dimples, curly hair, or a sense of humor. Lead your youngsters in a discussion about the differences among people by asking questions such as "Why do you think it is important for people to be different?", "Are you ever uncomfortable with your unique characteristics?", and "What would it be like if everyone looked and acted the same?" Close the discussion by having each child write a journal entry using one of the following sentence starters:

— "There's no one quite like me because...."
— "Being unique is a treat because...."
— "The things I like most about myself are...."

There's no one quite like me because I am unique! I have three dimples and I love peanut butter and pickle sandwiches.

Care To Contemplate?

Challenge your youngsters' critical-thinking skills at the completion of each chapter with the following questions.

Chapter 1: What do you think is in Sharon's recipe for freckle juice?

Chapter 2: Why do you think Sharon wanted the money before showing Andrew the freckle-juice recipe? Do you think that the freckle juice will give Andrew freckles? Why or why not?

Chapter 3: What do you think will happen to Andrew after he drinks the freckle juice?

Chapter 4: Andrew did not want to admit that he had been fooled by Sharon. How do you think Andrew will accomplish this?

Chapter 5: What do you think Miss Kelly's magic freckle remover really was? What do you think Andrew learned in this story? Do you think Nicky learned anything? Explain your answers.

The Weekly School Review

Date: _____

Reported by _____

Note To Teacher: Use this activity with "Extra! Extra! Read All About It!" on page 110.

111

Sizing Up The Story

Name _____

112

Complete each sentence about the story.
Cut on the dotted lines.
Staple the pages to the cutout in order.

1.

2. My favorite part

   was _____

3. My favorite
   character was _____

   because _____

4. The funniest part

   was _____

5. My advice to
   Andrew is _____

6. My advice to
   Sharon is _____

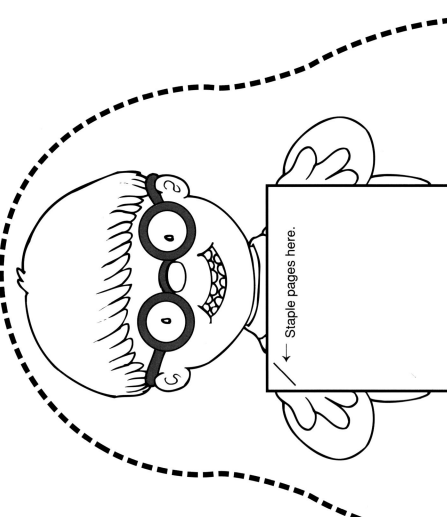

→ Staple pages here.

Freckle Juice

Note To Teacher: Use this activity after completing the book.

TEACHING *And* RESOURCE UNITS

Math

Five-Minute Fillers

Weather

Open House

Getting Ready For OPEN HOUSE

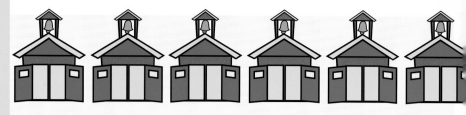

Without a doubt, Open House procedures vary greatly across the country. Thanks to our trusty subscribers, we have a wide variety of top-of-the-line Open House ideas and suggestions for your perusal. So whether you're looking for refurbishing ideas or a whole new look, you've definitely come to the right spot!

Kids At Work

Enlist your youngsters' help in creating a classroom full of busy workers! In advance, ask each student to bring a T-shirt from home. To make a busy worker, invert a large-size paper plate atop a second plate of the same size. Align the plates' edges and staple halfway around the rim. After positioning the staples at the top of the project, create a self-portrait by using markers and scraps of construction paper, fabric, and/or yarn to add facial features and hair. Next trace your forearm and hand onto a folded length of bulletin-board paper. Cut out the shape and decorate the two resulting cutouts as desired.

To assemble the project, slip a T-shirt over the back of a desk chair. Carefully pin or tape one arm cutout inside each sleeve; then position the cutouts atop the desk. Secure the paper-plate likeness atop the project as shown.

Debbie Tussey—Primary
West Irvine Elementary
Irvine, KY

Subject Displays

Give parents a clear picture of what their youngsters are learning with these student-made displays. Assign a group of students to each subject area; then ask each group to cooperatively create a display that reflects what has been or is being learned in its assigned subject area. Encourage students to use a variety of visual aids such as charts, posters, maps, models, and filmstrips. Audio aids can also be included. Exhibit the eye-catching displays around the classroom. Now that's impressive!

Jill Raveling—Gr. 3
Rudd Elementary
New Waverly, TX

Making The Connection

With all of the usual confusion of a big event like Open House, it can be difficult to figure out which child belongs with which adult(s). To clarify family connections for yourself as well as for other visiting parents, include the appropriate child's name on each adult's nametag. Presto! You'll have instant recognition!

Diane Fortunato—Gr. 2
Carteret School
Bloomfield, NJ

Enhancing Communication

A bulletin board featuring a photo-essay of classroom expectations and experiences is an ideal way to enhance communication with parents who have difficulty understanding the English language. Label each photograph with a simple sentence of explanation. After Open House, place the photographs and their corresponding captions in a photo album. The album can then be sent home to parents who were unable to attend the Open House festivities.

Marty Kafer—Gr. 1
English Language Development Center
De Vargas Elementary School
San Jose, CA

Hello! I'm Clare's dad, Fred Robbins.

Hi! I'm Mike's mom, Anita VanBeek.

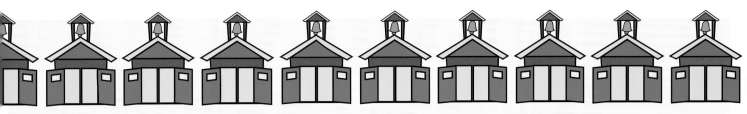

Bushels Of Fun

Students and their parents can easily sink their teeth into this Open House extravaganza. With your youngsters' help, decorate the classroom using an apple theme. (Ideas might include apple-shaped desktags, apple-shaped parent and student nametags, and a bulletin-board display entitled "Bushels Of Good Work.") Also label and suspend a large apple cutout above each of your learning stations. On the afternoon of Open House, display the nametags, a supply of safety pins, and an Open House checklist like the one shown. That evening, position yourself at the conference station. If desired provide a table of "apple-icious" snacks for your visitors to enjoy.

Angelia Morton—Gr. 1
Carpenter Elementary School
Nacogdoches, TX

In The Spotlight

On Open House night, what could be more appealing to parents than observing their children in a class mini-production of "Our Day At School." Send home special invitations encouraging parents to be present for this 15-minute portion of the evening. At the scheduled time have your youngsters take their seats. Ask all family members to stand at the back of the classroom. During the 15-minute time frame, guide students through a series of mini-lessons. If desired, have students perform a special song or fingerplay at the conclusion of the program.

Kay Wulf—Gr. 1
Cheney Elementary School
Cheney, KS

Pop Quiz!

Students will enjoy turning the tables on their parents with this Open House activity! With your youngsters' help, brainstorm a list of questions that could determine how well parents know their children. Questions might include "What is the name of your child's favorite book?", "What is your child's favorite food?", and "What does your child like to do in his or her spare time?" Use the list of questions to create a pop quiz for your Open House visitors. On the evening of Open House place copies of the quiz on your students' desks. Encourage all visiting parents to complete the quiz. Students will have a blast grading these papers!

Bonnie Coddington—Gr. 2, Voorhees School, South Bound Brook, NJ

OPEN HOUSE VISITORS

Students		
Moms		
Dads		
Sisters		
Brothers		
Grandparents		
Friends		

Open House Graph

Here's a nifty way to turn your Open House participation into a high-interest graphing activity. On a length of bulletin-board paper, design a graph like the one shown above. As visitors enter your room on Open House night, ask them to write their names on individual sticky notes and attach their personalized notes to the graph. The next day have students use the graph to answer questions about Open House attendance.

Lora McGinn—Gr. 1
Strawberry Park Elementary, Steamboat Springs, CO

Scheduling Conferences

Scheduling parent-teacher conferences is an enormous task. To lighten the load of this responsibility, give your Open House guests the opportunity to sign up for their conferences in advance. On Open House night display a sign-up sheet—complete with dates and times—for parent-teacher conferences. Ask each parent to sign up for the time that best fits his or her schedule. As conference time draws near, schedule those parents who were unable to attend Open House; then notify all families of their scheduled conference times. Involving your entire school in this scheduling system allows parents with more than one child to coordinate their conference times with ease.

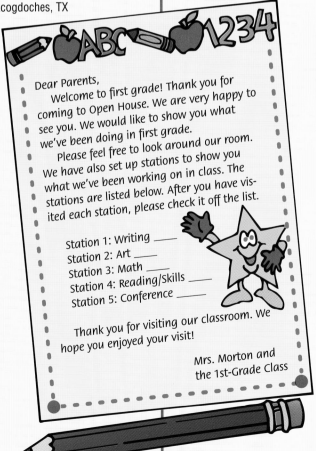

Dear Parents,
    Welcome to first grade! Thank you for coming to Open House. We are very happy to see you. We would like to show you what we've been doing in first grade.
    Please feel free to look around our room. We have also set up stations to show you what we've been working on in class. The stations are listed below. After you have visited each station, please check it off the list.

Station 1: Writing ____
Station 2: Art ____
Station 3: Math ____
Station 4: Reading/skills ____
Station 5: Conference ____

Thank you for visiting our classroom. We hope you enjoyed your visit!

Mrs. Morton and
the 1st-Grade Class

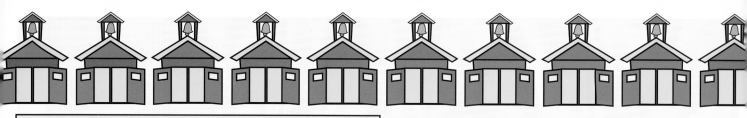

The Crane Family

This is our family.

This is my dad playing catch with me.

Here is a list of the things we like to do:
1. We like to go camping.
2. We like to play games.
3. We like to go fishing.
4. We like to work in the garden.
5. We like to play with our dogs.

This is a postcard from our summer vacation. We had a ball at the beach.

My brother's name is Jackson.

My mom is an artist. She is really good.

One-Of-A-Kind Family Book

Invite families attending Open House to participate in a special homework project. Explain that you would like each family to create a page for a class book. As you distribute 12" x 18" sheets of tagboard (book pages), suggest that photographs, student-created illustrations, and written descriptions be used to tell about a family and its special interests. (Be sure to inform families who were unable to attend Open House about the homework project.) Invite each student to share his family's completed project the day he brings it to school. Then laminate and three-hole-punch the completed pages, and compile them into a class book. Keep the book on display throughout the year.

Betty Pilato—Grs. 1–3, Dryden Elementary School, Cortland, NY

Open House Recording

Tape-recording your Open House presentation is a bright idea! Suggest that parents who were unable to attend Open House borrow the recording at their convenience. The tape recording also serves as a valuable source of information for parents whose children join your class in midyear.

Leigh Anne Newsom—Gr. 3

Open House Fund-Raiser

Join forces with your grade-level colleagues and plan this simple Open House fund-raiser. Ask each teacher to bring a plate of goodies to Open House. Display the goodies, napkins, a donation basket, and an eye-catching poster (that explains how the donations will be used) on a table near your classrooms. A pot of hot coffee and a supply of cups are also a nice touch. If desired, arrange for an attendant to be present. This is a great way to fund an author presentation, purchase additional arts-and-crafts supplies, or subsidize student prizes.

Sylvia Kabanuck—Gr. 3, Max Public School, Max, ND

Open House Raffle

If you're trying to increase your Open House attendance, a raffle just may be the ticket. Inform students and their parents that each person attending Open House may enter his or her name in a raffle. If desired, display the raffle prizes during Open House. Hold the raffle the next day and award the winners (or their family members) the prizes they won. And the winner of the glitter pen is....

Linette Farris—Gr. 1
John C. French Elementary School
Cuero, TX

Voluntary Contributions

Encourage classroom contributions without a lot of fanfare. During your Open House presentation, show your guests a basketful of colorful index cards. Explain that the cards are labeled with inexpensive items (such as paper plates, pipe cleaners, cassette tapes, and grading stickers) that will be used during the school year. Place the basket near the door and invite parents who are interested in making classroom contributions to choose cards before they leave. Each time a donation is received, send a personal note of thanks to the appropriate family.

Leigh Anne Newsom—Gr. 3
Greenbrier Intermediate
Chesapeake, VA

The Top Ten Reasons To Attend Open House

1. To see our pet hamster.
2. To meet our teacher.
3. To meet our principal.
4. To see our classroom.
5. To find out what we are learning.
6. To ask our teacher questions.
7. To see our school library.
8. To use our classroom computer.
9. To have a snack.
10. To have a nice evening away from home.

Top Ten Reasons

Here's a trendy way to promote Open House! Divide students into small groups and have each group brainstorm ten reasons why their parents should attend Open House. Compile the lists and remove any duplicate reasons. Then, by student vote, determine your youngsters' ten favorite reasons. Copy the resulting list on a sheet of paper entitled "The Top Ten Reasons To Attend Open House." Have students autograph the page; then send home a copy with each child. If desired display a poster-size list of the top ten reasons in your classroom and ask your Open House visitors to autograph the poster as they enter the room.

Katie Fairley
Water Valley Elementary
Water Valley, MS

Conference Requested

Use the conference request form on page 118 to show your enthusiasm for keeping the lines of parent-teacher communication open. Duplicate and cut apart a supply of the forms; then distribute approximately five forms to each family. (Later send forms home to the parents who were unable to attend Open House.) Encourage parents to complete and submit requests whenever they feel there are concerns that need to be discussed. Parents will appreciate the ease with which they can set up special conferences and your willingness to meet with them.

Chinita Hodo—Gr. 2
Redan Elementary School
Redan, GA

Lights, Camera, Action!

It's difficult to greet parents individually when they all arrive at one time. To help with this, create a video of a typical school day and have it playing continuously throughout Open House. New arrivals will be attracted to it right away, which can eliminate a line of parents waiting to speak to you. Start your video with a shot of your chalkboard that bears the message "Welcome To Our Class" along with the signature of each student. Conclude the tape by filming each youngster sharing a personal goal for the school year. You'll know this video is a big hit when parents ask if they can get a copy.

Marie Bovat—Grs. 1 & 2
Special Education
Paper Mill Elementary
Westfield, MA

My Weird Parents

Audrey Wood's wildly funny and affectionate story *Weird Parents* (published by Dial Books For Young Readers) expresses what most youngsters feel about their parents at one time or another—that they love them no matter how embarrassing they can be! After reading the story aloud, have each child think of one weird thing that an adult in his family does, like singing in the shower, wearing uncool socks with shorts, and kissing his child in public! Then have each student illustrate his parent doing something weird. One-sentence descriptions may be added below the illustrations, but all students' and parents' names should be omitted. Display the completed projects on a bulletin board entitled "Our Parents: They May Do Weird Things, But We Love Them Just The Same!" Also display Audrey Wood's book nearby. Your Open House visitors are sure to have a good laugh as they peruse this one-of-a-kind attraction.

Peggy Auvil—Gr. 3
Espy Elementary
Nixa, MO

Pam Crane

Reasons For Teaching

If you've been teaching for several years, this eye-catching Open House display may spark a myriad of memories. And even if you haven't been teaching for long, the display simply and effectively states your reasons for teaching. Mount the title "My Many Reasons For Teaching" on a bulletin board. Then display a group photograph of each class that you have taught. Beneath each photograph list the names of the individuals pictured. If you're an old-timer, be prepared for a few laughs and a bit of ribbing from the younger members in the crowd.

Phil Forsythe—Gr. 3, Northeastern Elementary School, Bellefontaine, OH

Top Secret!

When you openly display student work during Open House, you run the risk of judgmental onlookers comparing and contrasting the projects and papers on exhibit. To protect your youngsters' identities, assign each student a code name or number. Then, when papers are displayed for any special event, the identity of the author or illustrator is protected. Caution students to keep their pseudonyms confidential, sharing them only with family members. Students truly enjoy the mystery of it all!

Pam Negovetich—Gr. 3
Ready School, Griffith, IN

Classroom Computer

Be sure to have your classroom computer booted up with a game or activity favored by your young computer experts. Students will be eager to show off their computer skills and, better yet, challenge mom or dad to a quick game at the computer.

Patricia V. Smiley, Spiller Primary School, Wytheville, VA

Conference Coupons

Use with "Conference Requested" on page 117.

Conference Request

Student: _____

Concerns: _____

_____

_____

Preferred conference time: _____

Preferred day of the week: _____

_____
Parent's Signature

Conference Request

Student: _____

Concerns: _____

_____

_____

Preferred conference time: _____

Preferred day of the week: _____

_____
Parent's Signature

Conference Request

Student: _____

Concerns: _____

_____

_____

Preferred conference time: _____

Preferred day of the week: _____

_____
Parent's Signature

SHIVER ME MAPS!

Subscriber Ideas For Teaching Map Skills

Yo-ho-ho! Your adventure-seeking bucca-neers will find this treasure chest of mapping activities irresistible! So what are you waiting for, mateys? Dig in!

WHERE'S THE BOOTY?

Add excitement to map skills with a student-created treasure hunt! To begin, give each youngster a small treasure to hide within the classroom. (Treasures might include pencils, erasers, bookmarks, stickers, or duplicated awards.) On a sheet of drawing paper, ask each child to draw a map of the classroom and mark the location of his treasure with a large X. Also have each student write directions for how to find the treasure near the bottom or on the back of his map. Collect the completed projects; then randomly redistribute them to the students. Once you've determined that each student received a project other than his own, let the hunt begin!

Lisa Hash—Gr. 3
Austin Road Elementary
Stockbridge, GA

NORTH, SOUTH, EAST, AND WEST

Buccaneers review cardinal directions during this daily mapping activity. On a bulletin board mount a poster-board grid like the one shown, and pin a small shape (laminated for durability) to the grid. Each morning ask a different child to move the cutout around the grid according to your oral directions. Encourage the remainder of the students to listen carefully to your directions and monitor their classmate's moves. Consider directions like "Move the parrot one square north, two squares east, and three squares south." When the student's turn is over, he pins the cutout to its new location. After students become familiar with the activity, have them try their hand at providing the oral directions.

Susan Barnett—Gr. 3
Northwest Elementary
Huntington, IN

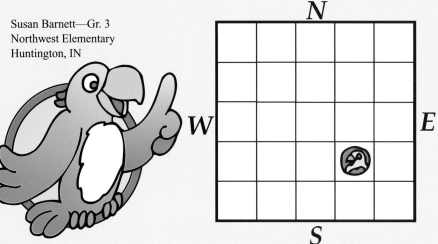

HOOKED ON MAP SKILLS

Keep your crew's map skills sharp with this hands-on approach to teaching map skills. Divide students into small groups and give each group a colorful, poster-sized map. (Maps of this type can be purchased at most school supply stores for modest prices.) Then have the students in each group work together to answer several map-related questions. Having a map for each small group of youngsters significantly increases the students' interest level and keeps them actively involved in the discovery process. Use the maps time and again by providing a new set of map-related questions for each use.

Nancy R. Zuellig—Gr. 2, Jackson Elementary School, Northridge, CA

WHERE IN THE WORLD?

At this mapping center, students try to track down their missing teacher! Each week, choose a geographical location to "hide out." Then, on each of several index cards, write clues that can be used to determine your location. At the center mount the clues and the title "Where In The World Is [your name]?", and display an atlas, a globe, and a variety of maps (such as city, state, and regional). Place a supply of paper slips and a small travel bag nearby. A student uses the clues and the resources at the center to determine your location. When a student thinks he's found your hiding spot, he writes his name and your geographical location on a paper slip, then tucks the paper inside the travel bag. At the end of the week, empty the travel bag and award a sticker or other small prize to each student who "found you." Then reprogram the center for a different geographical hideaway.

Carrie Damron, Anchorage Christian School
Anchorage, AK

119

CONTINENTAL EVENTS

Why not keep your youngsters abreast of current events while simultaneously reinforcing their map skills? Each morning cut from a current newspaper five articles that mention five different countries. Highlight the name of the country mentioned in each article before posting the cutouts alongside your world map. To complete the activity, a youngster writes the five countries' names on a sheet of paper, locates the countries on the world map, and writes the corresponding continents on her paper. Encourage students to scan the newspaper articles for clues pertaining to the locations of the countries and continents. If desired, also ask students to list the hemispheres where the countries/continents are located. At the end of the day, either check the papers as a class activity or collect them to grade later.

Julie Johnson—Gr. 3,
Colonial Hills Elementary, Houston, TX

A LITTLE HELP FROM THE NFL

You'll score big with this mapping activity! With your youngsters' help, create a resource list of the teams in the National Football League. (A list of team names can be found in The World Almanac.) List each team's name and its corresponding state and/or city on a length of bulletin-board paper; then display the resulting poster. Next give each child a duplicated map of the United States and a supply of small stickers. To complete the activity, a student attaches stickers to his map to show the locations of the NFL teams. For a fun follow-up to this activity, have each child choose a city within a state that does not have an NFL team. Then have each student create a poster unveiling a new football team. A student's poster should include the team's name, its corresponding city and state, and an illustration of its mascot.

Lisa Roeschley—Gr. 3
Elkton Elementary
Elkton, VA

PICTURE THIS!

Review states and their capitals again and again with this popular large- or small-group game! If you have a states-and-capitals puzzle, use the puzzle pieces to trace the shapes of the states onto construction-paper squares. (Otherwise refer to a United States map to complete your sketches.) Inside each outline write the name of the state and its capital city. Laminate the resulting game cards for durability; then store the cards in a large container. To play, select a child to be the game host. This student draws a card from the container and begins sketching the corresponding state on the chalkboard (using the outline on the card as a reference). At the same time, he calls on classmates who raise their hands to indicate that they can name the state he is drawing. The first player to correctly identify the state is given the opportunity to name its capital. If the student's response is correct, the round is over, and he becomes the new game host. If the student's response is incorrect, the game continues until a correct capital is provided. The student who supplies the correct capital hosts the next round of play.

Natalie Nastasi—Substitute Teacher
Randolph, MA

MAPS FOR THE TEACHER

Put your youngsters' mapping skills to the test with this motivational assignment. In a parent letter explain that you will be asking each child to draw a map that shows how to get from the school to her home. Specify that each child needs to know the name of each street or road that needs to be traveled on, whether right or left turns are necessary, and the address of her home. Also mention in the letter that when the maps are completed, you will be using them to deliver a small goodie bag to the doorstep of each youngster's home. Give the students several days to research and complete their mapping projects. Then begin to visit the students' homes in the order that you receive their completed maps. Each afternoon announce whose homes you plan to visit. Explain that if you do not arrive at a child's home by a certain time, you'll meet with the child the following school day to explain why. Then, if needed, meet with any children whose maps were incorrect. Point out where you got lost and let them submit corrected versions. This procedure guarantees that goodies will be delivered to every child's home.

Libby Price, Carmel, IN

AN ELEVATING EXPERIENCE

To give students firsthand experience with map elevation, have them make relief maps of the United States. To make a map of this type, trace a simple map of the United States on a sheet of bulletin-board paper, cut around the shape, and glue the resulting cutout atop a slightly larger piece of heavy cardboard. (Be sure to allow room for a map key near the lower edge of the project.) After studying a physical or a relief map of the United States, use newspaper strips and wallpaper paste to cover the paper cutout with papier-mâché so that the country's terrain is accurately represented. (For example, the Rocky Mountains in the West would have a greater elevation than the Appalachian Mountains in the east.) When the papier-mâché is completely dry, design a map key at the lower edge of the project; then paint the map according to the key. Students develop an awareness of the different elevations across the country and experience a wonderful sense of accomplishment when their projects are completed.

Dana Muraski—Substitute Teacher
Clifton Park, NY

MAP MURAL

With this hands-on idea, you can easily incorporate map skills into your next country unit. And in the end, students will have a greater understanding of the country they have just studied. Enlarge the appropriate country's shape onto a length of bulletin-board paper, write the country's name across the outline, and mount the resulting map so that it is within your youngsters' reach. Routinely refer to the map as you teach students about the country. The first time a specific city is discussed, ask a student volunteer to put the city on the map by drawing and labeling a dot in the appropriate location on the map. When geographical features are discussed, have students add them to the map. For example, students could attach and label blue-yarn rivers and brown-paper-triangle mountain ranges. In the end you'll have an informative student-made map. If space is available, consider keeping the maps on display throughout the year. If not, have a drawing and send each completed map home with a lucky winner.

Julie Johnson—Gr. 3
Colonial Hills Elementary
Houston, TX

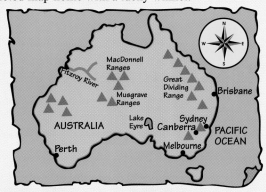

WHICH STATE IS MISSING?

If you have a map of the United States that has removable states, you have a ready-to-go mapping activity! Before your students arrive each morning, remove one state from the map. Challenge students to secretly record the name of the missing state on a slip of paper. Near the end of the day, have each youngster display his guess atop his desk. Carrying a supply of stickers or other small rewards, walk among the desks and present each student who made a correct guess with a prize. Then return the missing state to the map. Repeat the activity daily until each of the 50 states has been removed one or more times.

Paula Ciotti—Gr. 2, Lauderhill Paul Turner Elementary, Sunrise, FL

ONCE UPON A MAP SKILL

This unique approach to map skills has a very happy ending! To find the happy ending, follow up favorite storybook tales with mapping projects. For instance, after several readings of your favorite rendition of *Goldilocks And The Three Bears*, have your students create maps that show the story's setting. Give each student, student pair, or small group of students a large piece of bulletin-board paper. Students must show the places and things that are mentioned in the story on their maps; however they may embellish the maps with additional elements. For example, in addition to showing the woods, the Three Bears' cabin, and Goldilocks's house, students can also add a river running through the woods, a lake behind Goldilocks's house, and a mountain range to the south of the bears' home.
Be sure to request that each map include a map key, a map scale, and a compass rose.

If desired, have students write series of questions that relate to their maps and program corresponding answer keys. That will give you a ready-made map center for several weeks. Wow! That is a happy ending!

April Johnson—Gr. 3
Morningside Elementary
Perry, GA

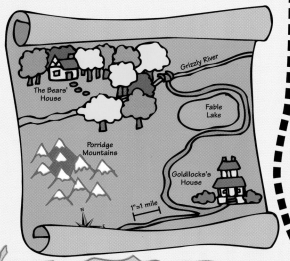

IN THE NEWS

This ongoing mapping activity makes "I've got a news spot!" a familiar classroom phrase. Laminate a large world map; then mount the map so that it is within your youngsters' reach. Also attach a sticker to the map to indicate the approximate location of your state or city. Each day allow time for students to report on current news events from around the world. Before a student shares his news story, have him attach a sticker to the map to show the geographical location or "news spot" of the event. (Provide assistance as needed.) If a sticker is already in place, ask him to point out the corresponding map location for his classmates. At the conclusion of each report, have students note the distance between the news spot and their state or city. If desired, provide an estimated number of miles or hours of travel time between the two locations.

Betty Crites—Gr. 2
Minier-Armington Elementary
Minier, IL

STEP-BY-STEP

This partner game helps students get in step with cardinal directions. Label each wall in your classroom with the appropriate cardinal direction. To play, one student in each pair secretly chooses an object in the classroom; then he guides his partner to the mystery object by giving him a series of directional clues. For example, a student might give clues such as "Take four giant steps west. Now take two tiny steps south." The student continues giving directional clues until his partner arrives at and identifies the secret object. Then the partners switch roles and play the game again.

Beth Davino—Gr. 1,
Acreage Pines Elementary,
West Palm Beach, FL

A CONTINENTAL APPROACH TO READING

Here's a unique way for students to travel around the world without leaving the classroom! With the help of your school's media specialist, collect a supply of books that have settings all over the world. For example *Mama, Do You Love Me?* by Barbara M. Joosse and *Possum Magic* by Mem Fox take readers north to the Arctic and south to Australia, respectively. When your supply of books is in place, ask each student to select a book from the collection, then read the story and prepare a review of it for his classmates. As part of the review assignment, ask each child to determine the continent where his story takes place.

When the reviews are ready, capture the action on video. In turn, ask each youngster to step up to a world map and use a pointer to direct his classmates' attention to the continent where his story takes place. Then have him present the book and give his review. After all the reviews have been presented, rewind the tape; then sit back and view it with your youngsters. What a trip!

Kathleen Darby—Gr. 1, Community School, Cumberland, RI

HIDDEN TREASURE

Students put their map skills into action to discover a hidden treasure box! In advance, decorate a cardboard box to resemble a treasure chest; then fill the chest with enough treats for each child. Hide the box in your classroom or elsewhere on the school grounds. Divide students into small groups and give each group a different teacher-made treasure map that leads to the hidden chest. On a given signal, send the groups off with their maps to find their way to the chest. When all of the groups have arrived at the chest, open the box and distribute the treasures found inside. Happy hunting, mateys!

Sr. Sandra Krupp—Gr. 1, Our Lady Of Loreto
Pittsburgh, PA

"I'M THINKING OF..."

Reinforce cardinal directions with this large- or small-group game. Without your youngsters' knowledge, identify an object within the classroom. Then give your students a series of directional clues to aid them in identifying the mystery object. For example a series of directions might be, "I'm thinking of an object that is south of the pencil sharpener, north of the window, and east of the bookshelf. What am I thinking of?" If desired, have a student confirm his hunch about the mystery object by first asking you a directional question such as "Is the mystery object east of your desk?" If the response is affirmative, the child makes a guess. Once the object is identified, choose another mystery object and begin play again. Soon your youngsters will be eager to choose mystery objects and deliver corresponding directional clues to their classmates.

Beth Davino—Gr. 1, Acreage Pines Elementary
West Palm Beach, FL

THE CREW'S ALL HERE!

Conclude your concentrated study of map skills with this fun-filled finale. In a parent note, request that students come to school dressed in pirate attire on a designated day. (Make plans to dress up on this day, too!) Plan a series of activities related to the pirate theme. For example, students could write and illustrate pirate adventure stories and treasure maps, enjoy a snack of peanut butter-and-*jellyfish* sandwiches, and paint colorful parrots during art time. Conclude the day with a treasure hunt such as the one described in "Where's The Booty?" on page 119.

Betsy Meyer—Gr. 1
Pulaski Academy
Little Rock, AR

BASEBALL CARD MANIA!

Coach your little sluggers into the major leagues with these mapping activities. With your students' help, collect a large supply of baseball cards. Then have students use several cards to complete a variety of mapping activities such as those listed below. Students can work independently, in pairs, or in small groups. Batter up!

- Locate the state or country where each player was born.
- Locate the state where each player now lives.
- Determine which direction a player would need to travel from his hometown to visit his birthplace.
- Determine which direction a player would need to travel from his hometown to visit your school.

Kathy Seals—Gr. 3
Park Lane Elementary
Lawton, OK

Cal Ripken

ONE STATE AT A TIME

Keep students involved in your state-by-state study with this cumulative display. Using an overhead projector, enlarge and then trace a map of the United States onto bulletin-board paper. Repeat the procedure a second time, changing only the color of the paper. Trim around one map and mount the resulting cutout on a bulletin board. Trim around the second map; then cut apart each state. Laminate the resulting cutouts for durability and store them in a large container. Every three or four days (depending on the number of days in your school year), ask a student to draw a state cutout from the container and attach it to the mounted map in the appropriate location. Then, before the next cutout is drawn, challenge students to find out the name of the state and its capital, and discover other points of interest within the state. Set aside time for youngsters to share the information they have learned; then use a permanent marker to label the cutout with the name of the state and its capital, and any other desired information. Continue in this manner until all 50 states are featured on the map. What an accomplishment for your students!

Jan Waring—Learning Disabilities, Roswell North Elementary, Roswell, GA

PUTTING THE SQUEEZE ON PROJECTIONS

This hands-on activity helps students understand how a sphere such as the earth can be represented as a flat surface. Using a fruit peeler and two oranges, demonstrate two methods of projection that are used. (See the illustrations.) After emphasizing that it's impossible to make a flat map of the earth that shows all distances, directions, shapes, and areas as accurately as a globe, ask students why flat maps are necessary. Then let each student try his hand at projection by peeling an orange (with a fruit peeler) in one of the manners you have demonstrated. The juicy conclusion to this activity is obvious. Yummy!!

Pam Miller—Grs. K–2 Special Education
Carnall Elementary
Fort Smith, AR

FROM MEXICO TO CANADA

Put this idea into action, and by the end of the year your graduates will know a wealth of information about the continent of North America. To begin, draw the outline of North America on a large sheet of poster board or plywood. Involve your youngsters in using papier-mâché to construct the continent's physical features. Students can also use tempera paint to "colorize" the resulting geographic details. As the year progresses, have your youngsters embellish the project. For example a study of the Oregon Trail could result in the trail being painted on the map. Or a transportation unit could include adding major highways to the map project. Whether the facts pertain to the past or present, there will be a place for them on your map!

Janice C. Simon—Gr. 3
Bay Minette Elementary
Bay Minette, AL

FOLDERS WITH DIRECTION

What better place for students to store their map-related projects than in map-covered folders! Give each child a discarded manila folder and outdated map. (Inquire at a local travel agency for outdated maps or solicit them from your students' parents.) Then, following your step-by-step demonstration, each student uses his map and glue or tape to cover his folder, inside and out. (If needed enlist older students to provide individual student assistance.) After students have personalized their folders, laminate them for durability; then instruct students to store their map-related activities and projects inside. At the conclusion of your map unit, staple or sew each child's papers inside his folder. Each resulting booklet is a travelogue of mapping experiences.

Cheryl Phillips—Gr. 1
Marshallville Elementary
Orrville, OH

MARSHMALLOW MASTERPIECES

If your youngsters are learning about landforms, here's a hands-on approach that's sure to make a sweet impression. Have each child draw the outline of a different state on his own sheet of poster board. Then, using a terrain map as a reference, have each student use marshmallows to design a topographical representation of the state and a corresponding map legend. Students will look forward to sharing their masterpieces with their classmates.

Phil Forsythe—Gr. 3
Northeastern Elementary School
Bellefontaine, OH

"In 1492, Columbus

A Look At Christopher Columbus And His Voyages

More than five hundred years ago, the Old World bumped into the New—and the futures of both were forever changed, forever linked together. Though Christopher Columbus never knew it, his voyages brought tremendous changes to the world. Bring the pageantry—and the debates—surrounding Columbus's voyage into your classroom with the following activities.

by Becky Andrew.

Background For The Teacher

For some, the anniversary of Columbus's maiden voyage is cause for celebration. But for others—particularly Native Americans and African Americans—it is an event to bemoan and protest. Why the difference in opinion?

Columbus's voyages greatly changed both the East and the West. New windows to science and knowledge were opened. Peoples, plants, animals, and diseases were intermingled between Europe, Africa, and the Americas. Tragically, entire populations of Native Americans were wiped out by diseases brought from the Old World. With local populations devastated, Africans began arriving to work as slaves.

Columbus's quest for a shorter route to the Indies changed the world forever. Rather than focus on the heroes and villains of this historic event, help students understand the facts about Columbus's voyages and the great changes that they brought.

> My big dream is to find a cure for AIDS.
> Melinda

One Man's Big Dream

Columbus was a man possessed by the dream of discovering a shorter route to the Indies and its treasures. His dream was so important to him that he spent years petitioning Europe's rulers for help.

Ask your students about their biggest dreams. Find out what incredible feats they would like to have others remember as their accomplishments. Then on her paper, have each student copy and complete the sentence starter "My big dream is to _____." Edit the sentences for spelling; then have each child copy and personalize her final work on a white construction-paper cloud cutout. If desired, have each student add a border of silver glitter to her cutout. Invite each youngster to share her big dream as you mount her cutout on the display titled "Sail On, Columbus." (See page 7.)

Sail On

After seven years of petitioning, Columbus finally convinced King Ferdinand and Queen Isabella of Spain to finance his westward journey. His ships—the Niña, the Santa María, and the Pinta—were from 82 to 74 feet long. The sails were brownish because they were woven of flax. All of the sails were decorated with crosses and symbols.

Let children hit the high seas on these seaworthy ships! For each child, duplicate the pattern on page 126 on white construction paper. Before students begin, explain that the parts of the ships above the waterline were usually painted bright colors. After students have colored and cut out their ships, give each child three craft sticks and a 3" x 9" strip of brown paper bag. Have each student cut his paper strip into three sails, then decorate the sails using crayons or markers. To complete his ship, have each youngster glue a sail to the end of each craft stick, then glue the opposite ends of the sticks to the back of his ship cutout. See page 7 for an eye-catching bulletin board display.

The World Is Much Bigger Than That, Chris!

Most educated people of Columbus's day knew that the earth was round. What they didn't know was how far the ocean stretched. Columbus thought that he would have to sail west 4,400 kilometers to reach a group of islands near Japan. The distance was actually 20,400 kilometers. Columbus also never expected another continent to be between Europe and these islands.

Help your class visualize the discrepancy between Columbus's estimate and the actual distance. Have students lay 44 paper clips end to end in a hallway. Beside this column lay 204 paper clips end to end. Have students compare the distances. Follow up the activity by having students explain their answers to questions such as "Even though Columbus made a mistake, would you call him a success?", "If Columbus had known how far the distance really was, do you think he would have set sail at all?", and "Would you have set sail with Columbus?"

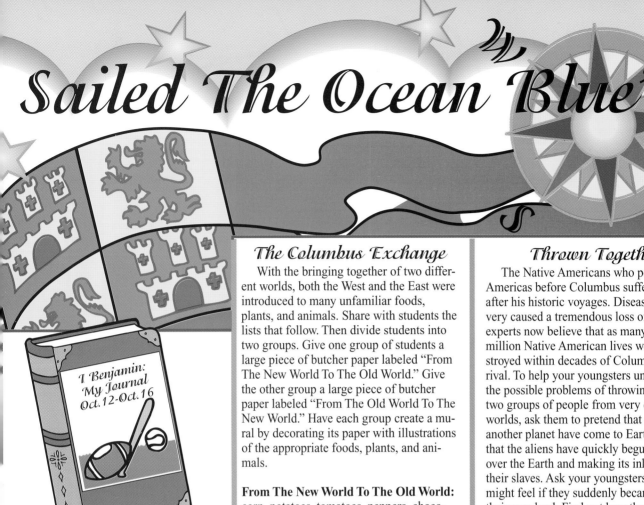

Sailed The Ocean Blue"

Dear Diary

Like any good captain, Columbus kept a ship's log detailing his first voyage. It is from a version of this diary that modern man learned of Columbus's maiden voyage.

Students can learn more about this method of recording history by creating their own personal logs. Start by sharing *I, Columbus: My Journal 1492–3* edited by Peter and Connie Roop (Walker Publishing Company, Inc., 1990), which includes edited excerpts from Columbus's log. Then using the patterns and instructions on page 127, prepare each student set of duplicated patterns. To make his personal log, a student cuts out his patterns, staples the log pages between the two covers, and personalizes the front cover of his resulting booklet. Each day during the week of Columbus Day, have students write in their logs. Encourage youngsters to detail each day's events, share their feelings, and/or respond to things they have read. Be sure to take time to read through the logs and add your own comments.

The Columbus Exchange

With the bringing together of two different worlds, both the West and the East were introduced to many unfamiliar foods, plants, and animals. Share with students the lists that follow. Then divide students into two groups. Give one group of students a large piece of butcher paper labeled "From The New World To The Old World." Give the other group a large piece of butcher paper labeled "From The Old World To The New World." Have each group create a mural by decorating its paper with illustrations of the appropriate foods, plants, and animals.

From The New World To The Old World:
corn, potatoes, tomatoes, peppers, chocolate, vanilla, tobacco, beans, pumpkins, avocados, peanuts, pecans, cashews, pineapples, blueberries, sunflowers, petunias, black-eyed Susans, dahlias, marigolds, wild rice

From The Old World To The New World:
horses, cattle, pigs, sheep, chickens, honeybees, wheat, barley, sugarcane, onions, lettuce, okra, peaches, pears, watermelons, bananas, olives, lilacs, daffodils, tulips, daisies, dandelions

Thrown Together

The Native Americans who populated the Americas before Columbus suffered greatly after his historic voyages. Disease and slavery caused a tremendous loss of life. Many experts now believe that as many as 40 to 50 million Native American lives were destroyed within decades of Columbus's arrival. To help your youngsters understand the possible problems of throwing together two groups of people from very different worlds, ask them to pretend that aliens from another planet have come to Earth. Explain that the aliens have quickly begun taking over the Earth and making its inhabitants their slaves. Ask your youngsters how they might feel if they suddenly became slaves in their own land. Find out how they would feel being loaded into a spaceship and flown to the aliens' planet. Help students compare this scenario with what actually happened when the Native Americans first came into contact with Columbus and his followers.

Reading About Columbus

Several books about Columbus and his voyages have recently been published. Ask your media specialist for assistance in locating several of these books. For starters, try the following titles:

- *Follow The Dream: The Story Of Christopher Columbus* written and illustrated by Peter Sis (Alfred A. Knopf, Inc., 1991)
- *A Picture Book Of Christopher Columbus* written by David A. Adler (Holiday House, Inc., 1991)
- *The Discovery Of The Americas* written and illustrated by Betsy and Giulio Maestro (Mulberry Books, 1991)
- *In 1492* written by Jean Marzollo (Scholastic Inc., 1991)
- *Encounter* written by Jane Yolen (Harcourt Brace Jovanovich, Publishers, 1992)
- *The First Voyage Of Christopher Columbus 1492* written and illustrated by Barry Smith (Viking Penguin, 1992)

Art project

Sail On!

Make a ship that look like the ships Columbus sailed!

Steps:
1. Color and cut out the ship
2. Cut three sails from light brown paper.
3. Draw and color a design on each sail.
4. Glue each sail to one end of a craft stick.
5. Glue the other end of each stick to the back of your ship.

Now you're ready to set sail!

Finished ship

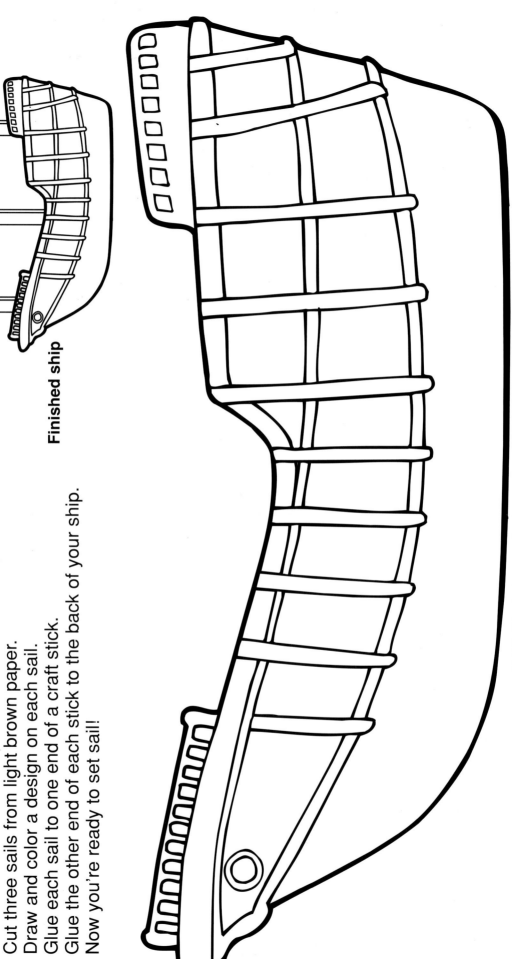

Note To The Teacher: Use with "Sail On!" on page 124.

Cover

Duplicate two copies on tan construction paper for each child.

Patterns

Use with "Dear Diary" on page 125.

Log page

Duplicate five copies on white paper for each child.

Pokin' Around The Pumpkin Patch

Harvest a crop of fun-filled learning with real pumpkins! Enlist the help of your students, a local grocer, or your school's parent group in gathering a class supply of small pumpkins. Then use the following tips and hands-on activities to cultivate math, observation, and writing skills.

ideas by Felice McCreary, Buda Intermediate, Buda, TX

The Perfect Patch

A pumpkin patch is the perfect spot for storing pumpkins when they are not in use. Choose a location that's large enough to house a class supply of pumpkins. To prepare the patch, have students cut out and attach construction-paper pumpkin leaves to lengths of yarn; then display the resulting greenery in the patch. If desired, enlist your students' help in creating an eye-catching scarecrow to guard the classroom crop.

Before students place their pumpkins in the patch, have each child dangle a numbered tag from his pumpkin's stem. To make the tags, hole-punch a class set of construction-paper leaf cutouts and label each one with a different number. Each student chooses a cutout, threads a length of yarn through the hole, and ties the yarn ends. The pumpkin owners should remain anonymous until the first activity has been completed. Be sure that you have a pumpkin in the patch, too!

Prizewinning Pumpkin Journals

In the activities that follow, students are asked to record information in journals. With your students' help, you can make the needed journals in a jiffy. You will need a class supply of pages 130 and 131, four sheets of blank white paper per child, two 9" x 12" sheets of orange construction paper per child, and several tagboard templates in the shape of the large pumpkin shown on page 130. Each student will also need scissors, crayons or markers, and access to a stapler.

To make a journal, a student uses a template to trace a pumpkin shape on each sheet of unprogrammed paper. He cuts out the pumpkin shapes—including the duplicated ones—and stacks the resulting cutouts in the following order: orange cutout, two white cutouts, cutout A, cutout B, two white cutouts, orange cutout. After aligning the cutouts and stapling the stems together, he personalizes his journal cover.

My Journal

Charlie Crow

Activity One: Whose Pumpkin Is It?

Sharpen your students' observation and writing skills by having each child write a detailed description of her pumpkin. At the pumpkin patch—without revealing which pumpkin is hers—a student carefully studies her pumpkin. Back at her desk, on a blank journal page, she describes her pumpkin in detail. When the students have finished writing, each child takes a turn reading aloud her description and challenging her classmates to identify her pumpkin by number. When a child's pumpkin has been identified, she takes it to her desk. To keep the interest level high, have a student claim his pumpkin if it hasn't been identified after five guesses.

When the last student pumpkin is claimed, leaving only yours in the patch, ask students to name their pumpkins. Ask each student to write her pumpkin's name on its leaf-shaped tag.

Activity Two: Problem Solving With Pumpkins

Your pumpkin patch is packed with problem-solving opportunities! Pose several pumpkin-related word problems for your students to solve. Have students use their pumpkins to demonstrate how to solve the problems. Then have each student write and solve two pumpkin-related word problems on a blank journal page. Have each child take a turn reading aloud one problem he created. When a classmate supplies the correct answer, the student's turn is over.

Activity Three: Sizing Up Pumpkins

Divide students into small groups to complete the following measurement activities:

Circumference

Each group needs one measuring tape, pencils, and its pumpkins and journals. To begin, ask students to estimate the circumference of your pumpkin. Record several estimates on the chalkboard; then measure the actual circumference of the pumpkin and write this measurement on the board. Discuss the results as a class.

Next have each child turn to cutout A in his pumpkin journal and locate the circumference chart. On the chart, have each student list the pumpkin names in his group and log a circumference estimate for each one. Encourage students to apply the outcome of the previous demonstration to their estimates and to discuss their estimates within their group. Then, in turn and using the provided measuring tape, each group member measures his pumpkin's circumference. All group members record the resulting measurement on their circumference charts. Urge students to evaluate their estimates after each measurement is recorded, reminding them that unconfirmed estimates can be adjusted.

Height And Weight

Using the same teaching technique described in "Circumference," have students complete the height and weight charts in their pumpkin journals. Each group needs a ruler for the height activity and scales for the weight activity.

Activity Four: Sink Or Float

Divide students into small groups. Each group needs its pumpkins and journals, pencils, crayons or markers, a supply of paper towels, and a water-filled container large enough to hold the entire group's pumpkins. Ask students to turn to a blank page in their journals and answer the following questions: Do you think a pumpkin will sink or float in water? Why? Next have the students rest their pumpkins on top of the water without letting go of the pumpkin stems. On a count of three, have the students release their pumpkins. Discuss the results of the experiment as a class. Then ask each student to remove his pumpkin from the water and dry it off. Lastly have each child summarize and illustrate the activity in the remaining space on his journal page.

Activity Five: Counting Seeds

Before introducing this activity, prepare the students' pumpkins by creating a removable lid in the top of each one. Do the same to your pumpkin; then remove its lid, pulp, and seeds. Discard the pulp and count the seeds. Note the seed count; then store the seeds inside the pumpkin in a plastic bag. Replace the pumpkin lid.

Divide students into small groups. In addition to its pumpkins, journals, and pencils, each group needs a supply of paper towels and one resealable plastic bag per child. Using the teaching technique explained in "Circumference" (Activity Three), have students estimate and determine the number of seeds in their pumpkins. The chart for this activity is found on journal cutout A. However, unlike the previous exercises, allow group members to simultaneously scoop out their pumpkins and count the resulting seeds into their plastic bags. When the entire group has completed the exercise, each member can share his final count so that the rest of his group can record it on their charts. Send the seeds home with the students. Provide toasting instructions if desired.

Activity Six: Graphing The Results

Students may work individually or in groups to complete this activity. To begin, have students turn to cutout B in their pumpkin journals. Explain that each student will create a graph that compares the circumference, the height, the weight, or the seed count of six pumpkins. First have each student label his graph to reflect his graphing choice. For example, a student who is graphing pumpkin heights labels his graph "Comparing Pumpkin Heights" and "Number Of Inches." Then he programs the graph in one- or two-inch increments. To complete his graph, he records the names of six pumpkins along the lower edge and colors the graph to show the heights of the pumpkins listed. A student can use information from his height chart and/or gather new information from his classmates to complete his graph.

Pumpkins With Personality

For a fun finale to your pumpkin activities, let students decorate their pumpkins before they carry them home. Provide assorted arts-and-crafts supplies for the decorating endeavor. If desired, students can illustrate their decorated pumpkins on their remaining journal page. Students will be pleased as pumpkins to carry home these pumpkin projects!

Just Ripe For Reading

These picture books are perfect for a pumpkin-related unit!

The Pumpkin Blanket
Written & Illustrated by Deborah Turney Zagwÿn
Fitzhenry & Whiteside, 1990

The Pumpkin Patch
Written & Photographed by Elizabeth King
Dutton Children's Books, 1990

Pumpkin Pumpkin
Written & Illustrated by Jeanne Titherington
Greenwillow Books, 1986

Pumpkins: A Story For A Field
Written by Mary Lyn Ray & Illustrated by Barry Root
Harcourt Brace Jovanovich, Publishers; 1992

The Great Pumpkin Switch
Written by Megan McDonald & Illustrated by Ted Lewin
Orchard Books, 1992

Circumference

Pumpkin	Estimate	Actual

Height

Pumpkin	Estimate	Actual

Weight

Pumpkin	Estimate	Actual

Seed Count

Pumpkin	Estimate	Actual

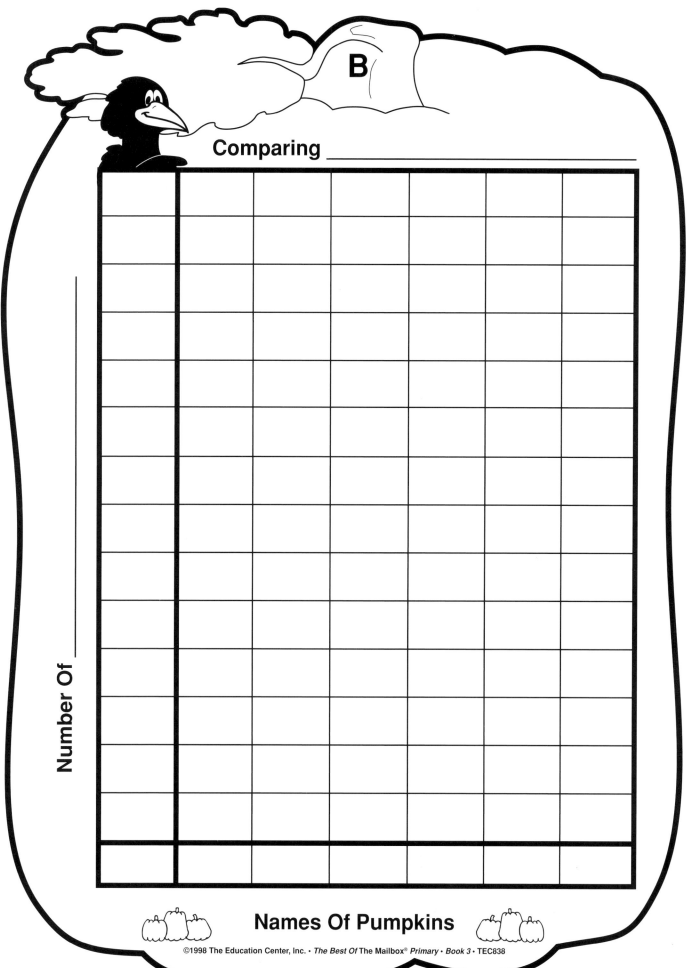

Comparing _____

B

Number Of _____

Names Of Pumpkins

WHOOOOOOO'S UP FOR PUNCTUATION PRACTICE?

Some days, does it seem as though your youngsters just don't give a hoot about punctuation? No need to stay up nights thinking of ideas when this topflight collection is right at your fingertips!

All Aboard!

Get students' punctuation skills on the right track by making this nifty punctuation train. To begin, draw and cut out a train engine, three boxcars, and a caboose from tagboard. Use a permanent marker to write the words "Today is" on the train's engine; then display the cutouts near the calendar. Program blank cards with the seven days of the week, the 12 months of the year, the numerals 1 through 31, and the two years within this school year. Using a red marker, insert commas after the days of the week and the dates; then place periods after the years. Attach the appropriate cards to the train. Each day have a student look at the current cards on the train and tell which ones need to be replaced. After the sentence is brought up-to-date, have the class read the information aloud. As they read, have students use hand signs to represent the punctuation marks. This daily review will keep your youngsters' punctuation skills on track!

Pamela S. Lasher—Gr. 2, Grand Rapids Baptist Academy, Grand Rapids, MI

Today is | Monday, | November | 6, | 1995.

It's A Holdup!

With this idea your students will be holding all the cards—period, question mark, and exclamation-point cards, that is! Have each student use three blank index cards and a dark marker or crayon to make punctuation cards. Once the cards are ready, students listen as you say a sentence. Each student decides which punctuation mark belongs at the end of the sentence and holds up the corresponding card. You can evaluate at a glance your students' punctuation skills.

Doreen Carlo—Gr. 2
Broadview Elementary
Pompano Beach, FL

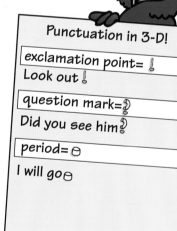

Punctuation in 3-D!

exclamation point= !
Look out!

question mark=?
Did you see him?

period= ⊖
I will go⊖

Munchable Marks

Try using 3-D punctuation marks in your classroom to reinforce students' punctuation skills. In advance, program a chart with sentences that end with periods, question marks, and exclamation points; but instead of writing the punctuation, glue the following items after each sentence: period = a miniature marshmallow, question mark = a piece of elbow macaroni and a small dried bean, exclamation point = a pretzel stick and a small dried bean. Discuss the chart with your students; then distribute glue and the food items to each student. Students refer to the chart and use the appropriate items to punctuate sentences in a writing assignment. After checking students' work, invite them to munch on leftover pretzels and marshmallows!

Leigh Anne Newsom—Gr. 3, Greenbrier Intermediate, Chesapeake, VA

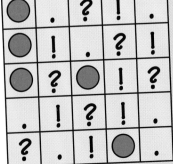

Lotto Fun

Reinforce punctuation skills by adding a new twist to the ever popular game of lotto. Distribute blank lotto cards and markers to your students. Have each child program the spaces with periods, question marks, and exclamation point. When the cards are complete, read aloud a sentence from a deck of unpunctuated sentence cards. Each student then decides which punctuation mark ends the sentence and places a marker on a space containing that mark. Continue reading additional sentences from the card deck. The first student to fill a row and say, "Lotto!" wins the game, if she can locate one used sentence card to match each of the punctuation marks in the winning row. Each child will be a winner when she discovers how much fun practicing punctuation can be!

Doreen Carlo—Gr. 2

Colorful Cards

Here's a bright idea for helping students polish their punctuation skills. Write several sentences on a transparency, omitting ending marks. Supply each student with one green, one blue, and one yellow index card. Have each student program his blue card with a period, his green card with an exclamation point, and his yellow card with a question mark. Using an overhead projector, display the first sentence on the transparency and ask each student to select the punctuation card that correctly fits the sentence. Ask each child to wait for your signal, then hold up the selected card. Reveal the remaining sentences one at a time for students to punctuate.

Tonya Byrd, William H. Owen Elementary, Fayetteville, NC

Annie Apostrophe

Your students will find that learning to use apostrophes is a breeze when they get a little help from a friend named Annie Apostrophe. Make Annie by cutting an apostrophe shape from tagboard. Add appealing facial features and laminate her for durability. On the chalkboard write a word or sentence in which an apostrophe is needed; then invite a student to insert Annie Apostrophe into the space where the apostrophe belongs. A little masking tape (or magnetic tape for a magnetic chalkboard) will keep Annie in place. Repeat this procedure until each student has had at least one turn to position Annie. After students become familiar with Annie Apostrophe, you might want to introduce them to her cousin, Connie Comma!

Julie Mazzarino—Gr. 1, American Heritage School, Plantation, FL

The ducks saw the child☐holding a bag of peanuts☐"Let's go☐" said the mother duck☐The three ducklings☐swam behind their mother☐

Transforming Textbooks

Get new uses from outdated reading books by using them for punctuation practice. Affix correction tape (or small pieces cut from white, self-adhesive labels) to cover the punctuation marks on a story page copied from an old basal reader. Once the punctuation marks are hidden from view, attach a few extra pieces of correction tape to act as distractors. Laminate the page. Place the page in a center along with a wipe-off marker and an unaltered duplicate of the page. Challenge students to take turns writing appropriate punctuation marks and referring to the unaltered page to check the accuracy of their work.

Cindy Lonergan—Special Education, Disney Elementary, Tulsa, OK

A machine makes your work easier☐. There are lots of different kinds of machines☐. The lever☐, inclined plane☐, screw☐, and pulley are names of some machines☐. Do you know the names of any other machines☐?

What A Combination!

When your purpose is punctuation practice, ensure meaningfulness by connecting punctuation, literature, and student writings. Ahead of time, determine which punctuation mark to emphasize; then write it on a chart similar to the one shown below. After introducing (or reviewing) the featured punctuation mark, challenge each student to browse through one of the books that he is currently reading to find an example of a sentence in which the punctuation mark is used. Write these examples on the chart. Discuss each sentence and its punctuation mark; then leave the chart on display for future reference. To extend the learning, ask each student to examine a sample of his previous writings and correct any punctuation mistakes that he now notices.

Mary E. Fagan—Gr. 1, Public School #9, Brooklyn, NY

PUNCTUATION	EXAMPLES
Question Mark ?	1. Well, what do you think? 2. Why not? 3. How about Dr. Grizzly? 4. Where have you been? 5. Who is that speaking?

Take Note!

Stick with this idea and your students will be punctuating pros before you know it! Write a class-dictated paragraph on chart paper, omitting punctuation but leaving spaces large enough to accommodate small sticky notes. As students read aloud the class paragraph, have them identify each place where punctuation is missing and attach a sticky note to that spot. On each note, have a student record the missing punctuation mark. After the entire paragraph has been correctly punctuated, have students reread it; then remove the sticky notes. Put the chart and a pad of sticky notes where students can again supply the punctuation.

April Johnson—Gr. 3, Morningside Elementary School, Perry, GA

Making Every Minute Count

Got a minute? We'd like to help you make the most of it! We received a wonderful response when we asked you and your colleagues what you do with a minute or two between activities. We feel certain that you'll use this collection of classroom-tested ideas time and time again!

Wiggle Away!

Here's a fun way to fill a few minutes between lessons and help your youngsters release extra energy. To begin, ask your youngsters to dance and wiggle around the classroom. After a short while signal the youngsters to stop; then have each child tell the person nearest him one special thing. For example you may ask youngsters to describe something that they enjoyed doing in school that day or explain what they plan to do after school. This type of interaction builds positive student relations and paves the way for peaceful transitions.

Maura Hendrickson
Hall County School Districts
Wood River, NE

News For Today

This time-filling activity encourages students to share their opinions about world, state, and local happenings. Keep a current copy of the daily newspaper in your classroom. When you find yourself with a few unplanned moments, read aloud a headline from the paper and invite students to share their views on the subject. Surprisingly enough, most youngsters will have opinions about current news events.

Marilyn Haynos—Gr. 3
Waverly Elementary School
Waverly, PA

Making A List

Reserve a portion of your chalkboard for this listing activity. On individual slips of paper, write several student-generated topics for making lists. Topics might include "Things Found On A Farm," "Items That Are Yellow," and "Three-Letter Words." Place the paper slips in a decorated container on your desk. When you have minutes to fill, choose a topic from the container and copy it on the reserved portion of your chalkboard. Then have students work cooperatively to reach a predetermined number of items as you list their answers. If the goal is reached, reward students with small treats, rewards, or a special class privilege.

Andrea Johnson—Grs. 1–3
Blanton Elementary School
St. Petersburg, FL

The mystery number is ___

Mystery Number

Improvise with this math game when you've got a few minutes between activities. Write a number on a scrap of paper. Tell your youngsters that you are "...thinking of a number between [insert number] and [insert number]." On the chalkboard, draw a corresponding number line. Record each youngster's guess on the number line and note whether the mystery number is greater than or less than this number. When the mystery number is guessed, confirm its identity by revealing the written number. Children love the game and gain valuable numeration practice.

Tammy Smith—Gr. 2
Crawford County R-II, Cuba, MO

Barry Slate

Magic Slates

Plan ahead and you'll be prepared to fill spare minutes productively. In a parent letter request that each youngster bring a Magic Slate to school. Each slate, which has two plastic writing sheets and a special pencil, can be purchased for less than one dollar and easily fits inside a youngster's desk. When you have extra time, ask students to pull out their slates and complete a variety of activities. For example, students could list two or three spelling words, solve a math problem, or demonstrate a cursive letter. After a child has completed the assigned task, he places his slate under his chin with his answer(s) facing out. A quick glance at the slates reveals which youngsters are proficient at the assigned task. To clean his slate, a student simply separates the two sheets of plastic and his writing magically disappears!

Susan Ream—Gr. 2, Artman Elementary, Hermitage, PA

Sign Language

Whenever you have a few minutes to fill or you need a few moments of silence, teach your youngsters the sign language alphabet. When all of the letters have been learned, students can learn to spell their names and a variety of other words. Who knows? Idle moments may be silently filled forever!

Jill Prucha—Gr. 3
Smithville Elementary
Smithville, MO

Give Me Five!

Have a few minutes to spare? No sweat! Play a quick round of Give Me Five. To begin play, declare, "Give me five!" Then challenge youngsters to name five similar items such as five presidents, five dinosaurs, or five flavors of ice cream. Randomly call on students to respond. When he is called on, a youngster immediately stands and answers. If the student provides five correct answers, he wins. If not, he sits down and another student tries to meet the challenge. Students quickly realize the importance of listening to their classmates' responses. Kids love this fast-paced game and they learn a lot too!

Linda Davis
St. Mark School
Indianapolis, IN

Memorize The Moments

Why not use those spare minutes to memorize organized information? A fun way to learn the 50 states is to memorize them alphabetically. To ease the burden of this awesome task, assign each youngster two states. When you have a few minutes to fill, have your youngsters practice reciting the names of the states in alphabetical order. With a little bit of practice, each youngster learns to provide the names of his two states at the appropriate times. And most likely, he'll learn several other state names in the process too. Alabama, Alaska, Arizona,….

Eileen Fancher—Gr. 3
Morris Street School
Dalton, GA

Tickets To Success

These trusty tickets are great time fillers. Label a decorated box "Tickets To Success." Throughout the year place cards that you have labeled with questions and answers in the box. Each question and its corresponding answer should reflect something that your youngsters have learned at school that year. Whenever a few extra minutes arise, remove a ticket from the box, read the question aloud, and challenge your youngsters to provide the correct answer. Students enjoy the challenge and the extra minutes speed by!

Loni Baker—Gr. 2
Lancaster Elementary School
Bluffton, IN

Mirroring Fun

Here's a totally quiet time filler that's like Follow The Leader. Instruct youngsters to mimic your actions. Then pose in a series of zany positions, moving from one pose to another without pausing. Continuous eye contact and unstoppable smiles make this transition activity a fun-filled diversion. Once students are familiar with the game, select individual students to lead their classmates in a series of silent antics.

Rachelle Rodriguez—Gr. 2
Liestman Elementary School, Houston, TX

What's Your Prediction?

When you're faced with a few extra minutes, grab your chalk and begin to draw. Your kids will love it! On the chalkboard, draw one part of an object such as a pencil. Then invite two students to predict what object you are drawing. If neither prediction is correct, draw another part of the object; then stop for two more predictions. The game continues in this manner until a correct prediction is made. Consider drawing objects related to your current theme or any of the following: star, house, car, stop sign, rocket.

Carolyn Wareham—Grs. 1–3 Music, Central Elementary, Spearfish, SD

Alphabet Categories

You'll have all hands on deck when it's time for a quick game of Alphabet Categories. To play, you need a deck of letter cards (one card per alphabet letter) and a deck of category cards. Divide students into two teams. In turn a player from each team draws a card from each deck. To earn a point for his team, the player must name an item in the category he drew that begins with the letter he drew. Keep an ongoing tally of points on the chalkboard. Declare the winner of the game after each student has participated or after one team has earned a predetermined number of points.

Sheryl Songer—Gr. 2
Roosevelt School, Hays, KS

A CONTINENTAL APPROACH
TO INTERNATIONAL GAMES

Playing games is an important part of childhood—and it's fu[n] besides! With this game plan, your students are introduced to games that are played in other parts of the world. As an added bonus, they learn about the seven continents, too.

DESTINATION: ASIA

Asia is the largest continent in both population and size. The continent covers almost a third of the world's land area!

Vietnam

You can expect squeals of laughter—and twisting and turning—as students play this game from Vietnam.

Catch A Carp's Tail
Number Of Players: six per line
Equipment Needed: none
To Play: Each group of six players stands single file to form a carp. With the exception of the first player in line (the head), each player places his hands on the hips of the player in front of him. To play the game, the head tries to tag the tail (the last player in line). The children in the middle of the carp must hang on tight to prevent the fish from pulling apart. When the head tags the tail, the tail moves to the head position and the game starts again.

Burma

This country in Southeast Asia is not quite the size of Texas, but it has almost three times as many people!

Hiding The Stone
Number Of Players: an even number, eight or more
Equipment Needed: a small stone
To Play: Divide students into two equal teams—A and B. Each team sits single file on the floor so that the resulting lines are parallel. All players extend their legs straight ahead of them. Except for the first player in each line, each player's feet should barely touch the back of the teammate who is seated in front of him. To begin play, hand the stone to the first player of team A. The objective is for the player to hide the stone under the knees of one of his teammates. To do this, the player goes up and down his line of teammates, putting his hand under the knees of each child in line. When he returns to his position, the first player of team B guesses where the stone was placed. If the player is correct, the player from team A who hid the stone must join team B. Then the player from team B who guessed correctly hides the stone under the knees of one of his teammates. However, if the player from team B guesses incorrectly, he must join team A, and the next player in line for team A gets to hide the stone. Play continues in this manner. The team having the most players when time runs out is the winner.

Denmark

Almost completely surrounded by water, Denmark is well-known for its fishing industry. This game from Denmark is quite fishy and fun!

The Fish Game
Number Of Players: an even number, eight or more
Equipment Needed: two chairs less than the total number of players
To Play: Pair students and declare one couple to be IT. This couple is called the whales. Each of the remaining couples secretly selects the name of a fish; then it positions a pair of chairs somewhere in the playing area and sits in them. To begin play, the whales march about the playing area, weaving in and out between the chairs, calling out the names of fish. If a couple's secret fish name is called, the pair must march in line behind the whales. After the whales have called out as many fish names as they know or want, they declare, "The ocean is calm!" This signals all seated players to march in line behind the whales. The whales lead the students for as long as desired, but when they suddenly call out, "The ocean is stormy!" all couples run to find chairs. The couples may not separate. The couple left standing becomes the whales for the next game. Be sure to have each seated couple secretly choose a new fish name before the next round of play begins.

DESTINATION: EUROPE

Unfortunately we can't provide a game from the more than 40 countries of Europe! However, your youngsters are sure to enjoy the following games from Denmark and Spain. Assist your students in finding these locations on a world map; then let the playing begin!

Spain

Spain is famous for its bullfights, castles, and sunny climate. This game can introduce students to several Spanish cities.

Come On Over!
Number Of Players: an even number, eight or more
Equipment Needed: none
To Play: Divide students into two teams; then line up the teams so that they face each other. There should be about ten feet between the two teams. Name each team for a different city in Spain, such as "Valencia" and "Madrid." The object of the game is for the citizens of one city to capture all the citizens of the other. To begin play, choose a player from Valencia to travel to Madrid. Each player from Madrid extends one hand, palm up. The visitor from Valencia walks down the line and rubs his hand over the extended palms. Eventually the visitor claps the palm of one Valencia player. This player chases the Madrid player as he runs for home. If the Valencia player tags the Madrid player before he reaches his team line, the Madrid player is taken captive and returned to Valencia with his captor. If the player is not tagged, the Valencia player returns home alone. Play continues with a Valencia player traveling to Madrid and repeating the same actions. The game is over when one city is captured, or time runs out, in which case the city with the most people is declared the winner.

DESTINATION: AFRICA

The continent of Africa is about four times the size of the United States. Within this vast continent there are more than 50 countries and territories! Help students locate the continent of Africa on a world map; then help them find the African countries where the next two games are played.

Egypt

This Egyptian tug-of-war game has been played in Egypt for centuries—and it is still played in Egyptian schools today.

Tug-Of-War
Number Of Players: an even number of three-player teams
Equipment Needed: a large grassy playing area, a long length of string or yarn, a whistle
To Play: Lay the length of string down the center of the playing area. Have half of the teams line up single file behind the string. On the other side of the string and directly opposite these teams, have the remaining teams line up single file. Have each team leader (the player closest to the string) clasp hands with the team leader opposite him, while the rest of the players hold onto the waists of the teammates in front of them. At the sound of the whistle, each team tries to bring its opponents across the string to its side by pulling and leaning backwards. When a team is tugged over the line, both teams involved sit down. When all the teams are sitting, the round is over. Then rotate the teams so that each team has a new opponent and play another round.

Ghana

Because of its warm climate, Ghana is home to many types of snakes. Here's a fun game that puts this cold-blooded reptile in the spotlight!

Big Snake
Number Of Players: ten or more
Equipment Needed: a large, defined indoor or outdoor playing area, several cones, a whistle
To Play: Choose one child to play the snake. Using the cones, the snake marks off a corner of the playing area as its home. The snake stays in its home as the rest of the players roam the playing area. At the sound of the whistle, the snake runs out of its home and tries to tag free players. A player who is tagged must join hands with the snake and become a part of its body. The snake's head (the original snake) and tail (the last player to join the snake) are the only students who may tag free players. If the snake's body pulls apart, blow the whistle and send the snake home. When the snake has regrouped, blow the whistle again to signal that the snake is rejoined and ready to play. Free players may try to break apart the snake's body. The game ends when everyone is caught or out of breath!

DESTINATION:

ANTARCTICA

Your visit to the bottom of the globe will be brief. Find Antarctica on a world map. Find out what your youngsters know about this icy wonder. Remind students that because of the extreme weather of Antarctica, few people live there—in fact, only a small number of scientists call Antarctica their home.

DESTINATION:

AUSTRALIA

Australia is unique because it is the only country that is a continent. As students locate Australia on a world map, inform them that Australia produces a large amount of our world's wool.

Sheepdog Trials

Number Of Players: eight or more, divided into teams of equal numbers of players

Equipment Needed: a large playing area, a defined starting line, two inflated balloons per team (provide a different color for each team), one jump rope per team, one 3" x 12" strip of cardboard per team

To Play: Create a starting line in the center of the playing area. Divide students into equivalent teams, and line up each team single file behind the starting line. Opposite each team, at the far end of the playing field, use a jump rope to form a pen. At the back of each pen, leave an entrance. Place two sheep (balloons) in front of each team and hand the first player in line a sheepdog (cardboard strip). On your signal, the first player of each team uses the sheepdog to guide his sheep down the course and into his team's pen through the rear entrance. The first player to have both of his sheep in the pen scores a point for his team. Continue play until all players have herded the sheep. The team with the most points wins.

DESTINATION:

SOUTH AMERICA

South America is the fourth-largest continent in the world and is home to almost a fourth of all the known animals in the world! Help students find South America on a world map; then give them map-related clues so that they can guess the country in which each of the following games is played.

Peru

This educational jump-rope game called "El Reloj" (EL ray-loh) is a popular children's game in Peru. The faster the game is played, the more exciting it becomes!

The Clock

Number Of Players: eight or more

Equipment Needed: a long jump rope (15–20 feet)

To Play: Select two rope turners. As they practice turning the rope, have the remaining players line up single file about ten feet away from the turning rope. When the rope turners are turning the rope so that it swings in a complete circle and lightly touches the ground at the bottom of each turn, begin play. The first player in line runs through the rope without a jump. The second player runs in, jumps one time, and runs out as the players say, "One o'clock." The third player follows, jumps two times, and runs out as the players say, "Two o'clock." The game continues with this jump pattern until one player makes 12 consecutive jumps (12 o'clock). If a player touches the rope or misses the correct number of jumps, he exchanges places with a rope turner and the game begins again.

Bolivia

Players must keep their eyes on a handkerchief when they play this Bolivian game!

The Handkerchief Game

Number Of Players: nine or more

Equipment Needed: a handkerchief

To Play: Place a flattened handkerchief in the middle of the playing area. Divide students into four teams and one IT. Have each team sit in single file facing a different edge of the handkerchief. When the teams are in position, IT circles around the group and drops the handkerchief behind a player seated at the end of one team. The players on the team jump up and run around the group. IT takes a vacated spot. The last player to return is without a seat and becomes the new IT.

DESTINATION: NORTH AMERICA

The third-largest of the seven continents, North America spans from the icy Arctic to the warm tropics. After students have located the continent on a world map, help them find Canada and Mexico—since a game from each of these countries is provided. If desired, have students locate the United States, too; then take a bit of time to play some of your students' favorite games.

Canada

Many of the games that are played in Canada and the United States were played in the colonial days. These games have been played and taught and adapted so many times that today it's next to impossible to know where the games originated. This game from Canada may feel familiar to your students.

Pass The Broom
Number Of Players: eight or more
Equipment Needed: a long-handled broom, music that can be quickly stopped and started
To Play: Students stand in a large circle formation, facing inwards. Each student holds one hand behind his back. Pass a broom to one player. While the music is playing, the players pass the broom around the circle in a designated direction. The child who is holding the broom when the music stops must drop out of the circle. Continue play in this manner until only one student remains!

Mexico

The title of this next game brings to mind the beautiful parrots and other colorful birds that flourish in Mexico's lush rain forests.

The Little Parrot
Number Of Players: eight or more
Equipment Needed: a small object such as a pebble or beanbag
To Play: Students sit on the floor in a large circle, facing inwards. Give one player the small object. This student becomes player 1. She turns to the player on her right (player 2) and asks, "Won't you buy this little parrot?" Player 2 asks, "Does it bite?" Player 1 answers, "No, it does not bite," and hands the object to player 2. Player 2 turns to the player on her right (player 3) and asks, "Won't you buy this little parrot?" Player 3 asks, "Does it bite?" Player 2 does not answer the question, but instead turns to player 1 and asks, "Does it bite?" Player 1 answers, "No, it does not bite." Player 2 repeats the answer to player 3 and then hands over the object. Play continues in this manner, with the question "Does it bite?" always being referred back to the first player for the answer. The answer is likewise passed from player to player until it reaches the player who asked the question. The game is over when the last player in the circle turns to player 1 and asks her to buy the parrot—and she responds, "Yes! I will buy the parrot for it does not bite!"

WORD WATCHERS!

Double Draw

This booklet activity is highly adaptable and can be used for any subject, season, or holiday that has its own specialized vocabulary. Choose a topic and write vocabulary words related to the topic on individual slips of paper (one per student). Place the programmed papers in a decorated container and give each youngster a booklet page of the desired size and shape. A student draws a vocabulary word from the container and writes it near the top of his paper. Next he writes the word in a complete sentence and illustrates it. After each child has shared his completed booklet page, staple the pages in alphabetical order between a decorated cover. Keep these booklets on display in your classroom library.

Word Collages

Make use of discarded magazines and newspapers as you increase your students' word awareness. To make a word collage, a student looks through several discarded newspapers and/or magazines. Each time he finds a word that he thinks is interesting, he cuts it out. When he has a supply of word cutouts, he randomly glues them on a 12" x 18" sheet of construction paper. Encourage students to look for words of different sizes and colors, words that are written in unusual type styles, and words of various lengths. Once the collages are completed, have students discuss their projects with partners and find unfamiliar words in their dictionaries. Then as a class activity, have each youngster name and describe a favorite word from his collage. Display the completed projects on a bulletin board for all to enjoy.

Object Of The Day

As a part of your morning routine, display an object of the day. On the chalkboard write five words that describe the object. Elicit four of the words from your youngsters. Provide the fifth word yourself, attempting to list a word that is unfamiliar to most students. Use these five words throughout the day in your lessons and conversations, and encourage your students to do the same. By the end of the day, most youngsters will have familiarized themselves with a new vocabulary word. Enlist your students' help in providing objects for this activity.

Word Of The Day

This activity gives each student the opportunity to teach an interesting vocabulary word to his classmates. In a letter sent home, ask parents to assist their children in selecting interesting vocabulary words. Explain that each youngster must be able to say and write his vocabulary word and explain its meaning. Suggest that parents look for interesting words in the news media, in their vocations, and on product labels.

Ideas For Vocabulary Expansion

Words! Words! Words! Increase your youngsters' writing, speaking, listening, and reading vocabularies with these motivational activities and reproducibles.

ideas contributed by Joyce Swan

Character Studies

Increase your youngsters' descriptive vocabularies by taking a closer look at the characters featured in your current read-aloud. For each character, draw a simple chart like the one shown. On the left side of the chart, list the character's actions as described in the story. On the right side of the chart, list other words that describe these actions. Older students can complete this activity independently using the books they are currently reading.

Charlie

Things that Charlie did:	Other words to describe these actions:
did not spend money	stingy, tight, greedy
saved a friend's life	courageous, brave, clever

The Word Corner

For a fun free-time center, set up a Word Corner. At the center place a collection of games such as Scrabble®, Boggle®, and Spill and Spell®. Also keep several dictionaries at the center and encourage students to use them as they play the games. Add to your collection of word games throughout the year. Check yard sales for good buys on used games for the center.

Creative Vocabulary

Here's an activity your youngsters are sure to love. Make a list of unusual words that are unknown to most students. Periodically choose one word from the list and write (and underline) the word in a sentence on the board. Instruct students to read the sentence carefully as they try to derive the meaning of the underlined word. Then have each student draw and color a picture that shows what he thinks the word means. Encourage students to share their illustrations. Be sure to praise students for their creative thinking. Then conclude the activity by finding the correct meaning of the word in a dictionary. Here are a few sentences to get you started:

1. The old man was wearing a black <u>fedora</u>. *(a felt hat)*
2. Mary proudly wore her new <u>cerise</u> coat. *(red)*
3. The teacher scolded the <u>loquacious</u> students. *(talkative)*
4. No one liked the <u>stingy</u> king. *(unwilling to share)*
5. The beautiful <u>cob</u> swam slowly. *(a male swan)*

Fun With Words Through Literature

At the mere mention of Amelia Bedelia (the main character in a series of books authored by Peggy Parish), you'll probably hear squeals of delight from your students. Amelia's literal interpretations of words land her in some of the most outrageous situations. Discussing and predicting Amelia's antics are great ways to enrich students' vocabularies. Another fun book of a similar nature is *The King Who Rained* by Fred Gwynne. In this delightful book a young child visualizes what her parents tell in funny (literal) ways. Ask your media specialist for assistance in locating these and other books of this type.

Ruth Heller has also written a collection of colorful and rhythmic books that are superb for extending language. *A Cache Of Jewels & Other Collective Nouns, Many Luscious Lollipops: A Book About Adjectives, Kites Sail High: A Book About Verbs,* and *Merry-Go-Round: A Book About Nouns* are filled with endless language opportunities.

TRDavidson

Daily Vocabulary Builder

Increase your students' vocabularies with this daily activity. For each student, staple 26 blank pages between two slightly larger construction-paper covers. Then have each youngster label his booklet pages in alphabetical order. As a homework activity, give each student an index card and instruct him to cut an interesting word from a discarded item in his home (such as a magazine, newspaper, or cereal box) and attach the cutout to the card. Have students deposit their completed cards in a decorated container labeled "The Discovery Box." Each day, one student draws a card from the box. This student is responsible for discovering the meaning of the word he has drawn. At a predetermined time later in the day, the child writes the word and its definition on the board for his classmates. After briefly discussing the word, have each student copy the word and its definition on the appropriate page in his word booklet. Continue the activity thoughout the year, asking students to restock The Discovery Box as needed. By the end of the school year, students will have impressive word collections.

Leigh Anne Newsom—Gr. 3, Greenbrier Intermediate, Chesapeake, VA

Vocabulary Hunt

Write a word in each box.

an action word _____	a descriptive word _____	a noun that has five or more letters _____
a weather word _____	a two-syllable word _____	a feeling _____	a synonym for *said* _____
a one-syllable word _____	a synonym for *big* _____	a word used in cooking _____	a compound word _____	a homograph _____
a contraction _____	a noun that has less than five letters _____	a holiday word _____	a three-syllable word _____

Happy Birthday, Martin Luther King, Jr.

Martin Luther King, Jr., wanted people to be able to go place together, share food together, and love one another in peace. Because he worked so hard for freedom and helped so many people to gain it, we honor him every year on his special day. Use the following activities to celebrate the birthday of this great American.

A Place Setting Of Brotherhood

Illustrate Dr. Martin Luther King's life of serving others with this hands-on activity. Cover a classroom table with a white tablecloth (symbolizing peace); then decorate the table with red, white, and blue streamers (symbolizing unity). For each desired place setting at the table, label a set of six cards with the following; "a saucer of fairness," "a plate of justice," "a glass of righteousness," "a fork of patience," "a spoon of love," and "a bowl of opportunity." Attach each set of cards to the tablecloth in the appropriate locations (see illustration). Then, using tableware or poster-board substitutes, have students individually, in pairs, or in small groups take turns setting the table of brotherhood. As each individual piece of tableware is simultaneously placed upon the table, have students announce its significance. Once everyone has taken a turn, discuss the concepts of brotherhood that are symbolized at this special table.

Freddie Marie Maxie—Gr. 2, Moss Bluff Elementary, Lake Charles, LA
Brenda Robinson—Gr. 2, J. F. Kennedy School, Lake Charles, LA

"Freedom, Freedom, Let It Ring"

One of the most famous references from Dr. King's speeches was his call for freedom to ring throughout our country. This song—sung to the tune of "Twinkle, Twinkle, Little Star"—reminds us of Dr. King's greatest wish.

Freedom, freedom, let it ring.
"Let it ring," said Dr. King.

Let us live in harmony.
Peace and love for you and me.

Freedom, freedom, let it ring.
"Let it ring," said Dr. King.

Carol A. Caryl, Steele Elementary, Tucson, AZ

Dreams For The Future

To conclude your celebration, ask youngsters to think about their dreams for the future. Then have each student write his dream on a dove cutout like the one shown. After each child has shared his dream with his classmates, mount the doves on one half of a large bulletin board labeled "Children Have Dreams." Label the remaining half of the display "Parents Have Dreams Too." Send home a dove cutout with each youngster. Ask youngsters to share with their parents what they have learned and ask them to write their dreams for the future on the dove cutouts. When students return the cutouts, invite them to share their parents' dreams. Then mount the cutouts on the bulletin board.

Debbie Wiggins
North Myrtle Beach Primary
North Myrtle Beach, SC

Reading About Martin Luther King, Jr.

Use these books to enhance your study of this great civil rights leader.

- *Happy Birthday, Martin Luther King*
  Written by Jean Marzollo
  Illustrated by J. Brian Pinkney
  Published by Scholastic Inc.

- *Martin Luther King, Jr.*
  Written by Jacqueline Woodson
  Edited by Bonnie Brook
  Illustrated by Floyd Cooper
  Published by Silver Press

- *A Picture Book Of Martin Luther King, Jr.*
  Written by David A. Adler
  Illustrated by Robert Casilla
  Published by Holiday House, Inc.

- *Martin Luther King, Jr.: A Biography For Young Children*
  Written by Carol Hilgartner Schlank and Barbara Metzger
  Illustrated by John Kastner
  Published by Gryphon House, Inc.

- *Let Freedom Ring: A Ballad Of Martin Luther King, Jr.*
  Written by Myra Cohn Livingston
  Illustrated by Samuel Byrd
  Published by Holiday House, Inc.

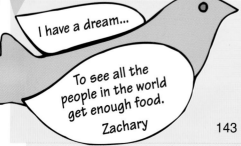

I have a dream...

To see all the people in the world get enough food.
Zachary

143

Hip! Hip! Hooray! It's The 100th Day!

How about that! It's the 100th day of school. Time *does* fly when you—and your students—are having fun. Celebrate your 100th day together with these fun-filled activities. Hip! Hip! Hooray!

ideas contributed by Ann Higgins, St. Davids, Ontario, Canada

Collecting 100 Items

In preparation for your 100th-day celebration, challenge each youngster to collect 100 items in the category of his choice. Specify that all 100 items must fit inside a small box or clear, nonbreakable container. On the 100th day, display the collections in a hallway or in your school library.

100 Feet

Just how long is 100 feet—student feet, that is? Provide your students with construction paper and scissors, and have them find out! Based on the number of students present, help the class decide how many shoe tracings each child will need to provide so that the total number of shoe cutouts will equal 100. Then have the students trace their shoes and cut out the shapes. Number the cutouts; then tape them end to end on a wall. Finally have your students measure the trail of cutouts. Compare its length to the actual length of 100 feet.

Spend It!

With this activity youngsters will discover some of the items they can buy with $100.00. Using play money, have the class count aloud 100 one-dollar bills. Then provide students with catalogs or sections of catalogs. Ask each student to find and cut out pictures of items that cost $100.00 or close to that amount. Have each student glue his pictures onto art paper and label them. Bind the pages together to create a class catalog of items that cost $100.00. Let's do some shopping!

bicycle

watch

coat

In 100 Years...

Help each student determine the year he will turn 100 years old. Then have him draw a picture of how he thinks he might look when he is that age. Encourage youngsters to write about their lifetime experiences or to describe what they think being 100 years old might be like.

Read On!

Youngsters will be surprised when they discover how many words they can read and spell. Ask the class to brainstorm a list of 100 words that they can read and spell. Challenge older students to list 100 science, math, or social studies words. One, two, three,....

The Pieces Fit

This hands-on activity is more than just fun! While participating, students will have hands-on experience with the number 100, and they will also strengthen their abilities to work cooperatively in a group. Divide the class into small groups; then give each group a 100-piece jigsaw puzzle to complete. Hey! Teamwork really counts!

Ten Groups Of Ten

Students are sure to give this idea a big thumbs-up! Provide each child with a piece of paper, a marker, and an ink pad. Have each child print his thumbprint onto his paper 100 times in groups of ten. As he prints each group, encourage him to circle the set and label it with the appropriate increment of ten. There you have it—ten groups of ten!

Measure It

Can't get enough of the number 100? Stretch out the fun of the 100th day with this measurement activity. Have students estimate which class-room items might be 100 centimeters long. Then provide students with measuring tapes to measure and verify their guesses. Record the actual lengths of the items on a chart for all to see.

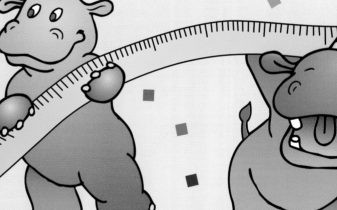

In 100 years, there will be robot salad bars.

Future Forecast

Help students calculate the year that it will be 100 years from now. Discuss ways the community might have changed. Also have students draw and describe items that might be invented during the next 100 years.

100 Good Deeds

Wrap up your 100th-day activities on a positive note! As a class, brainstorm a list of 100 good deeds. Challenge each youngster to commit to doing one or more of the good deeds listed. Your list of 100 will be only the beginning of many good deeds to come.

Abraham Lincoln

Well-known for his integrity, Abraham Lincoln fought to preserve the Union during the Civil War. Celebrate Lincoln's birthday with these activities and the reproducible on page 148.

A Penny For Your Thoughts

On the day you plan to celebrate Lincoln's birthday, place a penny on each child's desk before the students arrive. When they inquire about the coins, ask them to solve the mystery of why pennies would have a special meaning on this particular day. If students are having difficulty solving the case, take time to read aloud a book about Lincoln. Then throughout the day incorporate the pennies into several activities. For example, during math time divide students into small groups and have them arrange their pennies in sequential order by years. Or have students subtract those dates from the current year to discover how old their coins are. For a fun, following-directions activity, ask students to make rubbings of their pennies on selected assignments completed during the day. Vary the locations of the rubbings. If students are scheduled to play partner games during the day, have them flip their pennies to determine which player goes first. At the end of the day, let the youngsters take their pennies home.

Christine Tomlinson—Gr. 2 Continuous Progress, Ochovilla Elementary, Hawthorne, FL

Look At These Log Cabins!

This cooperative log-cabin project integrates Lincoln's birthday, recycling concepts, and critical-thinking skills. Enlist the help of your students in collecting paper-towel and toilet-tissue tubes for the project. Read aloud stories about Abraham Lincoln and call your students' attention to the illustrations of log cabins. Divide students into small groups and give each group a stash of cardboard tubes. Also make available supplies such as scissors, glue, paint, paintbrushes, sponges, construction paper, clothespins (to hold the cardboard logs in place until the glue dries), markers, crayons, and cotton balls. Ask each group to determine a plan for creating a log cabin and assign a specific function to each member. Suggest roles such as supplier, designer, gluer, painter, and decorator. Mingle among the groups, serving as a facilitator as the students work on their creations. When the log cabins are finished, ask each group to share its project and talk about its building experience.

Reading About Abe

Create further interest in our 16th president with these informative books.

- *Just A Few Words, Mr. Lincoln: The Story Of The Gettysburg Address* written by Jean Fritz and illustrated by Charles Robinson (Grosset & Dunlap, Inc.;1993)
- *Honest Abe* written by Edith Kunhardt and illustrated by Malcah Zeldis (Greenwillow Books, 1993)
- *Young Abraham Lincoln, Log-Cabin President* written by Andrew Woods and illustrated by Pat Schories (Troll Associates, 1992)
- *A Picture Book Of Abraham Lincoln* written by David A. Adler and illustrated by John & Alexandra Wallner (Holiday House, 1989)
- *Abraham Lincoln: President Of A Divided Country* written by Carol Greene and illustrated by Steven Dobson (Children's Press, 1989)

146

More Than Just A Hat

Lincoln used his black stovepipe hat for more than just a head covering! His habit of tucking bills, notes, and other legal papers inside his hat is a fond recollection of this great man. Students are sure to enjoy concealing notes and papers inside these unique presidential projects. To make a hat, cut away the flap of a 6" x 9" manila envelope before gluing the front of the envelope to a 9" x 12" sheet of black construction paper. Trim the construction paper to make a hat shape. Attach the top inch of a 6" x 9" piece of flesh-colored construction paper to the lower edge of the envelope; then turn over the project. Using crayons or markers, draw desired facial features and a scalloped beard on the flesh-colored paper. Trim away any excess paper below the beard and the project is complete.

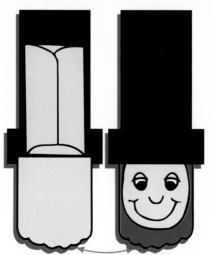

adapted from an idea by Cindy Bagocius—Gr. 2
McDowell School
Hudson, OH

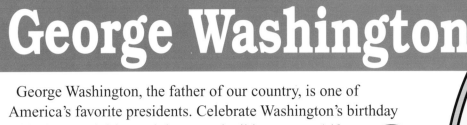

George Washington

George Washington, the father of our country, is one of America's favorite presidents. Celebrate Washington's birthday with these activities and the reproducible on page 148.

Quite A Guy!

(sung to the tune of "Yankee Doodle Dandy")
Here's a song of Washington,
General in the army.
Married Martha Custis and
He's father of our country!

Chorus:
Washington was quite a guy!
First president ever.
Would he let his country down?
No! Impossible! Never!

Surveyed the land when he was young.
Was honest in his youth.
Did he chop down a cherry tree?
He always told the truth.
(Repeat chorus.)

Two terms he served as president.
Would not be called a king.
Made it clear to all concerned
Democracy was his thing!
(Repeat chorus.)

He's honored with a monument.
He's on our dollar bill.
Could we, in time, forget this man?
Oh no! We never will!
(Repeat chorus.)

Sue Weisgerber—Gr. 2
South School, Mt. Carmel, IL

Easy Cherry Tarts

For a hands-on celebration of Washington's birthday, have students prepare these delicious cherry tarts. To make a tart, flatten a canned biscuit; then place a spoonful of cherry pie filling in the center. Fold the biscuit in half and press the edges together with a fork. Bake according to the directions on the biscuit can. By George! These tarts are tasty!

To Tell The Truth

Use the famous legend of George Washington and the cherry tree to talk about the importance of telling the truth. Conclude the discussion by asking each youngster to decide what he thinks is the most important reason for being truthful. To showcase your students' ideas in a cherry-shaped booklet, have each student write his reason on a precut circle of blank paper; then mount his cutout onto a slightly larger red construction-paper circle. Create a booklet cover like the one shown. If desired, laminate the students' pages and the cover for durability before compiling the project. Display the booklet in your classroom library for your students' reading enjoyment.

When I tell the truth I know I have done the right thing. by Ellen

Telling The Truth

If I tell the truth my dad doesn't get as mad. by J.D.

Reading About George

Create further interest in our country's first president with these informative books.

• *Young George Washington: America's First President* written by Andrew Woods and illustrated by John Himmelman (Troll Associates, 1992)
• *A Picture Book Of George Washington* written by David A. Adler and illustrated by John & Alexandra Wallner (Holiday House, 1989)
• *The Joke's On George* written by Michael O. Tunnell and illustrated by Kathy Osborn (Tambourine Books, 1993)
• *George Washington: First President Of The United States* written by Carol Greene and illustrated by Steven Dobson (Children's Press, 1991)
• *I Did It With My Hatchet: A Story Of George Washington* written and illustrated by Robert M. Quackenbush (Pippin Press, 1989)

Honest Abe

Abraham Lincoln loved to read.
Read the words.
Use the code to color the stars.

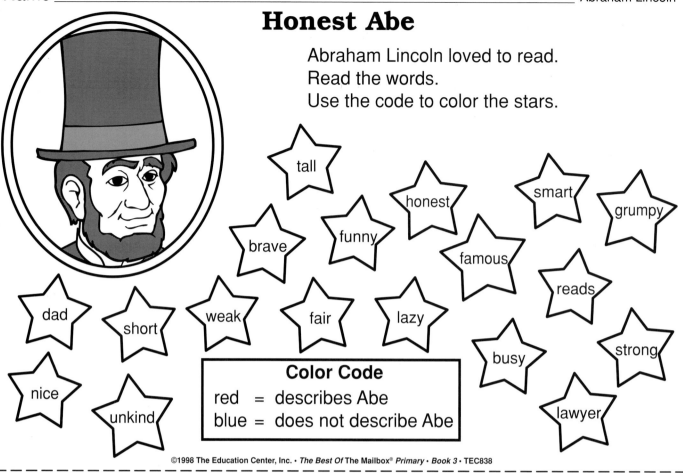

Color Code
red = describes Abe
blue = does not describe Abe

tall, brave, funny, honest, smart, grumpy, famous, dad, weak, fair, lazy, reads, short, busy, strong, nice, unkind, lawyer

Our First President

George Washington was very good at math.
Write a different math sentence on each line.
Use only the numbers and signs in George's hat.

+ − 7
2
3 6 = 5 1

_____   _____

_____   _____

_____   _____

_____   _____   _____

_____   _____

Bonus Box: How many more math
sentences can you make? Write them
on the back of this paper.

148

Making A Difference

African-American Trailblazers

African-Americans who have dared to fight racism and fulfill their dreams are at the heart of black history. Use these teaching suggestions and the centerfold cards to enrich your celebration of Black History Month.

Something To Talk About

Here's a teaching format that youngsters are sure to love. Pair students and have each twosome research a different African-American. Then ask each pair to present its information in the format of an interview. To do this, one student role-plays an interviewer and the other role-plays the African-American who has been researched. Encourage the students to dress for their parts. These high-interest presentations are sure to bring rave reviews. If possible, videotape the event. Move over Oprah! You've got plenty of competition headed your way!

Pamela Whitted, University School, Johnson City, TN

Charting African-American Contributions

Compile your youngsters' research efforts on an easy-to-read chart like the one shown. As each youngster makes a discovery, write it on the chart. Before long you'll have an abundance of information that can be used in a variety of ways. For example, each student can create a booklet of African-American contributions. To do this a student describes and illustrates a different contribution on each page of a blank booklet. Or challenge students to illustrate things that all people today can do that result from the efforts of African-Americans. Showcase these illustrations and a border of colorful hand cutouts on a bulletin board entitled "Applauding The Contributions Of African-Americans."

Agnes Tirrito—Gr. 2
Kennedy Elementary School
Texarkana, TX

African-American Trailblazers	
Name	Contribution
Rosa Parks	• Civil Rights Activist
Neal Loving	• Aviator
Harriet Tubman	• A Leader of the Underground Railway
Colin Powell	• Chairman of Joint Chiefs of Staff

A Celebration Of Differences

Celebrate the differences among people with this baking project. With your students' help, prepare a batch of your favorite rolled cookie dough. Then, using a cookie cutter, have each child cut out a body shape from the rolled dough. As the cookies bake, talk about how the cookies were made. Guide students to conclude that while the shapes of the cookies may vary, the cookies are all the same on the inside. When the cookies have cooled, ask each student to decorate a cookie to his liking. To encourage creativity, provide several colors of frosting and a wide variety of edible cookie decorations. Have each student display his work of art on a napkin at his desk. Provide time for students to admire their classmates' cookies. Lead the students to conclude that the differences among the cookies make them unique and special. Then, as the youngsters consume their creations, help them apply this important concept to the world around them.

Patsy Blakley—Gr. 2, Haskell Elementary School, Haskell, TX

Hot On Homework

Do your youngsters accept their homework assignments with all of the enthusiasm they'd have for foul-tasting medicine? Then try some of these creative approaches to make homework assignments more meaningful and pleasant for everyone involved. Before long, your youngsters—even you fire-breathing reluctant ones—can be hot on homework.

Brainteasers

Create enthusiasm for homework and increase parent involvement by putting a brainteaser or riddle at the bottom of each homework assignment sheet. Supply the answer at the bottom of the next homework assignment sheet, along with another brainteaser. Because solving this unusual challenge is likely to pique the interest of both the parent and the student, adding a brainteaser helps insure that every homework assignment sheet is read.

Sheila Monger
Gr. 2
Corlett School
Cheyenne, WY

Books To Go

Here's a system that assures that each student has an opportunity to read quality literature at home. Accumulate books for a classroom library; then encourage outside reading by sending a book home with each child on a regular basis. Busy families appreciate this method because it promotes good reading habits and saves them trips to the library.

Jane Hyla—Gr. 2
Seth Paine Elementary
Lake Zurich, IL

Variety Is The Spice

The key to successful homework assignments may be in the variety of learning experiences that they offer youngsters. So give homework that's very different from your classroom activities. For example, ask students to watch a special show on television and compare it to the book on which it was based. Give students as many hands-on assignments as possible. If your students are working on measurement, don't give them the usual worksheets. Instead have them use measuring cups and water to find the answers to several questions. Also have students complete experiments using appliances (such as freezers) that are difficult or impossible to use in the classroom.

2 half cups = 1 cup

Isobel L. Livingstone
Rahway, NJ

Show-And-Tell Fun

This show-and-tell alternative encourages creativity and critical thinking as it reinforces language skills. Each week, state a task or pose a question for students to answer during show-and-tell. Ask, for example, that each student bring in an object that begins with *ch,* or ask that he bring in something that relates to his favorite president. To complete the assignment, each youngster explains the relevance of his object and entertains the questions of his classmates.

Melinda Klinger—Gr. 1
Pine Valley
Colorado Springs, CO

Homework For The Family

Establish a routine of sending your youngsters home with family homework: challenging critical-thinking assignments that are to be completed with the assistance of family members. You'll find that parents enjoy the involvement, and youngsters get a kick out of the novelty of the idea. Homework's a lot more fun when everyone pitches in!

Lisa M. Borgo
North Caldwell, NJ

Open-Ended Assignments

Here's a great way to stimulate interest in your social studies and science units. Ask each student to bring from home several different items relating to one of your current units of study. The following day, have each youngster explain the relevance of his items and write about their significance to your unit of study.

Elaine Marie Deling—Special Education K–6
Everglades Elementary
Miami, FL

Bagging The Alphabet

Here's a great homework assignment for first graders who are ready for an alphabet/initial consonant review. Label each of 26 lunch bags with a letter of the alphabet. Distribute the bags to your students with the homework assignment of filling each bag with four items (or pictures of items) that begin with the bag's letter. When the bags are returned to school, have each child share the contents of his bag with his classmates.

Sue Dyett—Gr. 1
West Park Elementary School
Ravenna, OH

I Knew That

Here's a homework assignment that your youngsters will really get a kick out of! Have each youngster create a worksheet or quiz related to one of your current units. Then have him ask a parent to complete the exercise for homework. As a part of this assignment, he checks his parent's work and discusses any errors. How excited a youngster gets when he finds that he knows something that his parent doesn't!

Barbara Williams—Gr. 3
Bel Air Elementary
Evans, GA

Teacher Temporaries

Would your youngsters like a chance to switch roles with you? Sure they would! So try this fun role reversal. Give each student a homework worksheet with answers, many of them incorrect. Ask that each youngster find and correct the errors on his page. It's surprising how excited youngsters can get about filling your shoes.

Lisa M. Borgo
North Caldwell, NJ

Undercover Assignment

Secret homework assignments create just enough mystery to motivate youngsters. Program index cards or paper slips with assorted homework assignments. Give each child his assignment tucked in a sealed envelope labeled "Secret Homework" and decorated with a seasonal sticker. As this method creates homework excitement, it also allows you to tailor assignments to meet students' specific needs.

Sheila R. Chapman—Gr. 1
Atkinson School
Newnan, GA

Solo Assignments

Those of us who work can empathize with pressures experienced by the parents of our students who also have demanding schedules. So, every now and then, give homework assignments that purposefully exclude parent involvement. Ask the student to read to a stuffed animal, pet, sibling, or neighbor. Youngsters enjoy the change and respond well to the independence of shouldering the responsibility for completing their assignments.

Diane Afferton
Morrisville, PA

...and then the three little kittens...

Getting Real

Do your youngsters seem to be programmed by everything from Nickelodeon® to Nintendo®? Surprise them with a homework assignment that requires that they get outside for fresh air and exercise. Ask each youngster to play outside for 20 minutes and notice as many green things as he can find in that amount of time. The following day, have youngsters discuss their observations. The next time, vary the assignment by having youngsters notice animals, people, insects, or something related to your current studies. You'll quickly discover that these observations and discussions are much more fruitful than the usual paper-and-pencil tasks.

Diane Afferton

Yours, Mine, And Ours

With a little ingenuity on your part, homework can be a vehicle to promote parent/child interaction and build creativity. One example of such an assignment is to program a worksheet with two sets of ten circles and the question "How many different things can you make from a circle?" The child converts ten circles into drawings of objects while his parent does the same with the other set of ten circles. Another example is to ask each child to write and illustrate his favorite poem and ask his parent to do the same. When returned to school, these projects create a great deal of interest and reflect diverse input.

Lynne Spence—Gr. 2
McCoy Elementary
Aztec, NM

Hot On Homework

You can make homework a hot topic with this incentive program. Reward each child who meets his weekly homework goals with a hot prize. Some sizzling prizes include Hot Tamales® candies, Atomic Fire Ball® candies, and the awards on page 154. If your youngsters are having a hard time getting their homework in on time, try this technique. Soon your youngsters will be hot on homework, too!

Patty Quinn—Gr. 2, St. Jude's School and
Mary Ellen Bombara, Olney Elementary School
Silver Spring, MD

Swell Spelling

Here's a tip for converting spelling practice from drudgery into a dream. Pair each student with a partner. Then, for homework, have each youngster program an empty grid with the current spelling list and fill the remaining spaces with assorted alphabet letters. The following day partners exchange papers, and each student locates and circles the spelling words. Another option is to have each student prepare a fill-in-the-blank exercise for his partner to complete using the current spelling words. Reward hardworking partners with a treat at the end of a one-month partnership. Then assign new partners for the upcoming month.

Pam Negovetich—Gr. 2
Eldon Ready Elementary
Griffith, IN

Persuasive Tactics

This homework assignment is one that your youngsters will tackle gleefully. Explain that the assignment is to watch five television commercials, list persuasive words used in the commercials, note any product comparisons, and create a commercial for a favorite product. Encourage parent involvement. Getting youngsters to tune in to this assignment will be no problem at all.

Leigh Anne Newsom—Gr. 3
Greenbrier Intermediate
Chesapeake, VA

Awards

Use with "Hot On Homework" on page 153.

Don't mean to be braggin', but

_____
name

is

hot

on

homework!

_____
name

is hot

on

homework!

_____
name

is hot

on

homework!

Don't mean to be braggin', but

_____
name

is

hot

on

homework!

Lookin' For Loot!

Ahoy, mateys! If you're searching for ways to reinforce money skills, you'll find this booty of swashbuckling subscriber ideas as precious as gold!

A Penny A Day

A penny per day is a great investment in your youngsters' money skills. For this daily money activity, you will need a supply of play money and six resealable plastic bags. Label one bag "Pennies." Label the remaining bags "Nickels," "Dimes," "Quarters," "Half-dollars," and "Dollars." Beginning with the pennies bag, staple the plastic bags in order near your calendar display. Make certain that each bag can easily be opened and closed. Each day ask a different student to add a penny to the pennies bag; then as a class evaluate the contents of the bags and determine if coin exchanges are in order (for example, exchanging five pennies for a nickel or exchanging five pennies and a nickel for a dime). Conclude the activity by enlisting your youngsters' help in determining the value of the bagged money. As the year progresses, your students' money skills will grow right along with the amount of play money in the bags!

Barbara Turner—Gr. 2
North Central Schools
Pioneer, OH

Bags Of Money!

Money skills are in the bag at this kid-pleasing free-time center! Place a supply of play money at a math center; then for each student label one side of a paper lunch bag with eight or more different money amounts. Distribute the bags and have each student personalize his bag. When a student has free time, he circles one money amount on the side of his bag; then he goes to the center and fills his empty bag with a matching amount of play money. At the end of the day, have those students who completed the free-time activity exchange money bags. If the amount of play money inside the bag equals the circled amount, a student draws an X over the circle; then he returns the play money to the center and the empty bag to its owner. If the money amounts do not match, the student returns the bag of play money to its owner. When all the money amounts on a student's money bag have been crossed out, reward the student with a special privilege or a small prize; then present him with a new money bag!

Tamsin Monnoleto—Grs. 3 & 4
John Glenn School
Pine Hill, NJ

Spill The Beans

With this easy-to-make partner game, students practice their money-counting skills using lima beans. To make the game, give each student ten lima beans in a lidded container. Have each student use markers to program one side of his beans as follows: four beans with a blue dot, three beans with a red dot, and three beans with a green dot. Explain that a blue dot equals one cent, a red dot equals five cents, and a green dot equals ten cents. Then, playing with a partner, each student takes a turn shaking his container of beans, spilling them on the floor or a table, and determining the total value of the beans that have colored dots showing. The student who has the higher money value earns one point for the round of play. Students continue playing in this manner until a predetermined number of points are scored or game time is over. To increase the difficulty of the game, have each student label additional beans to represent quarters and half-dollars.

Donna Tobey—Gr. 1, Gulliver Academy, Coral Gables, FL

You're-In-The-Money Stories

Cash in with this soon-to-be-a-favorite, small- or large-group game! Ask each student to bring from home two quarters, four dimes, five nickels, and 17 pennies in a personalized, resealable plastic bag. Store the bags of money in your desk or another safe location until game time. You will also need a supply of paper tickets and assorted student prizes. Sort the prizes by value into three containers labeled "Three Tickets," "Five Tickets," and "Ten Tickets." To begin play, feature one student in a money-related story problem. Ask all students to solve the problem using the coins in their bags. Then ask the featured child to act out the problem and demonstrate how to solve it. Reward the featured child with a paper ticket if she correctly solves the problem. Continue in this manner until each child has acted out a money-related problem in which she is featured. Suggest that students store their paper-ticket winnings in their money bags. Plan to play the game two or more times per week. Set aside time each week during which students can cash in their paper tickets. This is one game students will be eager to play—even during indoor recess!

Karen Harper, Cary Reynolds School, Doraville, GA

Money Toss

Students work cooperatively to accomplish a valuable task with this coin-counting game. Divide youngsters into small groups. For each group tape a small bowl to the floor. Then affix a strip of tape to the floor approximately five steps away from the bowl. Place a variety of coins in a container next to the strip of tape. To play, one student sits by the bowl and is designated to be the counter. The remaining students are the *coin tossers*. In turn, each student randomly picks a coin, stands on the tape strip, and tries to toss the coin into the bowl. If the coin goes in, the counter adds the value of the coin to his count. If the coin misses the bowl, the coin is not counted. Each group continues to toss coins in this manner until the total value of the coins in its bowl reaches or surpasses $1.00. After the counter counts the change from the bowl for the teacher, a different team counter is determined and a new round of play begins.

Sharyl Zamb—Gr. 2, Earl Pritchett Elementary School, Buffalo Grove, IL

Punch-Out Coins

It's the end of the year and you have a class supply of punch-out coins from your students' consumable math workbooks. You feel guilty tossing them, but you know that your next class of students will have their own punch-out coin sets. This book-making activity is the perfect solution. Give each student a booklet of blank pages. After personalizing the front cover of his booklet, instruct each child to glue a handful of coins on the front of each booklet page, then write the total value of the coins on the back of the page. Check each child's booklet for accuracy; then send the completed booklets home with the students. Now students can keep their money-counting skills sharp over the summer!

adapted from an idea by Ursula Camenzuli—Gr. 1
Academy Street Elementary School
Bayport, NY

A Booming Business

Enhance your math program, foster community awareness, and build responsibility in your students—all by forming a classroom stationery company! As a class agree upon a company name; then make samples of the note cards and stationery that will be offered for sale. Every few days review the state of the company and discuss decisions that need to be made, such as buying supplies and filling orders. Each month, after the students have determined the amount of profit their company has made, have them donate a portion of the profits to a charity or organization. For example, students may decide to buy food for the needy or adopt a zoo animal. Use the remainder of the profits to purchase books for the students' reading enjoyment.

Maria D. Morris—Gr. 2
Tulsa, OK

Classroom Garage Sale

Culminate your money unit by having each child donate toys and books for a classroom garage sale. Display the items after labeling each one with a price tag. Position a toy cash register (or something similar) containing play money near the display. Give each student a resealable plastic bag of coin manipulatives. The manipulatives may vary, but the total value of the coins must be the same. Invite each student to shop for one item. After a student selects her item, she goes to the cash register where she pays the teacher or another classmate for her purchase. Repeat the activity again, inviting each student to shop for a second item. Students who have money remaining after their second purchases may return to the sale to spend the rest of their money. Children will love this shopping experience and gain a better understanding of money value. Store unpurchased items for a later sale or donate them to a local charity.

Linda Stiefel—Gr. 1
Walter Hall Elementary
League City, TX

Coupon Math

Inspire youngsters to write creative story problems with the help of grocery-store coupons. Give each child two coupons and challenge him to write a story problem about his trip to the store. In his story, the child tells the price of each item he buys, how much money he spends, and how much money he saves by using the coupons. Below his story problem, the student shows the math calculations that gave him the answers in his story. Then he glues the coupons to the back of his paper.

adapted from an idea by Cathy Pace—Gr. 2
Mount Pleasant Elementary
Mount Pleasant, NC

Wild About Weather!

Here's your chance to do more than just talk about the weather! Dip into this weather-wise collection of hands-on activities and discover a whirlwind of teaching success. And that's a forecast you can count on!

Hats Off To Weather!

Introduce your weather unit with this hats-on approach! In a large shopping bag, place an assortment of hats such as a rain hat, a stocking cap, a straw hat, a baseball cap, and a sun visor. Gather students around you, then remove one hat from the bag and place it on your head. Ask students to describe what the weather might be if a person chose to wear this hat. Retrieve another hat from the bag and place it on the head of a youngster. Ask students to describe the type(s) of weather this hat might be worn in. Continue in this manner until all of the hats are being worn. Ask students if they think weather forecasters or meteorologists predict the weather by observing the hats that people wear. Record your youngsters' thoughts about how weather is predicted on a large raindrop cutout and display the cutout for future reference. Then collect the hats and start observing the weather!

Paula L. Diekhoff, Warsaw, IN

Background For The Teacher

Weather is the condition of the air that blankets our earth. It is shaped by four "ingredients": the sun, the earth, the air, and water. These ingredients work together to make it hot or cold, cloudy or clear, windy or calm. They may produce rain, snow, sleet, or hail.

One universal aspect of weather is that it affects everyone. The type of clothing that we wear each day, how we spend our leisure time, and even our moods are tied into the weather. Weather also has a tremendous impact on farming, industry, transportation, communication, construction, and sometimes, our very survival.

A Writing Forecast

Your youngsters' writing skills can weather any storm with this colossal collection of journal writing topics. For added writing motivation, have each youngster design his own theme-shaped writing journal!

- Lost In The Fog
- The Raindrop That Was Afraid To Fall
- The Day There Was No Weather
- The Little Lost Cloud
- Trapped Inside A Raindrop!
- My Pet Tornado
- Silly Snow
- The Day It Rained Bats And Frogs
- The Wind That Was A Bully
- The Unforgettable Forecast

A Flurry Of Creative Expression

Many people believe that weather affects the behavior of animals and humans. Give your youngsters an opportunity to express their creative interpretations of different types of weather. If desired, play a recording of classical background music and have each youngster hold a crepe-paper streamer as she moves around the room, interpreting various weather conditions such as a cold wind, a thunderstorm, a hurricane, a flurry of snowflakes, a bolt of lightning, a gusty wind, a downpour of rain, a warm spring breeze, and a sunny day. Be sure to join in on the fun yourself!

Reading Thermometers

This quick and easy activity gives youngsters firsthand experience reading thermometers. Divide students into small groups and give each group an ice cube in a cup of cold water and an outdoor thermometer. Select one student in each group to hold the bulb of the thermometer between her fingers. This will cause the liquid in the thermometer to rise. Then ask the student to insert the bulb of the thermometer into the cup of water, causing the liquid in the thermometer to drop. Ask students to share their observations. Explain that holding the bulb of the thermometer increases the temperature of the liquid inside the thermometer. As the liquid is heated, it expands and rises in the thermometer tube. The cold water removes the heat from the liquid in the thermometer. When the liquid cools, it contracts and moves down the tube. Thermometers measure the temperature of air in the same way. Any increase or decrease in the heat content of air causes the liquid inside the thermometer to expand or contract. Now that students fully understand how a thermometer works, they'll enjoy monitoring the temperature of the air outside your classroom.

Clouds! Clouds! Clouds!

For an interesting and informative look at the different types of clouds and the weather that follows them, share *The Cloud Book* by Tomie dePaola (published by Holiday House) with your youngsters. At the completion of the book, write a student-generated list of cloud types on a large cloud cutout. If desired, write a brief description of each cloud type near its name. Then for each of several days, schedule a few minutes of sky-watching into your weather activities. Conclude each session by discussing the cloud types that were observed. As an added challenge, ask students to predict the weather conditions that will follow each cloud type.

When students are familiar with a variety of cloud types, have them create fold-out cloud booklets. To make a booklet, accordion-fold a 5" x 3' strip of blue bulletin-board paper to create a booklet that is approximately five inches square. On the front of the booklet, write your name and the booklet's title. On the bottom half of each booklet page, name and describe a different type of cloud. Then on the top half of the pages, create resemblances of the clouds using cotton balls, crayons, and glue.

How Weather-Wise Are You?

Thinking caps are a must for this weather-related challenge! Duplicate student copies of the activity on page 160. Have students search for the misused weather words independently or in pairs. After the words have been found and replaced, check the activity together.

For a fun follow-up activity, create a book of similar weather-teasers. To make a booklet page, have each child fold a blank 8 1/2" x 11" sheet of paper in half. Making certain that the fold is at the bottom of his paper, the youngster writes and illustrates a weather sentence containing a misused weather word. Next he flips his paper over so that the fold is at the top. Then he writes and illustrates the correct version of the sentence. Mount these papers on colorful sheets of 9" x 12" construction paper that have been folded in half. (See illustration.) Bind the booklet pages between a booklet cover entitled "How Weather-Wise Are You?" The completed booklet is sure to create a flurry of reading excitement!

Paula L. Diekhoff, Warsaw, IN

In A Fog About Fog

So what is fog anyway? Undoubtedly your youngsters will have a few ideas of their own. After students have had a chance to share their explanations, reveal that fog is actually a cloud that touches the ground. To make fog in a bottle, gather the following materials: a cup of hot water, a clear gallon jug, matches, a basketball or bicycle tire pump, and modeling clay.

Pour the cup of hot water into the bottle. Light a match, blow it out, and drop it into the bottle. Quickly seal the opening of the bottle with clay, leaving a small opening for inserting the air pump tube. Pump up the pressure inside the jar with about 15 to 20 strokes. Then remove the air pump, releasing the pressure. The air inside the bottle will instantly turn to fog! If you pump up the pressure again, the air will clear.

Why does it work? Increasing the air pressure warms the air inside the jar, allowing it to hold more water vapor. When the pressure is suddenly reduced, the water condenses into tiny droplets that produce fog. The smoke particles represent the dust particles that are present in the atmosphere.

Weather Bloopers

How weather-wise are you?
Cross out the weather word in each sentence
    that doesn't make sense.
Write the correct weather word in the cloud.
Use the answer bank.

1. A prediction about the weather is called a weather observation.

2. The atmosphere warms the earth.

3. During a storm you might see lightning and hear snowflakes.

4. When water freezes, it changes to fog.

5. Cirrus, stratus, and cumulus are types of frost.

6. A thermometer is an instrument for measuring rainfall.

7. Moving air is called snow.

8. A person who studies weather is called a barometer.

9. Hail is a cloud that touches the ground.

10. After the rain shower a colorful hurricane filled the sky.

11. Water freezes more rapidly in the sun.

12. Sleet, wind, hail, and snow are all kinds of precipitation.

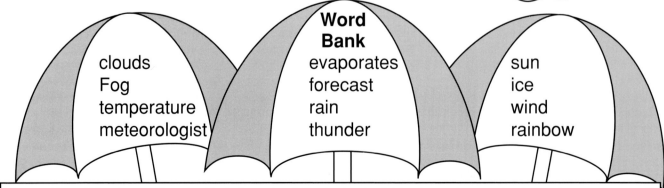

Word Bank

clouds	evaporates	sun
Fog	forecast	ice
temperature	rain	wind
meteorologist	thunder	rainbow

Bonus Box: What is your favorite kind of weather? On the back of this sheet, draw and color a picture of yourself doing what you like to do most in your favorite kind of weather.

Note To Teacher: Use this activity with "How Weather-Wise Are You?" on page 159.

Welcome To Mexico

Mexico is often described as a land of contrasts. To the north are dusty deserts; to the south are lush rain forests. There are hot, tropical coastlines. Flat plateaus are surrounded by high, mountainous areas. You'll also find huge cities and tiny villages—the populated areas and the pristine wilderness. Enlist your youngsters' help in finding Mexico on a physical map; then help the students locate the mountainous, flat, and coastal regions of Mexico along with its capital—Mexico City.

Next find your state on the map. Decide as a group if it would be better to drive or fly to this fascinating country. Propose a route of travel to and through Mexico and discuss the things that might be seen along the way. Conclude the lesson by reading aloud a book like *Mexico* by Karen Jacobsen (Childrens Press®, 1982) to give students more background information about our southern neighbors.

Marvelous Mexico

Travel to the land of sunshine and *sombreros*—Mexico. Use these across-the-curriculum ideas to teach your *muchachos* and *muchachas* about our neighbors south of the border. *Olé!*

ideas by Michele Converse Baerns and Stacie Stone

Grocery-Bag Garments

Typical dress in many parts of Mexico includes T-shirts, blouses, jeans, pants, skirts, and jackets. But in rural areas, many natives of Mexico still wear traditional clothing such as *guayaberas*—loose cotton shirts, *huaraches*—thick-soled sandals, or *huipiles*—cotton dresses trimmed with embroidered flowers. A wool scarf called a *serape* may be worn by a man on chilly nights. A *rebozo*, or shawl, is worn by a woman when she has visitors or goes into a village.

Dress up your study of Mexico by having students make their own serapes or rebozos. To begin have each student cut out the side panels of a large grocery bag so that it will lay flat. Then have the students use tempera paint and paintbrushes, markers, or crayons to decorate their serapes and rebozos. When the projects have dried, have students hole-punch a series of equally spaced holes along each end of their projects. Then, using three-inch lengths of colorful yarn, show students how to loop a yarn length through each hole as shown. When the serapes and rebozos have been completed, have students model their Mexican garb for their classmates. Plan for students to wear the garments again during a culminating activity like "It's A Celebration!" on page 165.

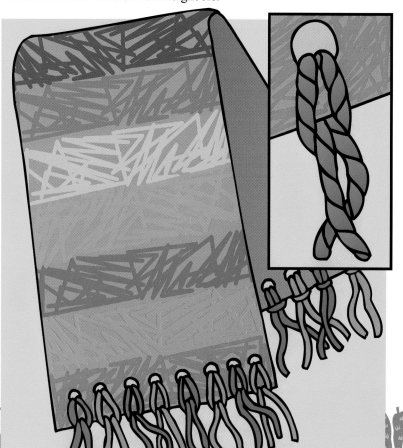

Mexican Munchies

Taquitos, tacos, tamales—mmm, tantalizing! Many of the foods from Mexico are made from corn. This is because corn, or *maize*, has been an important crop in Mexico for thousands of years. Corn is used—dried or fresh—in main courses, soups, desserts, and drinks. Most importantly, the corn is ground into flour and used to make tortillas—flat, pancakelike bread. Tortillas are eaten at almost every meal. They are the basis for other Mexican foods such as *burritos* and *quesadillas*. Use these recipes to give your students a taste of Mexico.

Quesadillas
(Makes 12 quesadillas)

You'll need:
12 tortillas (store-bought)
12 1-oz. portions of sharp cheddar cheese, grated
hot griddle
spatula

Directions:
Heat a tortilla on the griddle for about five seconds. Flip the tortilla. Spread one portion of cheese on the tortilla; then carefully fold the tortilla in half. Heat until the cheese melts. Repeat this process with the remaining tortillas.

Homemade Tortillas
(makes approximately 12 small tortillas)

You'll need:
1 cup masa harina (corn masa mix)
or 1 cup corn flour plus 1 tsp. salt
3/4 to 1 cup warm water
waxed paper
hot griddle
spatula
bowl

Directions:
Place all ingredients in bowl and mix together, using your hands. Divide dough into 12 balls. Press each ball between two sheets of waxed paper to flatten. Peel away waxed paper and place tortilla on ungreased griddle. Flip tortilla when edges begin to brown. Remove from heat when edges are brown.

Codex Books

Long ago the Maya were the most powerful group in Mexico. They were expert mathematicians, astronomers, and architects. One of the first writing systems in North America was developed by Mayans. It used pictures or symbols—called *heiroglyphs* or *glyphs*—to represent words and ideas. These glyphs were written on walls and in Mayan books called *codices*. Codices were different from modern-day books in that they were pleated and had to be unfolded in order to be read. Each codex told stories about Mayan gods and other significant people.

Students will enjoy creating a classroom codex that features people who are important to them. On a 9" x 12" sheet of white construction paper, have each student use crayons or markers to illustrate a significant person in her life. Then have each student write a sentence on her paper that explains *why* that person is, or has been, significant. To assemble the codex, position the student pages side by side. Place a 9" x 12" sheet of construction paper at the beginning and one at the end of the series of papers; then tape the long edges of the papers together. Fold the resulting booklet accordion-style. Decorate and write the title "Our Class Codex" on the front cover; then display the classy codex in your classroom library.

A Spectrum Of Spanish

Familiarize your youngsters with a bit of Spanish—the most commonly spoken language in Mexico. *My World Of Spanish Words* by Debbie MacKinnon (Barron's Educational Series, Inc.; 1995) is a wonderful classroom resource. The book's simple design and colorful photographs make it a terrific teaching tool.

When students are familiar with Spanish color words, they'll enjoy creating a Spanish color version of *Brown Bear, Brown Bear, What Do You See?* by Bill Martin Jr. (Henry Holt & Company, Inc.; 1992). Create the story as a class; then copy the text onto 12" x 18" sheets of white construction paper—patterning the format after the original story. Have the students illustrate the resulting pages; then bind the pages into a class booklet titled "Bear Moreno, Bear Moreno, What Do You See?"

Color Word Translations

brown	morena, moreno	**purple**	morada, morado
red	roja, rojo	**white**	blanca, blanco
yellow	amarilla, amarillo	**black**	negra, negro
blue	azul	**gold**	ora, oro
green	verde		

Casa, Sweet Casa

Homes throughout Mexico vary widely. City dwellers might live in modern homes and apartments. Others may live outside the city in colonial-style homes that share a courtyard with several other families. Many of these homes are built of *adobe*—sun-baked bricks of earth and straw. Mexicans who live in rural areas of Central Mexico also use adobe to build their homes.

This adobe brick-making opportunity is sure to thrill your future architects and builders! Each student needs a clean and empty eight-ounce milk carton, a plastic spoon, one-half cup of dry dirt, one-half cup of powdered plaster of paris, one-quarter cup of water, and a small amount of dry grass or straw clippings.

To make his brick, a student combines the dirt and plaster of paris in his milk carton; then he stirs in the water. He adds grass clippings to the mixture until it thickens. Then he uses his spoon to smooth the top of his project. Place the projects on a sunny shelf to harden and dry. (This will take several hours or overnight.) Then have each student tear the milk carton away from his project to reveal an adobelike brick.

If desired, students can decorate their projects to resemble adobe homes. Provide markers, paintbrushes and tempera paints, and other desired craft supplies for decorating purposes. Then have the students create a village by arranging their adobe homes on a sheet of poster board. To complete the class project, invite students to add construction-paper trees and roads, and a variety of other decorations.

Handwoven Baskets

Handwoven baskets are a popular craft item in Mexico. Your students are sure to be impressed with the results of this basket-weaving project! For each student you will need a clean and empty plastic margarine tub (or something similar—about 12 ounces in size) and three yards of raffia (available at your local craft store)—one yard of red, one yard of green, and one yard of natural. Prepare the containers for distribution by making an odd number of vertical cuts in the container. (The cuts should be about one inch apart and should stop at the base of the container. This will result in a series of plastic strips.) To begin his project, a student ties and knots one end of a length of raffia around one plastic strip—making sure his knot is on the inside of his container and the raffia is pushed to the bottom of the plastic strip. (Provide assistance as needed.) Then he weaves the length of raffia in and out of the strips of plastic until he uses the entire length—making sure the exposed end of the raffia is inside the container. He then repeats the process (starting where the last length of raffia ended) with the remaining lengths of raffia until the container is covered. After taping down any exposed ends of raffia inside his container, the student uses a permanent marker to label the bottom of his project with his name or initials. His handiwork is now ready to be displayed at your classroom market.

To Market, To Market

In villages all over Mexico, market day is a weekly highlight. People come to buy or sell food and items like baskets, rebozos, flowers, and clay figurines. Share the story *Saturday Market* by Patricia Grossman (Lothrop, Lee & Shepard Books, 1994) to give students a better understanding of the happenings at a local market. Then select students to move several unused desks to an area of the classroom to create a marketplace. While several students cover the individual desks with brightly colored paper, have a small group of youngsters design a sign that reads *"La Plaza*—The Market."

See "Handwoven Baskets," "Corn-Husk Crafts," and "Mexican Pottery" for craft ideas that can be displayed at *La Plaza*.

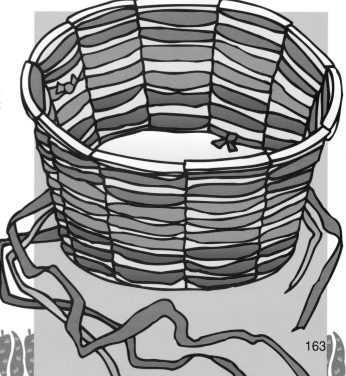

Corn-Husk Crafts

These "a-maize-ing" dolls will delight your little amigos. To make a corn-husk doll, each student needs one 6-inch and one 18-inch length of tan twisted paper, a one-foot length of yarn, a black felt-tip marker, and a scrap (about 3" x 6") of brightly colored fabric. Assist each student in untwisting his lengths of twisted paper. To make a doll, a student bends the 18" strip in half lengthwise without creasing the paper. Then he places the six-inch strip between the bent strip, creating the arms for his doll. To secure the arms in place, he holds one end of his yarn length at the back of his project; then he wraps the yarn length diagonally around the project, crisscrossing it as shown. When he approaches the end of the yarn, he ties a knot at the back of the project. Using the black felt-tip marker, the student adds facial features to his doll. To complete the project he drapes his fabric scrap around the doll's shoulders to resemble a rebozo or a serape. Display the corn-husk dolls in your classroom marketplace.

Mexican Pottery

Mexico is known for its brightly decorated pottery. Each student can create her own Mexican-style pottery using a three-inch ball of Crayola® Model Magic®, and permanent markers or acrylic paints and a paintbrush. After each student has molded her compound into the shape of a small animal, have her set it aside overnight so it will harden slightly. The next day, the student can decorate her figurine as desired. Add the colorful pottery to your marketplace display!

Michelle McAuliffe and Marsha Black, Greensburg, IN

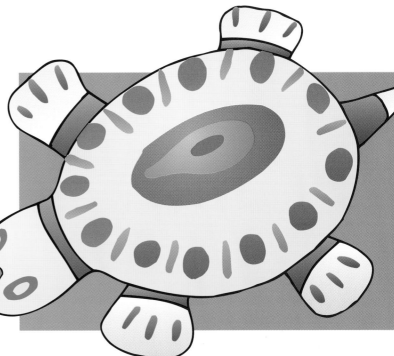

Fiesta, Fiesta!

People all over Mexico enjoy fiestas! Fiesta parties and festivals are held for a variety of reasons. A fiesta can be a birthday celebration, a tribute to a local hero, or an acknowledgement of an important day in Mexico's history. Many religious fiestas, like Christmas and Easter, are celebrated nationwide. While each fiesta is different, many begin at dawn with the ringing of church bells or an explosion of fireworks. Colorful parades, dancing, music, food and drink, rodeos, and/or bullfights may follow.

To learn more about some of the holidays for which people in Mexico hold fiestas, divide students into four groups. Have a different group research each of the following: Christmas traditions in Mexico, Easter traditions in Mexico, Mexico's Independence Day, and Cinco De Mayo. Then have each group present information about the holiday it researched. Conclude the activity by discussing how celebrations in the United States are similar to or different than celebrations in Mexico.

Comparing Cultures

Once students have been introduced to the culture of Mexico, have them compare life in Mexico to life in the United States. Display a chart like the one shown to initiate a discussion about a variety of topics. Ask student volunteers to record the observations of their classmates on the chart; then display the chart on a bulletin board. Invite students to add to the chart as they acquire more information.

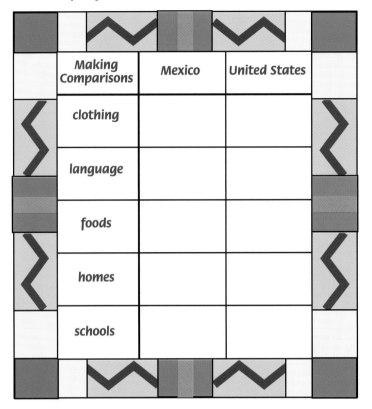

Making Comparisons	Mexico	United States
clothing		
language		
foods		
homes		
schools		

It's A Celebration!

Conclude your Mexico-related activities with a celebration of learning! Encourage students to invite their families to your classroom fiesta. The guests of honor can stroll through the classroom marketplace and view the student-made wares, then check out the student-created adobe village. As the visitors snack on a sampling of Mexican foods, the students can model the serapes and rebozos they made earlier in the unit. A presentation of the codex book and an oral reading of "Bear Moreno, Bear Moreno" will definitely be in order. If you are musically inclined, lead the students and your guests in a medley of songs (see "Song Collections") or add to the festive mood by playing selections from *Papa's Dream,* a recording that features traditional Mexican folk songs with a bit of classic rock 'n roll. (Available from Music For Little People at 1-800-346-4445: cassette #42562 @ $9.98; CD #42562D @ $15.98.) A fun time is sure to be had by all!

Song Collections

De Colores And Other Latin-American Folk Songs For Children
Selected, Arranged, and Translated by José-Luis Orozco
Illustrated by Elisa Kleven
Dutton Children's Books, 1994

This collection reflects all of Latin America across the pages, but author Orozco grew up in Mexico City. Combining his childhood recollections and adult research, this musician/author includes music notes. The verses are written in Spanish and English. Whimsical pictures dance over the brightly edged pages. Look for examples of architectural style, native instruments, and festival attire.

Los Pollitos Dicen: The Baby Chicks Sing
Collected And Adapted by Nancy Abraham Hall &
Jill Syverson-Stork
Illustrated by Kay Chorao
Little, Brown And Company; 1994

Music and bilingual text lie over lighthearted watercolors in this collection of traditional games, nursery rhymes, and songs from Spanish-speaking countries. An excellent resource that offers universal themes in appealing, singsong verse.

Outstanding Teacher Resources

Fiesta! Mexico's Great Celebrations
Written by Elizabeth Silverthorne
Illustrated by Jan Davey Ellis
The Millbrook Press, 1992

This book is an explosion of information on the various Mexican fiestas.

Mexico: The People
Created by Bobbie Kalman; with photographs
Crabtree Publishing Company, 1993

From The Lands, Peoples, And Cultures Series, this book looks at the way of life of Mexican people, including family life, education, religion, city and village life, and work. Two other books from the series—*Mexico The Culture* and *Mexico The Land*—are also packed with information for a study of Mexico.

A Taste Of Mexico
Written by Linda Illsley; with photographs
Thomson Learning, 1995

Through a study of the foods of Mexico, the country's culture and geography are explored.

Hot Off The Press!

Utilizing The Newspaper In The Classroom

Extra! Extra! Read all about it! Here's the inside scoop on using the newspaper in the classroom. We've gathered newsworthy tips and activities from a most reliable and respected source—our trusty subscribers—and we've published the best of the batch in this news-breaking collection. You can count on us to deliver!

Easy Does It

The format of newspapers makes them difficult for students to handle. To keep the oversized pages from slipping and sliding, place several staples down the left-hand edge of each newspaper.

Dee Ann Bates
Hawthorne Elementary
Oklahoma City, OK

Not Just For Grown–Ups!

Beginning readers often think that the newspaper is just for adults. Use this activity to convince your youngsters that they can read the newspaper, too! Have each student choose a different newspaper article and circle each word in the article that he can read. Then ask each student to count the number of circled words and write that number near the top of the article. By gum, students can read the newspaper!

Sally Bivins—Gr. 1, Apache Elementary School, Peoria, AZ

Front–Page News

Get the scoop on front-page news! Enlist your youngsters' help in comparing and contrasting a similar news story from two different newspapers. Read aloud the two articles; then as a class create a large Venn diagram that shows the similarities and differences between the two stories. This activity also works well with sports coverage and movie reviews.

Kelly Pflederer—Gr. 2, Academy Of The Sacred Heart, St. Louis, MO

Pam Crane

Comic Capers

This large-group sequencing activity leaves youngsters smiling from ear to ear! To prepare for the fun, each student cuts out her favorite comic strip from a discarded newspaper. She cuts apart the individual frames and mounts each one on a construction-paper rectangle; then she sequences the mounted frames and programs the backs for self-checking. Next she writes her name and the name of her comic strip on a library pocket before she randomly slips the pieces of her project inside. To begin the large-group activity, each student places her project on her desktop. The students then move from desk to desk along a prearranged route and work the projects their classmates have prepared. There'll be plenty of reading, sequencing, and chuckling taking place!

Marcia Dosser—Gr. 1
Eastern Tennessee State University School, Johnson City, TN

Attention–Grabbing Advertisements

Students may be surprised to discover the number of advertisements found in a newspaper. Display a few newspaper pages; then use a colored marker to circle the ads featured. As a class, critique the advertisements. Discuss what makes an effective ad and why the newspaper is a good medium for advertisers. Then challenge each child to create an attention-grabbing newspaper advertisement for a brand-new product or service. Set aside time for students to share their creative work; then showcase the ads around the school!

Lilly Schultz—Resource Teacher, Washington Elementary School, Auburn, WA

Movie Madness

Interpreting a movie schedule is a picture-perfect way for students to practice reading and interpreting information. Give each group or individual a similar movie listing from the newspaper. Pose a series of questions that require the students to interpret the information at hand. Be sure to include some problem-solving challenges as well!

Lilly Schultz—Resource Teacher

News And Views

Reinforce comprehension, critical thinking, and writing skills with this newsworthy idea. Each week bring to school a different newspaper article that you feel will be of special interest to your youngsters. Read the article aloud; then discuss it as a class. Pose several questions that require students to think critically about the information presented. In conclusion have each child write a paragraph that describes and defends his opinion about the news topic. Mount the completed paragraphs along with the featured news article on a bulletin board entitled "News And Views."

Laura Horowitz—Gr. 2
Plantation, FL

Classy Classifieds

Put your youngsters' writing skills to the test when you ask them to pen classified ads! Distribute several pages of classified ads for students to study. Discuss the kinds of information included in the ads and why some ads are more appealing than others. Also read aloud your local paper's guidelines for writing a classified ad. Then have each student write a brief ad in which he is selling or seeking an item or a service. After a student's ad has been proofread by a classmate, he copies it on a two-inch-wide paper strip. Collect the paper strips and mount them on blank paper as shown. Draw lines as needed; then photocopy a class supply of the project for your youngsters' reading enjoyment.

Pam Doerr—Substitute Teacher, Elizabethtown District, Elizabethtown, PA

Scavenger Hunt

Youngsters love scavenger hunts—so you can count on an enthusiastic response when you suggest this activity! Each student needs a newspaper, a copy of page 170, scissors, and glue. A student finds each requested item in his newspaper, cuts it out, and glues it in the corresponding box. To reprogram the scavenger hunt, photocopy the page and white-out the boxed text. Make this your master copy. Then program a copy of the master and duplicate student copies. Using this technique, you can create a different newspaper scavenger hunt each week!

Dee Ann Bates, Hawthorne Elementary, Oklahoma City, OK

Picture This!

High-interest newspaper photos make excellent springboards for creative writing. Cut out and code a supply of newspaper photos and their accompanying text. Store the text for later use. Each child chooses a photo and writes a brief news article about the pictured event. Remind reporters to address the elements of *who, what, when, where,* and *how* in their stories. Have each reporter mount the final draft of his article and its corresponding photo on construction paper. Then display each completed project along with the original newspaper text. You can bet this bulletin board will be read through and through!

Valerie Suttmiller—Gr. 2, Incirlik Elementary School, Incirlik, Turkey

Dear Editor

The local paper in Danville, Illinois, publishes a children's editorial section. Each week a topic or a question is provided and children are encouraged to submit written responses of 50 words or less. The students enjoy the writing challenge and they are always eager to read the replies that are published. If your local paper is unable to offer this educational opportunity, consider publishing a weekly classroom (or school) newspaper that offers a similar writing opportunity. Hot off the press! The first edition of the *The Students' Tribune!*

Mary Park—Learning Disabled Grs. K–8
Daniel School, Danville, IL

Comic Booklets

Use the Sunday comics to turn a parts-of-speech review into a barrel of laughs! To make a comic booklet, label a 6" x 9" rectangle of construction paper for each part of speech to be reviewed. Staple the resulting pages between construction-paper covers. For each booklet page, locate one comic-strip frame that has a written example of the featured part of speech. Use a crayon to underline the example; then cut out the frame and mount it on the appropriate booklet page. To complete each page, write a brief definition of the spotlighted part of speech. Add a title and byline to the booklet cover, and this newspaper project is complete!

Susan M. Stires—Gr. 3, Alamo Elementary School, Wichita Falls, TX

Tracking Down Numbers

Energize a math review with a number search! Each youngster needs crayons and a few newspaper pages. Challenge students to find numerals based on certain criteria. Directions could include, "Use a red crayon to circle a three-digit numeral that has a six in the tens place," and "Draw a green box around a numeral that is greater than 75." Provide a greater challenge with directions like "Find two numbers whose sum equals ten. Draw a yellow star on each number." The possibilities are endless! Be sure students understand that this activity includes an element of chance like the game of bingo. This will prevent students from feeling frustrated if they cannot find all the numbers.

Kelly Malandra—Gr. 3, Lorane Elementary School, Exeter Township, PA

Making Comparisons

Comparing newspapers from different communities provides a wealth of learning opportunities. As a class choose several communities from which you'd like to obtain newspapers. Divide the class into small groups; then ask each group to compose a letter that requests a sample newspaper and offers to pay for the requested newspaper and mailing costs. Mail the letters to the communities on your class list. (Most libraries have a reference, such as *Editor & Publisher International Year Book* or *Gale Directory Of Publications And Broadcast Media,* that lists the names and mailing addresses of newspapers.) When each paper arrives, compare and contrast its news coverage to that of your local paper for the same day. Students will enjoy comparing the comics, the weather, and the movie selections, too. Be sure to send a thank-you note to each newspaper that participates in your project.

Pam Doerr—Substitute Teacher, Elizabethtown District, Elizabethtown, PA

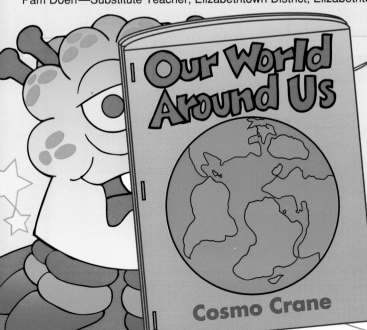

A Continental Study

Learning the continents of the world is in the bag with this individual booklet project. To make a booklet, stack eight flat paper bags; then staple the bags together along the left-hand edge. Personalize, attach a cutout of the world, and write the title "Our World Around Us" on the top bag. On each of the following bags, attach and label a cutout of a different continent. To complete his booklet, a student cuts out newspaper articles and determines where each news event took place. Then he slips each article into the appropriate continent bag. Encourage youngsters to find five or more articles per continent.

Patti A. Devall—Gr. 3, St. Anthony Grade School, Effingham, IL

169

Name _____

A Nose For The News

Five Compound Words

Your Age

Three Color Words

Three Numbers Larger Than 50

An Animal

Five Contractions

Two Rhyming Words

Four Odd Numbers

Two Different Countries

A Day Of The Week

©1998 The Education Center, Inc. • *The Best Of* The Mailbox® *Primary • Book 3* • TEC838

Note To Teacher: Use with "Scavenger Hunt" on page 168.

Buzzing Into Summer

Your happy hive will be humming with excitement when you try these teacher-tested ideas to end the school year.

Summer Fun List

This nifty list of summertime activities can keep youngsters as busy as bees when school lets out! Ask students to brainstorm things to do and titles of good books to read during summer vacation. Write the students' suggestions on chart paper, labeling each child's suggestion with his name. Then type the completed list and make student copies. Encourage students to refer to their list of peer suggestions when they're looking for something to do this summer. That all-too-common summertime phrase, "I'm bored!", will become a thing of the past!

Kelly A. Wong—Grs.1 & 2
Berlyn School, Ontario, CA

Autograph Celebration

Your youngsters will be buzzing about these student-made autograph booklets long after the school year is over. To make the front cover of the booklet, glue colorful tissue-paper squares on a 9" x 12" sheet of construction paper so that the squares slightly overlap. Then, using a paintbrush, brush a thin layer of diluted glue over the tissue paper. This will result in the colors bleeding together for a pretty effect. When the cover is dry, hole-punch two holes in the left margin. Then use the cover as a guide to punch holes in a supply of blank paper and a 9" x 12" construction-paper back cover. Stack and align the project. Thread a length of yarn through each hole; then securely tie each length's ends. Have each child write his name and grade on the front cover of his completed autograph book; then provide time for each student to gather written messages and autographs from his classmates.

Kristin McLaughlin—Substitute Teacher
Boyertown Area Schools, Boyertown, PA

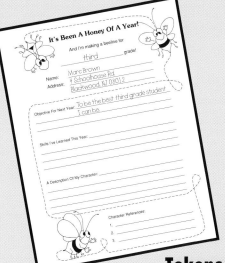

Making A Beeline

Creating a resumé is a fun and effective way for students to reflect on their growth during the past school year. Duplicate student copies of a resumé like the one shown. Before students begin the activity, talk about their next year's goals. Ask students to brainstorm the skills they've learned during the past year as you write their ideas on the chalkboard. You may also want to provide a sample character description to help students generate their own ideas. And lastly remind students that their character references should be three adults whom the students feel know them well. After students have completed their resumés, set aside time for students to share their impressive work. If desired, photocopy each student's resumé so that he may present a copy of it to his next year's teacher!

Anne Marie Fluck—Gr. 2
Loring Flemming Elementary, Blackwood, NJ

Tokens Of Thanks

How can you show appreciation for your "un-bee-lievably" helpful volunteers? Present each volunteer with one of the following inexpensive and easy-to-make gifts:
- an addition flash card with the message "Thanks for adding so much to our school."
- a crayon with the message "Thanks for bringing color to our students' lives."
- a glue stick with the message "Our volunteers help us stick together."
- a pair of scissors with the message "I just couldn't cut it without you!"

Your volunteers will "bee-m" with delight after receiving one of these gifts!

Barbara McCreary—Gr. 5
Ridge Elementary School, Henrico County, VA

Travel Brochures

Once your youngsters have created these travel brochures, they'll be eager to share them with students who plan to enter your classroom or grade level next fall! Explain that the purpose of a travel brochure is to enlighten its reader about the area or place featured on the brochure. Show students several travel brochures that you've obtained from a travel agency. Then challenge each youngster to create a brochure in which your classroom (or grade level) is the travel destination. As a class, brainstorm ideas for the travel brochure. Include the topics that are listed on the brochure on page 175. Write the students' ideas on the chalkboard; then give each youngster a copy of page 175 to complete. When the pages are finished and cut out, demonstrate how to fold the brochure along the thin lines so that the programming remains on the inside. Then have each student unfold his brochure, flip it over, and print "Take A Trip To _____" on the far right panel. To finish his brochure, a student decorates the two remaining panels with illustrations of favorite activities, projects, or events; then he refolds the brochure.

Mary Ann Reed—Grs. 2–6 Math Resource
West Wyomissing Elementary
West Lawn, PA

Sweet Awards

Supplement your academic end-of-the-year awards with sweet treats that highlight positive personality traits. Awards could include the following:

- a package of LifeSavers® for the student who is always willing to help
- a Snickers® candy bar for the student who has a great sense of humor
- a Bit O' Honey® candy bar for the student who exhibits kindness toward others
- a 3 Musketeers® Bar for those students who stick together through thick and thin
- Hershey's® Hugs® and Kisses® for all students!

Diane L. Bishop—Gr. 2
Assumption Catholic School
Denver, CO

Memory Day

Invite the families and friends of your busy bees to an end-of-the-year Memory Day! For this special occasion, display photographs around the classroom that feature your students engaged in a variety of school-related activities. Also enlist your youngsters' help to create a colorful chalkboard display. To do this, write the title " 'Sea' What We Have Learned" on the board. Then ask each child to draw two sea animals on the chalkboard and write one sentence that describes something he learned this year. Provide colored chalk for the activity. During the Memory Day event, invite students to share memory booklets that they have designed. For a fun finale, show a video that contains a compilation of events from the past school year. Student-made refreshments could also be served!

Linda Valentino—Gr. 2
Minisink Valley Elementary School
Slate Hill, NY

End-Of-The-Year Memoirs

Here's a honey of an end-of-the-year writing activity! On the chalkboard write a student-generated list of favorite events, activities, and projects from the past school year. Then give each student a blank writing booklet in which to pen her memoirs of the past school year. Instruct each student to write the title of her book on the first booklet page. Next ask each child to think of someone who encouraged her this year or helped make her year extra-special; then have her write a dedication to that person on page two of her booklet. On page three, have each student list the events, activities, and/or projects from the class-generated list that she plans to write about. This page will become her table of contents. When the student has finished writing her memoirs, have her number her booklet pages and complete her table of contents, then illustrate her booklet cover to her liking.

Mrs. S. Mates—Gr. 2
Public School 206
Brooklyn, NY

Student Surveys

On a scale of one to five, this activity rates a five! Enlist your students' help in naming subject areas learned, and activities and projects completed during the past school year. List the students' responses on the board. Type the list and duplicate a copy for each student. Then, using a scale of one to five, ask the students to score each activity on their lists—with five being the best score. Collect the surveys and use them to determine which activities and topics were most popular among your youngsters. Utilize this information as you make teaching plans for the following year.

Mary Jo Kampschnieder—Gr. 2
Howells Community Catholic, Howells, NE

Showcase Tea

Looking for a "bee-autiful" way for students to share their writing talents? Try having a tea party. To inform parents of the special event, have each student create an invitation to be sent home. On the day of the tea party, enlist students' help in covering tables with floral fabric or colorful paper and placing a potted flower atop each table. As guests arrive, have a recording of classical music playing. During the party have each child share a favorite piece of original writing from the past school year. If time allows, invite parents to write stories under their youngsters' guidance. These writing efforts can also be shared. Conclude the event by serving cookies and tea or apple juice.

Terry Gross—Gr. 2
Asher Holmes Elementary School
Morganville, NJ

End-Of-The-Year Notes

The recipients of these warmhearted thank-you notes are sure to be "bee-dazzled" by your youngsters' kind words. Ask students to name school personnel whom they would like to thank for helping to make their school year run smoothly. Write the students' ideas on the chalkboard. Be sure to include your school principal, secretary, nurse, custodians, and cafeteria workers. Next ask students to describe how each of these people has helped to make their school a better place. List the students' ideas near the appropriate name(s) on the chalkboard. Then, on provided writing paper, ask each student to write a thank-you note to one of the people listed on the board. Take measures to be sure that a fairly equal number of notes are being written to each spotlighted person. After the thank-you notes have been edited and illustrated, bind the thank-you notes for each deserving person between student-decorated construction-paper covers. Plan to present these booklets of heartfelt thank-you notes during the final days of the school year.

Christina MacTaggart—Gr. 2
Hemby Bridge School
Indian Trail, NC

Buzzing Down Memory Lane

Here's a picture-perfect way to end the school year. Give each student a copy of a multiple-picture frame like the one shown. Ask each student to print his name and the school year in the rectangular shape at the bottom of the sheet. In each of the remaining spaces, instruct the student to draw pictures of various events or activities that have taken place during the school year. Then have each student cut out his project and glue it on a 9" x 12" sheet of colorful construction paper. Laminate the projects for durability; then have each student take his impressive picture frame home as a reminder of his fun-filled year.

adapted from an idea by Kate Cassorla—Grs. K–1
Yavneh Hebrew Academy
Los Angeles, CA

End-Of-The-Year Party

No need to buy paper supplies for your end-of-the-year party. Use the leftover paper products from your Valentine's Day, Easter, Halloween, or Christmas parties. This economical idea will give students a chance to recall the fun times that they had during the parties at which the paper products were originally used. Remember when we searched for the missing pumpkin during the Halloween party?

Diane Fortunato—Gr. 2
Carteret School, Bloomfield, NJ

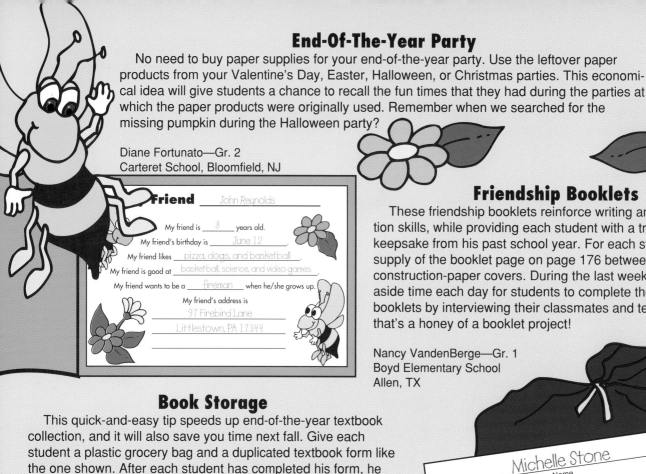

Friend   John Reynolds

My friend is ___8___ years old.
My friend's birthday is ___June 12___
My friend likes ___pizza, dogs, and basketball___.
My friend is good at ___basketball, science, and video games___.
My friend wants to be a ___fireman___ when he/she grows up.
My friend's address is
___97 Firebird Lane___
___Littlestown, PA 17344___

Friendship Booklets

These friendship booklets reinforce writing and communication skills, while providing each student with a treasured keepsake from his past school year. For each student staple a supply of the booklet page on page 176 between slightly larger construction-paper covers. During the last week of school, set aside time each day for students to complete their friendship booklets by interviewing their classmates and teacher. Now that's a honey of a booklet project!

Nancy VandenBerge—Gr. 1
Boyd Elementary School
Allen, TX

Book Storage

This quick-and-easy tip speeds up end-of-the-year textbook collection, and it will also save you time next fall. Give each student a plastic grocery bag and a duplicated textbook form like the one shown. After each student has completed his form, he secures his textbooks inside his plastic bag and tapes his completed form to the outside of his bag. Collect the labeled bags and store them for the summer. In the fall distribute a bag of books to each student in your class. Instruct each student to carefully remove the textbook form from the bag and write his name on the bottom line. Collect the forms and presto—you have a record of which textbooks each student has in his possession!

Sandra Morris—Gr. 3
Champion Elementary School
Warren, OH

Michelle Stone
Name
1998–99 School Year
Math   # 28
Science   # 14
Social Studies # 8
Health   # 2
English   # 5
              1998–99
Name

It's "Bee-n" A Honey Of A Year!

If you're looking for a unique way to review skills and concepts taught during the past school year, then look no further. Here's a honey of a game that's intended to do just that. Duplicate two copies of the open gameboard on page 177. Program the open spaces on each gameboard with a different set of review challenges. Then duplicate each version of the gameboard for one-half of your students. Pair students and give each twosome one copy of each gameboard version, a coin, and two game markers. Instruct each student to color one gameboard. If desired have each student glue the gameboard he colored onto a 9" x 12" sheet of colorful construction paper. Then each pair chooses one of its gameboards and begins play. When the winner of this game has been determined, the twosome plays a second game using its other gameboard. Each pair may continue alternating play between its two gameboards until game time is over.

Michele Anszelowicz—Gr. 1
Mandalay Elementary
Wantagh, NY

It's "Bee-n" A Honey Of A Year!

Start

Name 3 compound words.

Tell a number sentence that equals 17

Buzz ahead one space.

Name the days of the week in order.

Say the sounds of 5 long vowels.

Name these words in ABC order.
egg bed foot

Directions for two players:
1. Place your markers on Start.
2. In turn, flip the coin and move:
   Heads = 1 space
   Tails = 2 spaces
3. Read and answer or do what is written on the space. If your answer is approved by your partner, you may stay. If your answer is not approved, return to your original space.
4. The first player to reach Finish wins.

Oops! Lost your stinger. Go back one space.

Name the months of the year.

Name two authors we studied.

What country is north of the United States?

Buzz ahead one space.

Name one animal that lives at the South Pole.

Count by 5's to 100.

Finish

Draw a picture of something you needed to know this year.

Things you will need to know...

Things you get to do while you're there...

What you will learn...

Draw a picture of something you learned this year.

Use with "Friendship Booklets" on page 174.

My Friend _____

My friend is _____ years old.

My friend's birthday is _____.

My friend likes _____.

My friend is good at _____.

My friend wants to be a _____ when he/she grows up.

My friend's address is

_____

_____

_____

My Friend _____

My friend is _____ years old.

My friend's birthday is _____.

My friend likes _____.

My friend is good at _____.

My friend wants to be a _____ when he/she grows up.

My friend's address is

_____

_____

_____

It's "Bee-n" A Honey Of A Year!

Start

Buzz ahead one space.

Directions for two players:

1. Place your markers on Start.
2. In turn, flip the coin and move:
   Heads = 1 space
   Tails = 2 spaces
3. Read and answer or do what is written on the space.
   If your answer is approved by your partner, you may stay.
   If your answer is not approved, return to your original space.
4. The first player to reach Finish wins.

Oops! Lost your stinger. Go back one space.

Buzz ahead one space.

Finish

Note To Teacher: Use with "It's 'Bee-n' A Honey Of A Year!" on page 174.

"bee-dazzled"
us with

perfect attendance

during the _____ school year!

_____
signed

_____
date

©1998 The Education Center, Inc.

Thank you for
"bee-ing"
a honey of a student this year!

_____
signed

_____
date

©1998 The Education Center, Inc.

Here's something to buzz about!

_____

found sweet success in

_____ *grade.*

Congratulations!

©1998 The Education Center, Inc.

_____

has been as
busy as a bee
all year long!

_____
signed

_____
date

©1998 The Education Center, Inc.

LIFESAVERS....management tips for teachers

Paper Collection

Review cardinal directions with your students while collecting class assignments. Have your students pass their papers to you by following your oral directions. Use directions such as, "Pass all papers to the north. Now pass all papers to the east." Continue giving directions until all papers end up in your hands.

Gina Parisi—Gr. 2
Demarest School
Union, NJ

Storing Letter Cutouts

Here's a tip for organizing your bulletin-board letters. Sort letters by style, size, and/or color; then place each group of letters in a gallon-size, resealable plastic storage bag. Three-hole-punch the plastic bags as shown and place them in a three-ring notebook. Store the binder in a handy location. The next time you need letter cutouts, you'll have them neatly organized and ready to use!

Angela Virostick
West Hill Elementary
Sharon, PA

Friendship Fishbowl

Choosing partners or teams for class activities is fun with this fishy procedure. Cut out a supply of construction-paper fish shapes. Personalize one cutout for each student, then place the cutouts in a fishbowl. To create a student group, simply draw the desired number of cutouts from the fishbowl. This method ensures random grouping of youngsters.

Diane Fortunato—Gr. 2
Carteret School
Bloomfield, NJ

Clever Cleanup

If you need help keeping your classroom tidy, enlist the help of litter-eating Egabrag (*garbage* spelled backwards). Cut the shape of a dust ball from gray construction paper; then add facial features and the message "Please feed Egabrag!" Use clear Con-Tact® covering to attach the cutout to your classroom trash can. When you start to see signs of classroom litter, a gentle reminder such as, "Did I just hear Egabrag's tummy growl?" will have students cleaning up in no time!

Jo Fryer—Gr. 1
Kildeer Countryside School
Long Grove, IL

Nameless Papers

Here's a fun way to remind your students to write their names on their papers. Place an ink pad and a rubber stamp near your turn-in basket. If a child has written his name on his paper, he may stamp his paper before he turns it in. This silent reminder works wonders!

Linda S. Bowen—Gr. 1
Mannford Elementary
Mannford, OK

Planning For A Substitute

Making advance plans for a substitute is a snap with this reusable lesson planner. Write or type your daily schedule on a series of large index cards. Where appropriate, leave blank lines for writing specific information. (See illustration.) Laminate the cards. Using a hole puncher, punch a hole in the left-hand corner of each card; then bind the cards together on a metal ring. Using a wipe-off marker, write the lesson plans your substitute will need on the cards. When you return, wipe away the programming and store the lesson planner for future planned absences.

Chris Noel—Gr. 3
Monrovia Elementary School
Monrovia, IN

Learning Center Record Keeping

To make sure youngsters have equal opportunities to use your learning centers, try this record-keeping system. Place a class roster at each center. After completing a center, a child crosses off his name. A student may repeat a center after all of his classmates have had a chance to participate.

June Blair—Gr. 1, Franklin Elementary School, Reisterstown, MD

Absent Folders

Use these colorful file folders to organize work for students who are absent. Label each of several folders "Absent Folder"; then write a cheery message eon each one. Laminate the folders for durability; then store them in a convenient location. When a student is absent, place an "Absent Folder" on his desk. Ask a student helper to place the absent student's assignments in the folder throughout the day. When a parent or sibling comes to retrieve the student's work, or when the student returns to school, the missed assignments are in one handy location.

Tricia Peña—Gr. 3
Acacia Elementary
Vail, AZ

Assistance Needed

Use this handy display to avoid interruptions while conferencing with individuals or small groups. Have each student trace one of her hands onto tagboard and cut out the resulting shape. Visually divide a display area into multiple sections; then personalize one section for each student. (Sections must be large enough to display hand cutouts.) Attach a Velcro® dot to the center of each personalized section; then attach the matching Velcro® dot to a hand cutout. Store the cutouts in a basket near the display. When you're busy, a student who needs your assistance attaches a hand cutout to her personalized section. As soon as you're available, glance at the display to see who needs your attention.

Laura Mihalenko—Gr. 2
Truman Elementary
Parlin, NJ

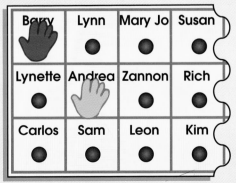

Tracking Student Progress

Keep an up-to-date record of your students' individual progress right at your fingertips! Purchase a flip-top photo album like the one shown. Personalize a card for each student and insert each card in a plastic sleeve. When you wish to make a note about or check on a student's progress, his card is readily available.

Paige Brannon, Pitt County Schools, Greenville, NC

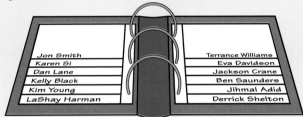

Files At Your Fingertips

How often do you momentarily misplace notes from parents because they accidentally become buried under other school-related paperwork? This easy filing system can put a stop to these frightful moments. Label a hanging file folder for each student; then place the folders in a hanging file box that you have positioned within an arm's reach of your desk. When a student hands you a note from her parent(s), read the note; then immediately place it in the student's file. If you need to retrieve the note, you'll know right where to find it.

Leslee McWhirter—Gr. 1, Mendel Elementary, Houston, TX

Sharing Sessions

Just in time—a great idea for managing student sharing sessions! Each day set aside time for a predetermined number of students to share their "egg-citing" news. Display an hourglass egg timer; then, as each student starts to share his news with the class, invert the timer. If the sand in the timer runs out before the youngster is finished, inform him that his sharing time is over and ask him to wrap up his story. Before you know it, students will be summarizing their stories so that they can make the most of their sharing sessions.

Judith Casey—Substitute Teacher: Grs. K–4
Chatham School District
Chatham, NJ

181

Nifty Neatness Awards

I use Nifty Neatness Awards to encourage neat work in my class. Students know that each day (or every other day), one assignment is eligible for Nifty Neatness Awards—but they aren't sure which one. I secretly choose one set of papers from all of the assignments I collect. Each student who completes that assignment neatly is awarded a neatness certificate, which I staple to the top of his paper. When papers are returned, students remove their awards and save them. After earning ten awards, a student is eligible for one of a variety of privileges such as skipping an assignment, being the teacher's helper for the day, or having extra free time.

Dianne Neumann—Gr. 2
Frank C. Whiteley School
Hoffman Estates, IL

Desk Groupings

Colorful adhesive dots can help keep student desks organized. Choose one desk in each group and affix two adhesive dots to the floor beneath its front legs. Ask the appropriate students to keep these desks properly positioned atop the dots. Instruct the remaining children in each group to align their desks accordingly. Replace and reposition the dots as desired.

Tamra Oliver—Gr. 2, Margaret Beeks Elementary, Blacksburg, VA

Grade-Book Tip

This color-coded system allows you to quickly identify which grades in your grade book indicate test scores, homework assignments, or daily work. Before recording a set of grades, use a highlighter and the following code to color the grade-book column you are about to use: yellow=homework assignments, green=daily work, orange=test scores. This system streamlines grade averaging and is helpful when evaluating students' study habits.

Barbara Gusler—Gr. 3
Bent Mountain Elementary School
Bent Mountain, VA

"Book-keeping"

Keep information about your favorite read-aloud books organized with a personalized card system. On an index card, write the title and author of each book; then note where this book can be found (school library, public library, personal collection) and your students' reactions to it. On the back of the card, list activities that you've done to accompany the story. Put the cards in a recipe box on your desk to keep the information at your fingertips. To remember when you last read the book, pencil the date you complete it on the card.

Renee Sebestyen—Gr. 2
Bayfield Elementary
Durango, CO

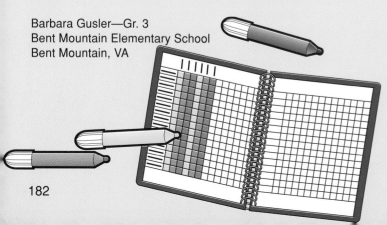

Circle Of Friends

Begin each day on a positive note with this daily sharing plan. Every morning gather students in a large circle. Beginning with the student to your left and proceeding clockwise, each child either shares an item or idea with his classmates in one or two sentences or he passes. Then ask the students to join hands and pass a silent hand squeeze around the circle. Lastly, deliver a positive thought for the day and dismiss the students to their desks. This sharing plan saves time, teaches students to summarize their thoughts, and creates a positive learning atmosphere.

Mary Beth Ghoreyeb—Gr. 2
Brewster School
Durham, CT

Happy Birthday To You

With all that you have to do in a day, remembering your students' birthdays can be a challenge. If you utilize a little spare time this summer, you will be ahead of the game. As you relax, fill out a class set of birthday cards with best wishes and your signature. In the fall, when you learn the names of your students, address the envelopes. Organize the cards by month. Now that you are so well prepared, you will really feel like celebrating.

Mary Dinneen—Gr. 2
Mountain View School
Bristol, CT

OUR READERS WRITE

"Job-osaur"

This classroom helper display is certain to be a huge success. Label each of several dinosaur cutouts with the name of a different "job-osaur." "Job-osaurs" might include "Line Leaderosaur," "Messengerontus," "Boardosaurus Rex," and "Snackodactyl." Mount the cutouts on a bulletin board or wall. Personalize a name card for each student. Each week attach a different student's name card to each "job-osaur." "Dino-mite"!

Amy Barsanti—Gr. 1
St. Hilda's and St. Hugh's School
New York, NY

A Puppet Reminder

Pencil sharpening can be quite a distraction during the school day. To prevent students from constantly sharpening their pencils, try this idea. Tell the children when they are allowed to sharpen pencils. During the times that pencil sharpening is not allowed, place a hand puppet on the pencil sharpener. The puppet acts as a silent reminder of your pencil-sharpening directions.

Sarah S. Moncho—Gr. 1
Ross Jeffries Elementary School
Orlando, FL

Welcome To Our Room

Moving to a new school can be a stressful experience for a child. Your class can help newcomers feel right at home by giving them welcome sacks. At the beginning of the year, have students decorate white paper lunch sacks. Fill the sacks with items similar to those provided for the class on the first day of school—pencils, erasers, crayons, stickers, a list of needed supplies, a copy of the class rules, and a class schedule. You may even wish to include a welcome letter dictated by your class and signed by each student. When a new student arrives, select one youngster to present him with a welcome sack and serve as his buddy for the day. New youngsters will surely feel lucky to have made a move to such a warm, thoughtful classroom.

Kathy Blocker, Forest North Elementary, Austin, TX

Placemat Nametags

Create durable, eye-catching nametags in a jiffy. Purchase inexpensive vinyl placemats in solid colors. Cut the placemats into strips that fit a die-cut machine. Cut shapes from the strips, one thickness at a time; then label each shape with a permanent marker. Using a hole puncher, punch two holes near the top of each shape. Thread a length of colorful cord through the holes; then tie the cord ends. This may be the only set of nametags that you'll need to make all year!

Kristin Smith—Gr. 2
Sunset Valley Elementary
Austin, TX

Daily Reading Plan

This reading incentive plan makes reading a family affair! Duplicate a supply of blank calendar sheets; then help each child make a reading calendar for the entire school year. (See the illustration.) In a parent letter, explain that the goal of the reading plan is for the child to read or be read to for approximately 20 minutes per day. When the daily goal is met, the student checks or initials the corresponding calendar space. At the end of the month, any child who returns a calendar with 20 or more spaces filled is presented with a certificate and earns a prize from the classroom prize box. Read on!

Anne Seil—Gr. 2
Sonoma Country Day School
Santa Rosa, CA

Spelling Directories

These nifty books make learning to spell difficult words a bit easier. At the beginning of the year, request that students bring to school programmable telephone directories that feature alphabetical tabs. Before a student requests a word's spelling, he opens his directory to the appropriate page. If the word is not already listed, he asks to have the word entered in his directory. Students enjoy using their spelling directories and quickly become very resourceful spellers.

Susan D. Stillerman—Gr. 1
Oak Grove School
Poughkeepsie, NY

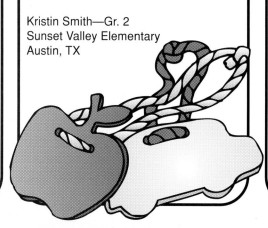

Oral Reading Tip

Have some fun and get positive results with inexpensive plastic fingers like the one shown. You will need one plastic finger per student. When oral reading practice is scheduled, distribute the plastic fingers to your youngsters. Students slip the appendages onto their index fingers, then use them to follow along as their classmates read orally. During the Halloween season you can find the plastic fingers on the costume aisles of most major discount stores.

Jill Hickey—Grs. K & 1
BonDeCroft Elementary School
Sparta, TN

Neighborhood Lotto

This simple twist on the game of lotto leaves more students feeling like winners. To play Neighborhood Lotto, distribute a lotto card and a supply of markers to each student. You will also need a supply of stickers to give away as prizes. Before play begins, announce that three games will be called before players must clear their cards. In addition, each time a winner is identified, the students who sit to the left and right of him win, too! Students love the results of this game variation. After three games are played and the game winners have been rewarded, have students clear their cards for another rousing trio of games.

Sue McDowell—Grs. 3–4
Kennedy Elementary School, Willmar, MN

Volunteer Bag

A volunteer bag makes it easy for school volunteers to lend a hand without disrupting the class. Fill a tote bag with scissors, glue, markers, and other school supplies; then put the bag in a special place. Before a volunteer comes, add a list of instructions and a special treat or thank-you note to the bag. When the volunteer arrives, direct her to the bag. She'll find everything she needs to assist you and a special treat for herself!

Kathleen M. Taylor—Gr. 2
Running Brook Elementary
Columbia, MD

Padded Dice Plates

Get on a recycling roll by making padded dice holders from plastic frozen-food containers. Simply cut a piece of felt to cover the bottom of a clean plastic container. When your students are playing a dice game, ask them to roll their dice in a padded container. The felt padding will make for a much quieter game.

Ann Margaret Neal—Gr. 2, San Antonio, TX

Where In The World?

Improve geography skills by imitating Carmen San Diego. Mount a United States map on a bulletin board along with the title "Where In The World Is Your Teacher Today?" Each morning post several clues that reveal which state you are hiding in that day. Clues might include a river, mountain range, or lake located in the state, or the name of the state flower or capital. For additional reference, provide map-related books near the display. Students will look forward to revealing your location at the end of the day. After your location has been confirmed, students can color in the corresponding state on their own duplicated maps.

Kim Hermes—Gr. 1, Furry Elementary, Sandusky, OH

Open House Checklist

With a special checklist to guide him, a student can give his parent a personalized tour of his classroom and school. Duplicate copies of a checklist similar to the one shown. Before Open House, have each student complete a copy of the checklist and place it on his desk. During Open House each student uses his checklist to give his parent a guided tour of the classroom and school. With this proven method, parents will be sure to see all of the important places and things.

Sandy McCann—Gr. 2
Aiken School
Pittsburgh, PA

Open House Checklist
Guide _Sara_

❏ my desk
❏ reading area
❏ centers
❏ science experiment
❏ good work display
❏ writing folder

"Class-y" Stationery

Your correspondence will make quite an impression when it's written on this one-of-a-kind notepaper. Using a pencil, have each child draw and personalize his self-portrait on a small square of white paper. Carefully cut out and glue the projects along the side and bottom borders of an 8 1/2" x 11" sheet of white paper. At the top of the paper, write "A Note From Room ___." Keep a duplicated supply of this stationery on hand for writing thank-you notes, reminder messages, and invitations.

Gail Thomas—Gr. 1
Norrisville Elementary
White Hall, MD

A NOTE FROM ROOM 2

Liam
Jesse
Holly
Stephanie
Ross
Jan

Magnetic Study Lists

Encourage students to practice spelling and vocabulary words at home with these magnetic reminders. Each week after students have carefully copied their word lists for home study, attach a small strip of magnetic tape to the back of each student's paper. Ask each child to attach his word list to his family's refrigerator as soon as he gets home. Now a student *and* his family members have a visual reminder of the youngster's study assignment.

Valerie Canady—
LD Teacher
Boulevard Elementary
Kokomo, IN

Edible Cornucopias

This year stir up a batch of thankful thoughts and a batch of tasty treats for your Thanksgiving celebration. In advance send home a parent letter asking each youngster to bring one thankful thought and one cupful of "cornucopia filling" to school on a designated day. Provide a list of suggested fillings such as raisins, nuts, popped popcorn, bite-size cookies, and small candy pieces. You will also need one waffle cone per child. On the day of your celebration, ask each child to share his thankful thought. Then stir together the youngsters' ingredients and serve each student a portion of the mixture in a waffle cone. Now that's a tasty cornucopia!

Elaine Clarke—Gr. 1
St. Patrick School
Terre Haute, IN

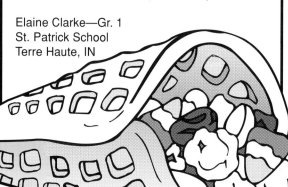

Books For Behavior

Reinforce your youngsters' positive behaviors and pique their interest in reading with a monthly book drawing. Each time you place a book order for your students, order several extra books for the monthly drawings. (If desired, apply your bonus points to these purchases.) At the start of each new month, display a new selection of books on the chalkboard ledge. Throughout the month, present tickets for the book drawing to students displaying positive classroom behavior. Have students sign their tickets before placing them in a designated container. On the last school day of the month, draw one ticket for every book on display and present the books to the appropriate youngsters.

Laura Mikalenko—Gr. 2
Truman Elementary School
Parlin, NJ

Class Picture Puzzles

Preserve favorite classroom memories with class picture puzzles. To make a puzzle, have a favorite snapshot of your students enlarged; then mount it on a sheet of cardboard and laminate it for durability. Cut the mounted photo into jigsaw-style pieces. Or, if desired, have a similar puzzle made commercially at a photo shop. Place the puzzle pieces inside a gift box; then attach the original snapshot to the lid. Students will enjoy piecing together memories throughout the year.

Tina Merdinyan—Gr. 2
Kimball Elementary School, Seattle, WA

Tennis-Ball Protectors

With the advantage of tennis-ball protectors, students can slide their chairs across the floor quietly and easily. To make a set of protectors, cut a slit in each of four old tennis balls; then slide them onto the legs of a student's chair. With these protectors in place, students can move their chairs with a minimum of noise and effort.

Angeli Crumbley
Redan Elementary
Redan, GA

I Am Thankful For...

This November, take time to reflect on each student's positive qualities. Program a chart "I am thankful for...."; then list each student's name and an attribute of his that you are thankful for. Display the chart along with a photo of each student. You'll find that you have quite a lot to be thankful for!

Julie Bulver—Gr. 1
Brooks Elementary
Des Moines, IA

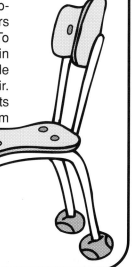

I am thankful for...

Sarah's storytelling
Tisha's helpfulness
David's quietness
Anthony's neatness
Leon's smile
Lamar's singing
Carrie's sweetness
Tyler's memory
Beth's jokes
Matthew's politeness
Tiffany's manners
Ashley's enthusiasm
Emily's dancing

Suspenseful Scoring

Add a little suspense to classroom games with this scoring twist. Decorate the lid of an egg carton as desired; then press a sticky dot into each egg cup. Label each dot with a number of points; then place a penny inside the carton and close the lid. When a team answers a question correctly, have a team member shake the carton. Open the carton and remove the penny to reveal the number of points; then add that number of points to the team's total. And the winner is…

Martha J. Alfrey—Gr. 1
Rose Hill Christian School
Ironton, OH

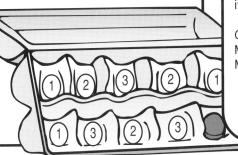

Clear Pocket Book Display

This clever bookbinding idea allows you to assemble class books, then take them apart without damaging individual pages. To make a book, bind together several clear 10" x 12" plastic sleeves. (Plastic comb binding is desirable.) Slip a decorated construction-paper cover into the first and last sleeves; then slip a child's story page into each remaining sleeve. Because the plastic sleeves protect your students' stories, the stories will be in perfect condition when it's time to take them home.

Cam Gerdts—Grs. 1 & 2
Minnesota Lake Elementary
Minnesota Lake, MN

Storing Bulletin-Board Borders

Here's a hassle-free method of storing your collection of bulletin-board borders. Wrap each border around one section of a cardboard wrapping-paper tube. Secure each border with a rubber band. This convenient storage technique keeps your borders in top-quality condition and makes them easy to access.

Karen Killian
Eden Christian Academy
Wexford, PA

Durable Gameboards

Vinyl placemats make terrific backgrounds for student gameboards. Draw a trail game on a placemat using a permanent marker or glue a paper game design to a placemat and cover the surface with clear Con-Tact® paper. These gameboards can be easily cleaned and conveniently stored.

Dolores Joiner—Gr. 1
Furry Elementary
Sandusky, OH

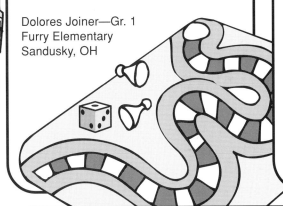

Are You Learning?

Children seem to have an uncanny talent for memorizing song lyrics. So why not capitalize on this talent when teaching the purpose of adjectives? Students will enjoy learning the following lyrics, sung to the tune of "Are You Sleeping?"

Adjectives, Adjectives
Describe a noun!
Describe a noun!
Tell us shape and color.
Tell us size and number.
Spice up a sentence!
Spice up a sentence!

Ann Margaret Neal—Gr. 2
Encino Park Elementary
San Antonio, TX

Homework Pass

Students unite to improve homework habits with this motivational strategy. The class goal in this activity is to earn the letters of the words HOMEWORK PASS. A letter is earned each day that all students complete and return their homework. When all of the letters have been earned, each child receives a homework pass, which can take the place of one homework assignment.

Barbara Williams—Gr. 3
Bel Air Elementary, Evans, GA

Self-Esteem Stockings

'Tis the season to boost self-esteem with these holiday stockings. Give each child a large paper stocking with his name printed at the top. Have students lay the stockings atop their desks. Then, rotating from desk to desk, have each student write a personalized compliment or holiday wish on each classmate's cutout. Focusing on the positive helps your students have a happy holiday season… and creates nice gifts for them, too.

Sara Horton—Gr. 1
St. Alban's
Waco, TX

Sing A Song Of Vowel Sounds

Remembering the sounds of vowels is much easier for children when the sounds are put to music. Teach your students to sing the following song to the tune of "Frère Jacques." Create additional verses with the other vowels and sing, sing, sing!

A makes two sounds.
A makes two sounds:
Ā and Ă—Ā and Ă.
Ă stands for apple.
Ā stands for apron.
Ā and Ă—Ā and Ă.

Betty Caskey
West Side School
Magnolia, AR

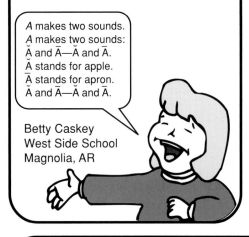

Happy New Year!

Add splashes of color to your January bulletin board with this festive tip. Before mounting your bulletin-board paper, splatter several colors of paint onto the paper. When the paint is dry, mount the paper onto your display area for a bright confetti background. Continue creating exciting backgrounds throughout the year by sponge-painting designs such as hearts for February, shamrocks for March, and ducks for April.

Eileen F. Knox—Gr. 2
Halle Hewetson School
Las Vegas, NV

Powdered Paint Prescription

If you're tired of mixing powdered paint, here's a solution you'll love. In each of several small containers, mix a different color of powdered paint with water. Keep the containers uncovered and allow the mixtures to dry. To use the paints, a student dips his paintbrush in water and then brushes it across the dried paint color of his choice. These paints keep messes to a minimum, and they can be used time and time again.

Sharon Hintz—Grs. 1–3
Beacon SDA School
Lewiston, ID

Your Opinions, Please

Let your children express themselves daily with this thought-provoking graphing activity. To make the graph, attach two columns of adhesive dots (one dot per student in each column) to a large T-shaped poster-board cutout. (See the illustration.) Laminate the graph; then display it in a prominent place near your door. Label a clothespin for each child and clip the clothespins along the top of the graph. Using a wipe-off marker, label the graph with a question and two answers. Each morning, a child reads the question of the day and places his clothespin on an adhesive dot in the column of his choice. Later in the day, have students interpret and discuss the graphing results.

Jill Russ—Gr. 1, West Side Elementary, LaGrange, GA

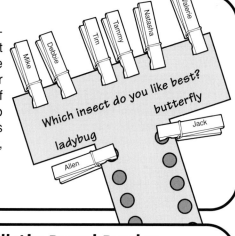

Tabs For Tape

How often do you lose the end of a roll of masking tape? Here's a quick and easy way to solve this problem. Attach a plastic tab from a bread bag to the end of the tape. Remove the tab each time you use the tape and replace it when you're finished.

Gina Parisi—Gr. 2
Demarest School
Bloomfield, NJ

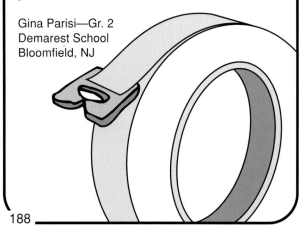

Fancy Bulletin-Board Border

Try this tip for a unique, three-dimensional bulletin-board border. Cut 12" x 18" sheets of construction paper into equal strips. To attach the border, staple one end of a strip to the edge of your board. Create the first wave by gently pushing the strip toward the stapled end and stapling it. Continue in this manner until the opposite end of the strip is reached. Then use the same technique to attach each succeeding strip until your border is completed.

Mary S. Casey—Gr. 2
Lawton Elementary School
Oviedo, FL

Edible Area And Perimeter

Students can really sink their teeth into this measurement activity! Purchase a supply of frozen waffles or prepare several waffles in advance. Carefully cut the waffles into a variety of shapes like the ones shown. Shortly before the activity, warm the waffles and give each child several waffle shapes on a paper plate. To introduce *area,* have the children count the total number of squares in each of their waffle shapes. To introduce *perimeter,* have students count the number of squares around each shape's outer edge. At the conclusion of the lesson, students may eat their waffle shapes!

Debra Vance—Gr. 3
La Jara Elementary
La Jara, CO

Kindness-Counts Box

Encourage students to acknowledge their classmates' acts of kindness with this positive procedure. When a student receives a kind deed from a classmate, he writes the student's name on a slip of paper and places the paper in a box labeled "Kindness Counts." At the end of each week, draw a name from the box. The student whose name is selected becomes the teacher's special assistant for the next school week.

Dawn Lindboe—Gr. 3
Five Points Elementary
Lake City, FL

Cups, Pints, And Quarts

Are your students puzzled when it comes to measuring cups, pints, and quarts? Help your students solve the mystery with these individual measurement puzzles. To make a puzzle, fold a sheet of paper in half and then in half again. Crease the folds; then unfold the paper and confirm that you have created four nearly equal boxes. In blue crayon, write "CUP" in all four boxes as shown. In red crayon, write "PINT" two times as shown with the letters "PI" in one box and "NT" in the adjacent box. In green crayon, write "QUART" in large letters across the horizontal fold line as shown. Then cut the boxes apart on the fold lines to make a four-piece puzzle. By assembling the puzzle pieces and completing the words, your students will be able to distinguish the number of cups in a pint and the number of pints in a quart.

JoAnn Nagy—Gr. 2, Powers Elementary, Amherst, OH

CUP	*CUP*
PINT	
QUART	
PINT	
CUP	*CUP*

Valentine Boxes

Tissue boxes make sturdy storage containers for your students' valentines. Have each student use markers, construction-paper cutouts, strips of lace and ribbon, and other appealing materials to decorate a tissue box. If a handle is desired, staple each end of a sturdy length of yarn inside the opening of the box. Happy Valentine's Day!

Debbie A. Oda—Grs. K–6
Rowland Heights, CA

Cherries For George

This February, celebrate George Washington's birthday with these individual, no-bake cherry snacks. To make one snack, spread cream cheese on one side of two vanilla wafers. At the top of each wafer, press a pretzel stick stem into the cream cheese. Arrange the wafers on a paper plate so that the pretzel stems meet. Using cherry pie filling, spoon one cherry and a bit of filling atop the cream cheese on each wafer. As a final touch, place two spearmint candy leaves near the tops of the stems. Yummy!

Marcia Miller
Merritt Elementary
Mt. Iron, MN

Keeping In Touch

With this tip, it's easy to keep in touch with students who move away during the school year. Keep a supply of self-addressed, stamped postcards in your desk. Before a student moves away, have her choose a postcard to take with her. Ask the student to write and mail the postcard from her new home. Remind the student to include her new address so that students may respond to her note. This type of correspondence can help the student make a smooth transition into her new school and neighborhood.

Sheila Monger—Gr. 2
Corlett Elementary
Cheyenne, WY

Round Off!

Rounding off numbers is fun with this activity. Give each student a piece of art paper and the sale section of a newspaper. Have the students cut out and glue a predetermined number of prices onto their papers. Underneath each price have the students write the price rounded off to the nearest dollar.

Patricia Mauldin—Gr. 3
Fair Elementery Shool
Pascagoula, MS

Social Studies Idea

A simple pasting activity can help your students understand the concepts of city, state, country, and continent. Give each child four pieces of different-colored paper, cut to these dimensions:

yellow: 1 1/2" x 3"—label with the name of your city
green: 3" x 5"—label with the name of your state
orange: 5" x 9"—label with the name of your country
blue: 9" x 12"—label with the name of your continent

Have each child label his yellow piece of paper as designated, then glue it on top of the green piece. After labeling the green piece, the student glues it on top of the orange piece, and so on until the project is complete. This handy visual reminder makes learning a sometimes difficult concept a snap!

Donna Koscianski—Gr. 3
Indian Avenue School, Bridgeton, NJ

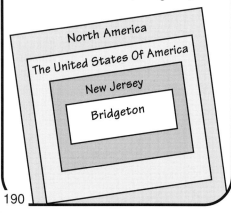

Phonetic Travels

Turn your students into armchair travelers with this fun phonics-review game. Each day choose a travel destination. On a map locate the city, state, or country you plan to visit; then challenge students to pack appropriate items for their trip. To be appropriate, an item must have the same beginning sound as the destination. For example, if students are visiting Michigan, items such as milk, money, mittens, and a microphone may be packed. After each student has identified an appropriate item, have him illustrate and label it on a sheet of drawing paper. Each day compile the completed projects into an appropriately labeled booklet.

Vickie Genovese—Gr. 2, Parkside Elementary, Solon, OH

M Is For Michigan

A Recipe For Mom

Cook up a wonderful Mother's Day gift with a fun poster project! Begin by showing students examples of real recipes. Brainstorm with the class "person ingredients" that could be included in a recipe. Let each child use markers to write a recipe for her mother on a large piece of poster board. After adding illustrations, have the student draw a portrait of her mom on the poster. This is also a great idea for Father's Day!

Diane Cantor—Gr. 1
Gurney Primary School, Chagrin Falls, OH

Recipe For
My Mom,
Charlotte

Curly brown hair
2 sparkly green eyes
1 cute nose
1 smiling red mouth
2 deep dimples
1 cup of brown freckles
1 teaspoon of being a clown
Mix all ingredients until well blended. Enjoy!

Auntie Nym's Antonyms

Help students remember the meaning of *antonym* with this fun association activity. Show youngsters a picture of an elderly woman and introduce her as your Auntie Nym. Then tell your children a series of silly stories that describe Auntie Nym's *opposite* behavior. For example, tell youngsters that one time Auntie Nym invited you to her home for a hot breakfast and she served cold cereal. Then explain that another time she agreed to come by your house after school and she arrived before school! After several tales of opposites, introduce youngsters to the term *antonym*. Without a doubt, the mere mention of antonyms or Auntie Nym will have students thinking about opposites!

Katherine Gegner—Gr. 2
W. M. Bass School, Lynchburg, VA

Priceless Student-Teacher Gift

Enlist your colleagues' help in creating this unique farewell gift for your student teacher. Ask each member of the teaching staff to complete a form like the one shown. If desired, laminate the completed forms for durability; then three-hole punch the pages and compile them in an attractive binder. A quick flashback to that first year of teaching is all it takes to realize the value of this gift.

Leigh Anne Newsom—Gr. 3
Greenbrier Intermediate, Chesapeake, VA

Name_____
Grade_____

One activity that I always do that really works:

Tell about a good discipline technique:

Describe a beginning-of-the-year activity that you can do each year:

End-Of-The-Year Keepsakes

Students and parents will be delighted with the results of this end-of-the-year keepsake project. Give each child a half-sheet of paper with space for an illustration and manuscript lines. Have him write a few sentences about his favorite school memories, then draw a picture to resemble himself in the space provided. Photocopy pairs of student pages side by side on single sheets of paper; then duplicate each full page for each student. Have each student place his pages between two construction-paper covers, then decorate his front cover as desired. No doubt these books will really be treasured.

Karen Brighton Gesl—Gr. 2
Indian Head Elementary, Indian Head, MD

My favorite memory of second grade was when we hatched chicks from eggs.
Kyle Beck

My favorite memory was when our class got the most points at Field Day.
Jacob Prillaman

A Sunny Message

If you're looking for a unique way for your youngsters to express their gratitude to a parent volunteer, school secretary, or other deserving person, this bright idea is for you! From yellow paper cut a large circle; then cut out a yellow, triangle-shaped ray for each student. Add facial details and a desired message to the circle cutout. Then have each student decorate his ray with a brief message or an illustration. Attach the rays to the circle as shown. There'll be plenty of bright, sunny smiles when your youngsters present their special thank-you.

Lara O'Brien—Gr. 2
Lexington Park Elementary
Lexington Park, MD

Dear Ms. Owens
You are "sun-sational"!

Melts-In-Your-Mouth Science

What do peanut M&M's® and the earth have in common? They both have three layers! After instructing students about the earth's *core, mantle,* and *crust,* have them brainstorm a list of items that have three layers. Give each child some peanut M&M's®; then explain that the candy represents the earth: The colorful candy shell is the crust, the milk chocolate is the mantle, and the peanut inside is the core. Finish the lesson by letting students eat their candies. What a delicious way to add a little science to the day!

Barbara Hamel
Joshua Intermediate School, Joshua, TX

Weird Paper Day

Don't be shocked if students write more on Weird Paper Day. On a day set aside to be Weird Paper Day, provide your students with various types, sizes, shapes, and colors of paper. For example, make available calculator tape, different sizes of cardboard, die-cut notepads, neon-colored paper, poster board, newsprint, and typing paper. Then let the writing begin. This idea may be just what students need to rejuvenate their creative-writing juices!

Sheila R. Chapman—Gr. 3
Elm Street School
Newnan, GA

Division Is A Family Matter

Teach your students this mnemonic device to help them remember the steps used in long division. The first letter of each name corresponds with the first letter of its related step.

Daddy = divide
Mommy = multiply
Sister = subtract
Brother = bring down
and sometimes
Rover = remainder

Rona Mendelson—Gr. 3
Estes McDoniel Elementary
Henderson, NV

Summer Fun Boxes

Provide each of your students with a special box of supplies to spark summertime creativity. Supply each youngster with a shoebox and have him color and decorate it. Towards the end of the year, gather classroom quantities of items such as memo pads, pencils, simple recipes, packages of Kool-Aid®, crayons, paper, and glue. Place one of each item in each student's box for him to take home for summertime fun. Glue a copy of the poem shown to the top of each box.

Janet Lewis—Gr. 1
Buford Elementary School, Flowery Branch, GA

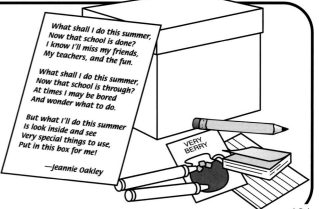

What shall I do this summer,
Now that school is done?
I know I'll miss my friends,
My teachers, and the fun.

What shall I do this summer,
Now that school is through?
At times I may be bored
And wonder what to do.

But what I'll do this summer
Is look inside and see
Very special things to use,
Put in this box for me!

—Jeannie Oakley

VERY BERRY

Answer Keys

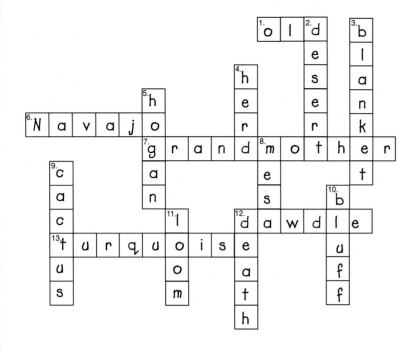

Crossword puzzle answers:

old

Navajo

grandmother

turquoise

dawdle

Down and across words include: desert, blank, her, hog, can, cac, tus, loom, message, breath, buff, mouth

(Items listed should be illustrated.)

TV	dime	Golden Ticket	bowl of soup
tube of toothpaste	wad of chewed gum	peanuts	news-paper
several candy bars	Wonka Bar	bread	dollar bill

1. A prediction about the weather is called a weather ~~observation~~. *forecast*

2. The ~~atmosphere~~ warms the earth. *sun*

3. During a storm you might see lightning and hear ~~snowflakes~~. *thunder*

4. When water freezes, it changes to ~~fog~~. *ice*

5. Cirrus, stratus, and cumulus are types of ~~frost~~. *clouds*

6. A thermometer is an instrument for measuring ~~rainfall~~. *temperature*

7. Moving air is called ~~snow~~. *wind*

8. A person who studies weather is called a ~~barometer~~. *meteorologist*

9. ~~Hail~~ is a cloud that touches the ground. *Fog*

10. After the rain shower a colorful ~~hurricane~~ filled the sky. *rainbow*

11. Water ~~freezes~~ more rapidly in the sun. *evaporates*

12. Sleet, ~~wind~~, hail, and snow are all kinds of precipitation. *rain*